0404.15 HOURS

Suddenly the night was torn by the rapid fire of the lieutenant's M16A1 on full auto. A burst of stark white light from Jose's parachute flare illuminated the VC from the far side.

Controlled pandemonium erupted as the rest of the squad opened fire. Several VC were knocked out of one sampan as the loads of #4 buckshot slammed into them. A blast roared out as the middle sampan was nailed with an MK 3A2 grenade. Splashes and noises were everywhere as tracers streaked toward the confused enemy. A sampan was suddenly blasted into two pieces as it was struck squarely by a 40-mm high explosive grenade.

As suddenly as it began, the firing stopped, as if on command. The entire event took only six minutes from start to end with 45 seconds of firing.

SEALS IN ACTION

KEVIN DOCKERY

AVON BOOKS ◆ NEW YORK

To Elaine
It could not have been done without you

AVON BOOKS, INC.
1350 Avenue of the Americas
New York, New York 10019

Copyright © 1991 by Bill Fawcett & Associates
Interior line illustrations courtesy of William Wardrop
Maps courtesy of James Clouse
Published by arrangement with Bill Fawcett & Associates
Library of Congress Catalog Card Number: 90-93556
ISBN: 0-380-75886-5
www.avonbooks.com

First Avon Books Printing: February 1991

AVON TRADEMARK REG. U.S. PAT. OFF. AND IN OTHER COUNTRIES, MARCA
REGISTRADA, HECHO EN U.S.A.

Printed in the U.S.A.

WCD 20 19 18 17 16 15 14

The author wishes to gratefully acknowledge all of the people who assisted in the creation of this book. Most especially thanks goes out to all of the SEALs and UDT men, both past and present, who helped supply the information that went into this, their history. Thanks to the officers and men of the Navy Special Warfare Training Center in Coronado, California. . . . HOO YAH!

Contents

The Trident

The Special Warfare insignia—or Trident, as it is known among its wearers—is the only outward sign that an individual Navy man is a SEAL. Authorized by the Department of the Navy in 1970 for wear on the service dress uniform, the Trident is a gold metal pin for dress wear and a patch of black embroidery on a green background for wear on subdued (camouflage or fatigue) uniforms. The insignia is normally worn on the left breast of the uniform above any service ribbons or other decorations.

Special warfare insignia

The symbolism of the insignia represents the three mediums in which the SEALs operate as well as their branch of the services. The central part of the insignia is an anchor, clearly identifying the branch of service as the Navy. Behind

1

and above the anchor is an eagle—with its wings out-spread—representing the air medium as well as the strength and courage of the SEALs. Each of the eagle's talons is reaching around and in front of the anchor. The eagle's right talon is holding a trident, representing the sea—the trident being symbolic of Neptune, the Roman god of the sea who used a trident as his scepter. In front of the trident, the eagle's left talon is holding a cocked flintlock pistol by the barrel. The pistol represents the land on which the SEALs operate and the fact that it is cocked indicates the SEALs' constant state of readiness for action. Only when an individual has successfully completed the Basic Underwater Demolition/Seals (BUD/S) course as well as six months of probation and training with a team is he authorized to wear the Trident, indicating his place in the Special Warfare Community.

The SEALs are part of a naval tradition that began during World War II. In many ways today's SEALs are part of an unbroken tradition born in the desperate battle to defeat the Axis powers. From the beginning, the SEALs have shown the courage, verve, and initiative that continue to be an integral part of the profile of all the Navy Special Forces.

The NCDUs

On May 6, 1943, Admiral Ernest J. King, Chief of Naval Operations (CNO), issued a directive for the immediate formation of Naval Demolition Units. Lieutenant Commander Draper L. Kauffman, founder and commander of the Navy Bomb Disposal School, was assigned the task of training the new units and was given a free hand in locating the school, recruiting men from in or out of the Navy, and obtaining whatever material or equipment he might need to achieve this goal. As the school was being set up, an emergency team of volunteers was assembled from the Dynamiting and Demolition School at Camp Perry, Virginia. This thirteen-man original team was joined by a number of already demolition-qualified volunteers and the entire assemblage was placed under the command of Lieutenant Fred Wise of the Navy Seabees. This small unit was to receive an accelerated course in underwater demolition and rubber boat handling before being shipped out. Training completed, the unit received immediate orders to the Mediterranean Theater under the official title of Naval Combat Demolition Unit (NCDU). Upon arrival in Africa, the unit was to assist in the invasion of Sicily.

The Sicilian invasion, Operation Husky, took place on

July 10, 1943, and involved enough Allied naval forces to surround one third of the island. The landing sites turned out to be defended by emplacements and troops but almost no obstacles were found to have been placed in the water or on the beaches. Heavy enemy air attacks sank several major ships and many small landing craft were sunk close to the beach. The NCDUs did not act in their trained role during the initial phase of the landings because of a simple lack of targets. To minimize clogging of the all-important supply landing sites by sunken craft, the NCDUs were ordered to demolish wrecked Allied boats. Some of the unit's men were sent inland to help eliminate cleared enemy strong points and blow up the remaining structures. After several days of clearing channels and blasting inland obstacles the NCDUs were returned home, bloodied by a combat of sorts—but not the sort they had imagined.

Most of the remaining men of the Sicilian NCDU reported to Fort Pierce, Florida, where they became instructors at the new NCDU school. The NCDU teams were filled with volunteers from the Navy Seabees, Bomb and Mine Disposal (Kauffman's old unit), and the Navy/Marine Scout and Raider personnel who were already based at Fort Pierce. The training of the new units began in July 1943, with heavy initial emphasis placed on the physical capabilities of the men.

This initial period of intense physical training proved to the individual who stuck through that he was capable of ten times the physical output he originally thought possible. The theory behind this level of physical demand had been initially developed by the Navy/Marine Scouts and Raiders. Kauffman agreed with the basic idea and ordered his Scout and Raider instructors to design the physical training program for the NCDUs. The press of coming events caused the pace of training to be accelerated. This intense period of training became known as Motivation Week—a term that has since been changed to Hell Week. During the six-day Motivation Week, the men were driven to their limits of endurance. Impossible objectives were expected to be reached. Lack of sleep and constant harassment made the men groggy and prone to mistakes, and any mistake was grounds for immediate expulsion. It took a maximum amount of fortitude and motivation to pass the course without quitting. The value of the program proved so great that Hell Week is still the most significant part of today's Special Warfare training.

The rigors of this grueling program caused 40 percent of the original volunteers to quit of their own choice. The survivors became completely confident of their abilities to endure and accomplish any possible task. The training course's mind-numbing conditions and impossible demands are what most credit for sustaining the men of the NCDUs during their most important operation.

Swimming was, of course, required training but did not receive the emphasis we would expect today. Such little importance was actually given to developing swimming skills that the men only had to swim a few hundred yards to qualify. Underwater swimming was not a familiar sport in the early 1940s and most of the instructors at the NCDU school were not acquainted with its peculiar demands. When masks and swim fins were first tried out by the NCDU instructors, who had never used such things, they were quickly discarded as of little practical use. The fins caused severe leg cramps in the men who improperly used them and the masks flooded and choked the users who had no knowledge of the simple clearing procedures easily taught today.

The major emphasis in training was given to demolitions of beach obstacles of varying types and under the most trying conditions imaginable. Further difficult training took place in the form of field exercises in the wide tracts of heavy swampland around Fort Pierce. The swamps were filled with alligators, rattlesnakes, cottonmouths, bloodthirsty insects, and other hostile forms of life. The men had to endure this while trying to cross open stretches of water, bogs, and jungle, all the time trying to remain undetected by watchful "enemy" personnel. Many of the men had never seen swamps like those in Florida—dark, deep water between lumps of soggy land. Footing was always treacherous and they were forced to learn how to judge the safety of crossing an area. The bellow or grunt of an alligator, combined with the slither and splash of a water snake, constantly served to remind the men that they had to watch for more than just the "enemy" instructors.

Men already exhausted from effort would have to stop and decide how to slip past experienced instructors. Sinking deep into the stinking mud or dark waters, the recruits scarcely dared to breathe, while men searched for them nearby. The pressure of the mission forced them to move, and soon they'd feel the crushing disappointment of having been caught by a better skilled and more patient instructor.

Capture could mean being forced to repeat the entire exercise or, worse, could prevent the hapless recruit's teammates from reaching their objective. The men of the NCDU had to prove they were made of sterner stuff than the average sailor and were forced to learn from their mistakes. The men knew that there would soon be a real battle to fight, and that there were more lethal things to face than an irate instructor . . . but not by much.

The result of this training was a supremely capable and rugged individual, confident in the most hostile of environments and able to demolish almost any type of obstacle with explosives he carried.

Graduates of this training program were formed into six-man teams. Each team consisted of five enlisted men led by either a commissioned officer or a petty officer. Most of the graduated CDUs were immediately sent to England in preparation for a large operation. Due in no small part to the overwhelming secrecy surrounding Operation Overlord (D day in Europe), most of the general staff and all of the lower ranking officers had no idea what to do with specialized Naval Combat Demolitionists. The result of this lack of knowledge was the breaking up of the teams, with most of the members being sent to outlying posts to perform other duties such as guarding ammo dumps and gates. After some time passed, orders indicating the NCDU's mission were finally issued. The units gathered together at Falmouth, England, for further training under the command of Lieutenant Robert Smith.

Gathering at Falmouth and being attached to the Fifth Corps Special Engineering Task Force, the CDUs were finally given some specific intelligence as to the type and quantity of obstacles they were expected to clear. The Allied High Command's obsession with secrecy about the Normandy invasion prevented any real target intelligence from being given to any unit, including the NCDUs, for fear the Germans might catch some unguarded word. It is to be commended, and to the men's credit, that no NCDU, or later UDT, was ever charged with a breach of security.

The primary and most difficult of the obstacles the NCDUs would face was something referred to as "Element C," popularly called the "Belgian Gate." This obstacle was a large, heavy construction of steel beams bolted together to form a ten-feet-high by ten-feet-wide flat-faced section of "picket fence." Each section was fourteen feet deep with a steel brace to support the structure, which weighed over two and a half tons per section. Sections were attached together, forming long obstacles that could be quickly moved into deeper water by means of muscle (conscripted labor) and the rollers attached to each section's base

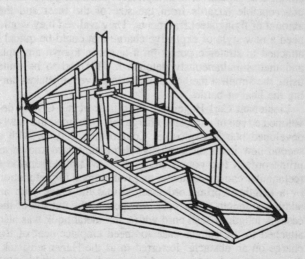

Element "C," the primary obstacle at Normandy Beach that the NCDUs were intended to destroy

and support. These gates formed a formidable defensive obstacle, especially since mines were discovered attached to the tops of the "pickets." Installed at the low-tide mark they would impale or sink any landing craft attempting to cross over them while still allowing defensive fire to be directed through the "pickets" against any infantry hiding behind them.

It was the discovery of these obstacles, as well as their numbers and effect, that had influenced Admiral King to issue the orders authorizing the CDUs. When the teams finally met the object they had been created to destroy, they realized with startling clarity the difficulty of the job. The simple size and strength of the gate, combined with its complex construction, ruled out using any demolition methods then known. New techniques were required to knock down the gates and other obstacles, and the job had to be done with speed! Initial attempts at blasting mock-ups of the Belgian Gates resulted in twisted masses of wreckage as impassable as the original obstacles. Using greater amounts of explosives to completely flatten the gates caused unacceptable hazards from the size of the blast and the amount of flying steel fragments. They realized they would need a new style of explosive charge that could be quickly attached to strategic points on a target in known amounts and then simultaneously detonated. This had to be done using the simplest method possible to prevent mistakes during the heat of battle.

Lieutenant Carl Hagensen, an officer of the CDUs, developed a type of explosive charge that combined the newly developed plastic explosive, Composition 2 (C2), with a second new item, the explosive detonating cord known as primacord. A two-pound block of C2 was placed inside a rectangular canvas container and was primed for detonation by a length of primacord inserted into the block with an additional length of the cord wrapped on the outside of the case. A length of sash cord with a flat metal hook was also attached to the canvas case to speed emplacement of the charge on an obstacle. Referred to as the Hagensen Pack, the new type of charge quickly proved that it could solve the demolition problem of the Belgian Gates. Sixteen of the packs could be quickly attached to strategic points on the gate's structure by using their attached sash cords and hooks. By connecting all of the packs' primacord lines to a master detonating line, any number of obstacles could be instantly reduced to a flat pile of rubble. Indeed, the charges proved so successful and generally useful that they soon became a standard naval demolition item, remaining in use today as the Mark 20 demolition charge, and still generally called the Hagensen Pack.

By February 1944, the ten CDUs in England were split into three sections for further training. Two sections were sent to the southern coast of England, one to Fowey and the other to Salcombe. The remaining section was stationed at Swansen in Wales. By the end of February, eight more units had arrived from Fort Pierce. They were split up among the already stationed units. In late March, the CDU units were preparing to gather for the invasion when new intelligence arrived that drastically changed the situation. A large increase in coastal activity by the Germans had been detected with a concurrently large increase in the number of obstacles emplaced on the planned invasion beaches. The number of obstacles caused sudden increased demand for qualified demolition specialists, and the sixteen CDUs from Fort Pierce suddenly found themselves en route to England. New types of obstacles were found to have been emplaced including steel or concrete tetrahedrons (pyramids), steel "hedgehogs" (six-pointed tripods), and concrete "dragon's teeth," with almost all of them mined.

The new emplacements were the direct result of Hitler's placement of Field Marshall Erwin Rommel as commander in charge of the Atlantic Wall. To further complicate the situation, the officers of the CDUs were finally told the tidal times and changes at the planned invasion beaches. These changes raised the water level twenty-five feet and went from low to high tide in less than three and a half hours. The Navy men immediately became very concerned and quickly pointed out the severe difficulties in conducting so massive a demolition project in so short a time. The problem was considered such an important point that the date and time of the invasion were changed to the early part of June to give the CDUs the maximum amount of time between tides. At a hectic four-day conference between high-ranking officers and engineers, who met during the last week of March 1944, a complete change in the size and organization of the Combat Demolition Units was finished and put into effect.

The CDUs were changed from the original six-man teams into five-man teams. To each of these smaller teams were attached three Navy seamen and five Army combat engineers. The new thirteen-man units were led by Navy officers and were designated Gap Assault Teams (GATs). Within one year the naval teams had gone from being Naval Combat Demolition Units (NCDUs) to simply Combat Demolition Units (CDUs). The generalized CDU designation was more for security's sake. Finally, the CDUs had reached their designation of Gap Assault Teams (GATs). GAT was the term used for the combined Army/Navy team, with the Navy men still being referred to as the CDU when listed separately. Each GAT was assigned twenty-six Army engineers led by an Army lieutenant. The Navy team was to demolish obstacles in the tidal zone between high and low tides with the Army team to attack obstacles from the high-water line to the top of the beach. Navy teams were to use rubber boats while each Army team was assigned two tanks, for firepower, and either a bulldozer or a tank with a dozer blade attached (tank dozer). This reorganization resulted in forty units totaling 550 men.

Some of the new intelligence also resulted in a very unwelcome change in combat dress for the CDUs. Information was received that indicated to the High Command the very possible use of mustard gas and stronger poison gasses (nerve agents) by the Germans in defense of the beaches. Further intelligence received from France stated that some of the mines emplaced on the beaches and obstacles were filled with gasoline that would ignite and spread over the water when the mines were fired. A new uniform designed to combat the problem was issued to the vital demolition teams. It consisted of a hooded, fire-resistant fire-fighting suit impregnated with materials making it also impervious to mustard gas and other gases. In addition to the heavy suit, CDU members had to wear overboots (galoshes) and long canvas overstockings that were also treated against gas. All of this was worn over the normal combat uniform while wearing a gas mask. This ''uniform'' was carried along with the CDU's individual fighting load of almost ninety pounds, most of which contained explosives.

The intense physical training undergone at Fort Pierce paid off! The CDUs were able to stand the punishing pace while the Army engineers and Navy seamen were often unable to keep up. Split into two groups, one for Omaha Beach and one for Utah Beach, the men were placed under higher ranking commanders for the actual operations. Captain Thomas Wellings was put in charge of the Omaha group with Lieutenant Commander Herbert Peterson taking command of the Utah group. Both officers had received intense training at Fort Pierce so they were completely familiar with the capacity and capabilities of the men put in their charge. From the second week of April to May 22, the combined Army/Navy units trained as teams at Appledore, Devon, on the southwest coast of England. The training completed, the teams moved to their final staging area in Salcombe, where they divided into their respective groups in preparation for the upcoming invasion. Primary preparation for most of the men was the fabrication of the ten thousand Hagensen Packs necessary for the massive demolition project ahead. On June 1, the Utah Beach group moved to the marshaling area and their waiting ships, and two days later, on June 3, the Omaha group proceeded to Portland Harbor, Dorset, to board their transport craft.

The trip to the landing areas took place in horrifyingly bad weather. But the transport ships arrived, amazingly, at exactly their intended positions and on schedule. Their luck changed when several craft then foundered in the heavy seas and had to be towed back to England. The remainder were, for the most part, filled with exhausted, cold, and miserable troops attempting to enter their smaller assault craft in pitching seas. The intended plan for both beaches was for the first wave of assault craft to land infantry supported by amphibious tanks with the second wave carrying the demolition teams. The infantry/armor teams were to secure the beachhead and provide covering fire for the Gap Assault Teams while they destroyed the beach obstacles to make way for the main landing force.

The CDUs had faced severe hardships and some very real dangers while training for the invasion. The training facility at Fort Pierce had been little more than a few tents and prefabricated huts. As it was the men spent precious little time in the tents since field problems and other training kept them outside most of the time. Southern swamps can claim even the most experienced, and men had been lost in training accidents.

Alligators and rattlesnakes were ever-present lethal and respected enemies, and the instructors saw to it that the men were prepared for any foreseeable combat situation. But little had been offered in way of preparation for the ride into the beaches. The weather had been misjudged by the High Command and, as a result, the transport ships had been wildly tossed at sea for at least several days. Many of the men, including the seasoned Navy men of the CDUs, were cold, tired, and seasick. Transferring from the transports to the smaller Landing Craft Vehicle/Personnel LCV(P)s, for the trip to shore proved hazardous, with the rough seas pitching the smaller craft about while the men tried to board them by scrambling down cargo nets. The four-to-six-foot waves almost immediately swamped the dual-drive (DD) amphibious tanks as they left their ships; only four were known to have arrived with the first troops on Omaha in firing condition. The heavy waves caused by the ten-to-eighteen-knot winds blowing onshore from the northwest also created a heavy surf on many portions of the beaches. These were the conditions that prevailed as Operation Neptune, the amphibious phase of Operation Overlord, took place.

The cloudy skies over Normandy caused a gray light to shine on the invasion beaches. The dull light combined with the smoke from exploding shells limited visibility and, as a result, created hazardous conditions for the approaching landing craft. The high waves and onshore winds caused the CDUs to have a great deal of trouble maneuvering their explosives-laden rubber rafts through the surf. Several times German shells detonated the contents of a raft, obliterating the CDU team around it in a blinding flash and thundering roar. Landing craft, wallowing in the waves approaching the beach, would become large, slow targets for German guns.

In the several years leading up to D day, the Germans had done more than just line the beaches with obstacles and mine fields. Carefully constructed concrete emplacements were hidden all along the shoreline and nearby cliffs. Almost every emplacement had at least one machine gun. Cannons of every caliber were located along the beaches; 75-mm to 88-mm guns were placed in eight concrete casemates and four open positions along Omaha Beach. Thirty-five pill-boxes holding lighter artillery ran the length of Omaha, along with eighteen emplacements armed with antitank guns ranging from 37 to 75 mm in size. Mortar positions were interspersed among the larger emplacements. Each of the positions held a weapon of 50-, 80-, 100-, or 120-mm caliber, with many weapons having been captured by the Germans earlier in the war. Several hundred yards inland were forty rocket pits each able to launch four 32-cm rockets simultaneously. Throughout the beach areas were trenches, rifle pits, machine gun positions, and remote-controlled flamethrowers, all ready for immediate use. Five thousand yards to the west of Omaha was a battery of six 155-mm howitzers, easily within range of the entire beach. Further west were an additional four 155-mm guns as well as four 105-mm howitzers, all within range of a large portion of Omaha Beach.

The preinvasion ''softening up'' of Omaha and Utah beaches took 21,500 projectiles ranging in size from 75 mm to fourteen inches and 1,285 tons of aircraft bombs. All this ordnance would be used in the forty minutes before the landings, with the majority earmarked for Omaha Beach. So many shells and bombs struck the beaches that in aerial photographs taken after the landing the beaches resembled the crater-pocked surface of the moon! To this day Normandy farmers and beach users are still finding unexploded bombs and shells along the site.

The naval preinvasion bombardment of Omaha Beach was restricted to only thirty-five minutes of firing to limit the time the Germans had to respond. The bombing by B-26 Liberator heavy bombers was limited to sighting by instruments, a particularly inaccurate system, due to the weather. As a safety margin the bombers were ordered to release their bombs late so as to miss the beaches and offshore armada. The result of the bomb run and naval bombardment was little more than a disruption of German communications since most of the bombs and shells fell too far inland to have any effect on the heavy beach emplacements. The men of the German 726th Infantry regiment found themselves facing the oncoming invasion with their primary weapons intact. This resulted in the first waves of Allied troops facing murderously accurate fire from the German 88- and 155-mm guns while still a half mile from the beach. Several of the GATs' landing craft took direct hits. One landing craft had just dropped its ramp and the CDU men were struggling with their rubber raft when a German artillery shell came in through the open bow, detonating the explosives in the boat. It was not until the invasion was actually under way that the heavier Navy ships were allowed to move up and fire at targets of opportunity and the big German guns were finally silenced.

The members of one GAT, containing CDU 11, landed on their assigned beach at 0633 hours and found themselves ahead of the supporting infantry whose boats had been blown off course. Ignoring the heavy enemy fire and having no supporting fire of their own, the GAT set to work. CPO William Freeman was in command of CDU 11 and had worked out a change of plan with the lieutenant in charge of the Army portion of the team. Freeman's intent was to have the larger Army team demolish the obstacles from the low-tide to the high-tide marks since the tide was out and the twenty-six engineers could do the job more quickly. The thirteen men of the NCDU would assault the obstacles from the top of the beach down to the high-tide line, with the smaller team being somewhat of a lesser target to the German snipers. As the Army team began charging the Belgian Gates, placing their Hagensen Packs at the calculated positions, the NCDU found themselves facing a new type of obstacle.

This new impediment was a fifteen-foot-long timber set as a shallow ramp with the buried end facing the water. The higher end of the timber was supported by either a single thick post or two thinner posts set as an inverted V holding the higher end of the main timber five feet off the beach with a Teller mine at the top of the main post. These obstacles could sink or capsize landing craft and flip oncoming tanks over onto their sides.

As the CDU worked to set charges on all of the obstacles, some of the few DD tanks to reach the beach started to fire over the heads of the demolition men. Because the 75-mm cannons of the tanks were rather ineffectual against the protected German fortifications, the tanks only served to draw heavier fire down on the area where the CDU men were trying to work. Chief Freeman left his demolitions and, while under fire, ordered the tanks away.

As Chief Freeman returned to his task, the Army unit fired the purple warning flare indicating impending detonation. Freeman's team took cover as the gates blew and then immediately returned to their task, charging all of the obstacles down to the high-water line as the Army team began to charge all of the obstacles they could reach from the high-water line up. When the teams met, with all of the primary obstacles charged and ready for destruction, a new, unforeseen problem arose.

As the teams had been working, the infantry, which was to have provided their fire support, finally arrived, with the mostly green troops taking cover behind the obstacles ready for demolition. CPO Freeman and the engineer lieutenant broke cover to force the infantrymen away from the primed obstacles. As the fire drove down onto the beach from the cliffs, the infantry finally moved away from the charged obstacles, taking their wounded with them. At 0655 hours, the charges were blown, opening the first fifty-yard channel. At other locations the infantry refused to move from charged obstacles; one frustrated demolition man fired the delay fuse and then ran around telling the soldiers that the charge was going to blow. This finally caused them to move. At another location a late-arriving tank drove over the main primacord line, cutting it, so the charges could not be fired at all. Many of the major obstacles were not finally destroyed until several days later when Army engineer units cleared the beaches.

Though the channel was now cleared, their job was not completed. CPO Freeman and several others had to wade out into the oncoming tide to place the green-flagged channel-marking buoys indicating a clear opening for the oncoming landing craft. As the buoys were being placed, other men moved to the top of the beach to put up posts with triangles on them as additional markers for the cleared channels. All of this resulted in the first channel's being cleared in twenty-two minutes, with only five of sixteen planned channels being fully blown and an additional two channels being partially cleared in the morning's operations on Omaha.

This was an incredible accomplishment considering the environment in which the NCDUs were operating. Literally hundreds of explosions of all sizes were taking place all around them. The blasts came so close together that it seemed like one long roar! This kind of noise is so powerful that the body "locks it out." There is no obvious sound, only the feeling of the shock wave as it thuds into and through the body. More than one man's mind has come unhinged by this kind of treatment.

In addition to the explosions, there were thousands of jagged steel fragments flying through the air from the bursting shells. These whirring steel "buzzsaws," combined with the hundreds of high-velocity machine gun and rifle bullets fired by the Germans, made it lethal to crawl, let alone stand up from cover. On top of all this the air was thick with raised dust and sand, as well as the smoke and stink of burnt explosives. It was in this environment that the men of the NCDUs worked steadily, sometimes standing upright, correctly placing hundreds of explosive charges and connecting them together for detonation.

As the day progressed Freeman moved his men upward onto the beach, where they dug a trench to protect the wounded. As the trench was being dug, the men discovered that they were in a mine field. As the mines were uncovered the NCDU men simply placed them to the side and continued with their work. The NCDUs continued to work through the day, clearing the partially sunk landing craft that blocked the few cleared channels as well as salvaging explosives and equipment to continue operations. Chief Freeman's squad, reduced to four CDU men and seven engineers, cleared a second channel after the tide went out that afternoon and managed to evacuate their wounded by 1900 hours. Chief Freeman, who was wounded in the first twenty minutes of the landing, was awarded the Navy Cross and commissioned as an officer for his actions during Operation Overlord. The citation read:

> For extraordinary heroism as Leader of Naval Combat Demolition Unit TWO, attached to the ELEVENTH Amphibious Force during the assault on the coast of France, June 6, 1944. Braving heavy German artillery and small arms fire, Lieutenant Junior Grade (then Chief Gunners Mate) Freeman led his crew on to the assault beaches at H-hour plus three minutes in an attempt to blow a fifty-yard gap through the formidable beach obstacles. Although seven of the twelve-man unit were killed or wounded by the terrific gunfire, he succeeded in accomplishing this perilous and vital mission. Heedless of his own safety, he repeatedly exposed himself to intense gunfire to recover wounded personnel and bring them to a place of comparative safety. By his inspiring leadership, aggressive fighting spirit and unwavering devotion to duty, Lieutenant Junior Grade Freeman contributed directly to the success of his vital operations and upheld the highest traditions of the United States Naval service.

The vital operations of the NCDUs during the D day landings resulted in seven men receiving the Navy Cross as well as the unit receiving a Presidential Unit Citation. NCDU losses on Omaha Beach reached over 50 percent, with a high percentage of deaths due to the almost immediate loss of medical personnel in the landing. Of the 175 Navy men in the NCDU complement assigned to Omaha Beach, 31 were killed and 60 wounded.

At Utah Beach the situation was quite different, due in no small part to the first and second waves' landing almost a mile to a mile and a half to the southeast of the planned beaches. The Germans had not expected a landing on these beaches, so there were relatively few fortifications. This resulted in much lighter enemy fire than at Omaha Beach. Another positive aspect for the CDUs was the smaller number of beach obstacles encountered, few of which were mined. The first wave landed as planned, and the infantry, supported by twenty-eight DD tanks, provided covering fire that allowed the CDUs to operate with some protection. The engineer sections of the GATs did not show up until later in the morning and so the CDUs handled most of the demolitions themselves.

Since Utah Beach is located in the lee of the Cherbourg peninsula, there were much lighter waves to contend with than were encountered at Omaha Beach. The wind was offshore, slowing the advancing tide, so the eight operating CDU teams, working without their engineers, were able to open and mark eight channels within thirty minutes, as planned, and an additional six channels were marked before the tide prevented the teams from operating. Even with all this working for them, the NCDUs on Utah Beach received 30 percent casualties from the German fire.

The end result of Operation Neptune proved the usefulness and feasibility of the NCDUs as they accomplished a monumental task against heavy difficulties. The training given at Fort Pierce was also proved effective as the men were able to force themselves to consistently and accurately place more charges and demolish more obstacles as the situation warranted, although they were staggering from exhaustion. The NCDUs' most successful operation would also prove to be their last as a unit.

The lessons learned on the beaches of Normandy would not be forgotten. In the future, the NCDUs would be sent in before an operation began so that they would not have to contend with the infantry moving amongst them. The heavy protective uniforms and gas masks would be dropped in favor of simple fatigues and combat boots. The fragile marker buoys and lane-marking flags would be replaced by a better system. And last, the Army reinforcements would be dropped; the NCDUs and their descendants would become completely autonomous and dependant only upon themselves. From this beginning, the remaining men of the NCDUs and the new graduates of training would move on to Maui, Hawaii, for further training, a new mission, and yet another new name—the Underwater Demolition Teams, the UDTs

Tarawa

Rear Admiral Kelley Turner was the principal commander of the amphibious invasion of Tarawa and the Gilbert Islands, code named Operation Galvanic, and was responsible for the final decision to make the assault. Hydrographic information on the Gilbert Islands and especially on the coral atolls such as Tarawa, was extremely limited, with up-to-date intelligence being almost impossible to obtain.

The primary information sources were interviews with occupants of the atoll from before the war, as well as charts and tide tables provided by the British. The memories of individuals for the very specific type of information needed was an unknown factor, and some of the more important charts and tables dated from the Wilkes expedition voyage of 1841! The information that had been gathered was combined with photographic surveys by both aircraft and submarines and indicated to Turner that he might expect there to be up to five feet of water over the reefs surrounding Tarawa.

With this intelligence gathered Turner made his decision and the invasion was launched. The first waves of troops landed in the new, tracked landing craft, which were available in only limited numbers. Though the tracked craft ground their way over the coral reefs to the shore, the waves of troops following were carried in flat-bottomed landing craft known as Higgens boats. The Higgens boats ran solidly aground on the coral, which in some places was covered by less than two feet of water.

Combat-laden Marines left their grounded craft to wade the several hundred yards to shore. Along the way many of the men disappeared into unseen holes in the coral reefs or craters caused by the prelanding bombardment. The packs of supplies and ammunition which would have kept the men alive and fighting on the island acted as weights, dragging them to the bottom. Men were carrying one hundred pounds and more of weapons, radios, and equipment in harnesses that were not easy to slip off. More Marines drowned while trying to reach Tarawa than were killed by the Japanese in the fighting for the island.

The loss of fighting men's lives in just reaching the beach caused a tremendous uproar back home in the States as well as with the command and control staff. As a result of this, Admiral Turner became a strong advocate for the creation of a new "scout" type of unit. When the few teams of the NCDUs who were not assigned to Europe for D day started arriving in Hawaii in December of 1943, they were immediately seized upon by Turner, who saw them as the nucleus of his desired unit.

The admiral became instrumental in changing both the training and overall mission of the NCDUs and saw to it that they received immediate priority on whatever they might need. Through these means, the Underwater Demolition Teams came into being.

The UDT at War

The Marshall Islands—The Beginning

The problems of the Tarawa landings fresh in his mind, Rear Admiral Turner became the moving force behind the creation of the UDT. As commander of the Fifth Amphibious Force, Turner put forward a request for qualified demolition men to be trained as a new form of scout for use in the Pacific Theater.

The information on the tides and reef layout for the Tarawa landings had been considered the best available, and the admiral had ordered the landings in LCV(P)s that ran aground on the reefs offshore. Future assaults would have to have better information. To prevent a repeat of the Tarawa landings and fulfill Admiral Turner's request, two teams of recent graduates of the Combat Demolition Unit School at Fort Pierce were sent to Maui, Hawaii, in December of 1943 for further training. Following the outlines put forward by Turner and his staff, the units underwent a crash course of training in hydrographic reconnaissance, mapping, and other skills needed for their new duties.

All the volunteers were qualified swimmers and they received further training in distance swimming. The earliest teams did not receive a strong emphasis on swimming, which was not originally considered the teams' primary means of movement. The teams were expected to use small craft as well as rubber boats to recon an area, and the uniform for operations would still be combat fatigues, helmets, and boots. With only about four weeks to complete what would later in the war be a six-week course, the men of the CDU completed their training in time to be members of Admiral Turner's expeditionary force for the upcoming operations in the Marshall Islands. Along with their new assignment, the units received their new designation of Underwater Demolition Teams 1 and 2.

The first reported operations of the UDTs were during Operation Flintlock, the invasion of the Kwajalein atoll in the Marshalls. Both UDTs were considered "walking" UDTs at the time and wore normal combat uniforms including an inflatable life belt and a lifeline connecting each man to either his Inflatable Boat Small (IBS) or landing craft. Both the earlier NCDUs and the UDTs had been required to wear the safety line as they did not swim at their targets but rather waded in the combat uniforms with the boots protecting their feet from the sharp coral.

Goggles were also issued as an aid in underwater vision when investigating obstacles. Habitually the men of the UDTs were not armed except for a heavy knife, usually a Marine K-Bar or Navy Mark II. Direct combat with the enemy was considered far too great a risk for such highly trained men.

Kwajalein Atoll, consisting of one hundred islands and inlets, is the largest coral atoll in the world. The islands enclose an L-shaped lagoon sixty miles long by twenty miles at its widest point. Kwajalein Island itself is the largest of the Marshall Islands and is found at the southernmost point of the atoll. The Japanese had built an airstrip on Kwajalein capable of handling both fighter planes and bombers.

At the northernmost point of the atoll is Roi-Namur, two smaller islands connected by a causeway built by the Japanese before the war. Situated where it can control one of the six major passages into the lagoon, Roi was almost entirely an airfield, with Namur being a defensive position where troops were barracked.

Operation Flintlock involved two major amphibious

forces that conducted landings on thirty of the atoll's islands. Fighting took place on ten of the islands, with major resistance on three.

Admiral Conelly commanded the Northern Task Force assigned to the landings on Roi-Namur and Admiral Turner took direct command of the Southern Task Force that attacked Kwajalein Island itself. Each of the task forces received one of the new UDTs for use in the landings.

The invasion of Kwajalein Island took place at the same time as the operations at Roi-Namur. The day before the assault on Kwajalein took place, five smaller islands were captured to help secure the area and support the coming invasion. The islands of Gea and Ninne, flanking Gea Pass, v. ere captured so the pass could be used by the troop transports moving forces into the lagoon. The islands Enubu, Ennylabegan, and Gebb were also captured, with Enubu being quickly used as a base for the Army's 105- and 155-mm howitzers, which bombarded Kwajalein.

As the rest of these operations took place, a team of UDT personnel moved out in four LCV(P)s to reconnoiter the intended landing beaches on Kwajalein. The lead landing craft was stopped by the increasing number of coral heads in the water when it was only five hundred yards offshore. Though protected by a "beach umbrella" made up of the heavy naval bombardment of Kwajalein, the UDTs in their small craft were targets to any enemy guns on shore as well as vulnerable to the constant possibility of a "short round" from their own artillery. In spite of the dangers, the UDT performed their assigned tasks and more.

Two members of the team wore unauthorized swim trunks underneath their combat uniforms. When the landing craft could go no farther the two men stripped off their uniforms and dove over the sides of the craft and swam in much closer to the beach. Making notes of both the beach defenses as well as the number and location of further coral obstacles on plastic slates, the two men successfully returned to the landing craft without drawing any enemy fire.

The returning UDT members made their reports and, according to the intelligence they had gathered, the method of landing the invasion forces was changed. Originally,

Turner was going to use the LCV(P) landing craft, which can move a large amount of men and vehicles quickly to shore but needs deeper water than some craft. The LCV(P) can also run aground, as was solidly proven to Turner at Tarawa. Instead of the LCV(P)s, Turner would now send the first waves in with amtracs, which could crawl over coral obstacles with their treads but were available in much smaller numbers.

Immediately after the invasion of Kwajalein Island itself on February 1, the UDT returned to the island to blast channels through the coral, allowing reinforcements and supplies to be more easily unloaded on the beach as well as expediting the evacuation of casualties. During the battle for the island, UDT members also went on an unauthorized jaunt with the invading troops as free-lance demolitionists. The UDT was instrumental in demolishing a pillbox that was holding up the advance, but such actions were strongly discouraged by the higher commands as an unwarranted risk of key personnel.

D day for the Roi-Namur portion of Operation Flintlock started on January 31 with landings on the small islands on either side of Roi-Namur. The four smaller islands—Mellu, Ennuebing, Ennumennet, and Ennuburr, were captured to secure the upcoming operation, as well as to act as firing platforms for the Marines' artillery bombardment of the major target, Roi-Namur.

Due to the loss of men at Tarawa from the too-light preinvasion naval bombardment there was a strong wish among the naval commanders to avoid making such a mistake. Admiral Conelly ordered his ships to close in on the shore to support the landing troops with all the firepower they had. This action earned the admiral the nickname "close-in Conelly," which stuck with him to the end of the war.

The actual invasion of Roi-Namur took place late in the morning on February 1 with landings taking place on both islands simultaneously. The battleship *Mississippi* had moved to within three thousand yards of the shore, where she could cover either island with her fourteen-inch guns.

The night before the invasion of Roi-Namur, the UDT

men performed reconnaissance of the intended landing beaches. Assisted by a contingent of Marine Scouts, the UDT members performed their mission in inflatable rubber boats, mapping and surveying the beaches and waters off the intended landing sites. All of the UDTs actions took place at night under the cover of the intense naval barrage of Roi-Namur.

The intelligence gathered by the UDTs and Marines allowed the planners to best assign the available landing craft to the beaches. Amtracs were used for the landings on Red Beach 2 and 3 on Roi, with the deeper waters off Namur allowing the larger LVTs to be used for the landings at Green beaches 1 and 2. Both on Roi and Namur, members of the UDT went ashore with the troops for an unauthorized, but useful, blasting spree at targets of opportunity.

Next on the timetable for the Marshalls was Eniwetok Atoll. Eniwetok is made up of over thirty small islands and islets surrounding the second-largest lagoon in the Marshall Islands. Shaped roughly like a square with one corner pointed north and the southernmost point being open with a passage into the lagoon, the atoll is the farthest west of the Marshalls and the closest to the Japanese mainland.

A captured Japanese naval chart gave indications as to the layout and depths of the Eniwetok lagoon and showed a channel, known as the Deep Passage, on the eastern side of the atoll. Engebi Island at the north end of the atoll held a large airstrip and this was considered the primary target of Operation Catchpole, the invasion of Eniwetok Atoll.

Major General Yoshima Nishida was in charge of the defense of Eniwetok for Japan and was forced to work under great handicaps from the lack of men and materials. Nishida had beach mines available to him but lacked the skilled manpower and time to fully utilize them. Put in charge of the atoll on January 4, Nishida was expected to build underwater beach defenses. The general instead spent the time and materials he did have installing and camouflaging interior positions and gun emplacements on the islands.

Rear Admiral Harry Hill was put in charge of the amphibious forces that were assigned to Operation Catchpole. The troops that would actually make the landings were from the 106th Army Infantry of the 27th Infantry Division and the Marine 22nd Regimental Combat Team. Neither the Marines nor, especially, the Army units had received sufficient training in modern amphibious operations before Operation Catchpole, many of the Marines having never even seen an amtrac.

Following procedures that had worked at Kwajalein, the invasion fleet moved to enter Eniwetok through both the Wide Channel and the Deep Passage. Obeying their orders to remain concealed, no Japanese emplacements fired on any of the American ships as they passed into the lagoon. The greatest difficulty encountered by the fleet as it entered Eniwetok was the discovery of a naval minefield, the first encountered in the Pacific War, inside the Wide Passage that took two hours to clear.

The fleet took up their positions in the lagoon, with the first landings taking place on February 17. American artillery was landed on Aitsu and Rujoru islets, which flanked Engebi. The UDTs performed their reconnaissance of the islets from rubber boats and found the way was clear, with the landings being quickly made and the artillery being able to fire sighting shots before nightfall.

During the night of the seventeenth, the UDTs again performed a recon, this time examining the waters surrounding Engebi while under the cover of a combined naval and artillery barrage. The UDTs reports said the waters off Engebi were clear of obstacles and of proper depth, so the Marines were able to land easily against light beach defenses on February 18.

Intelligence captured on Engebi indicated to Admiral Hill that the hardest fighting for the atoll would not be on Engebi but on Eniwetok and Parry Islands. This information changed the admiral's plan and a much greater force than he had originally intended would need to be landed on Eniwetok Island.

On February 18, the day before D day on Eniwetok, two amtracs, each with a UDT squad aboard, cruised across the invasion beaches Yellow 1 and 2 for two hours. Under the cover of the naval bombardment, the amtracs were able to cruise to within fifty yards of the shore. While close in, the

UDT members quickly stripped off their combat uniforms and dove over the sides of the amtracs. Using their goggles to see, the UDTs attached warning buoys to coral heads that were too near the surface to clear the landing craft. The men also marked the clear channels through the reefs intended for the next day's attack as well as made notes of what Japanese defenses they could see that escaped the bombardment. The next morning the UDTs assisted the invasion troops by guiding the first waves through the marked channels to the beaches.

Returning later, the UDTs blasted open channels and cleared anchorages for the larger support and supply ships to gain access to the beaches. It was during the invasion of Eniwetok that one UDT received its first casualty, one man wounded during the actual landings.

The last island to be captured was Parry, bordering the Deep Passage on its southern side. On February 20 units landed on the Japten islet north of Parry across the channel. The artillery quickly set up on Japten and proceeded to shell Parry for the next three days. Maps captured on Eniwetok detailed the Japanese positions and emplacements so that the artillery and naval barrage was able to concentrate on these targets.

At 0900 hours on February 22, units of the Marine 22nd Regimental Combat Team landed on Parry. The fighting lasted through the day and by noon on the twenty-third, Parry and Eniwetok Atoll were considered secured.

Though specific records are difficult to locate, it can be presumed that the UDT performed their reconnaissance at Japten and Parry as well as they did on the other islands of Eniwetok. Operation Catchpole was to be the last major operation in which the UDTs would operate as "walking" units. It was now time for the UDT to "get wet."

The Swimming UDT

The UDTs saw little major action during the spring of 1944—March through early June—and spent their time perfecting new techniques and equipment. The experience of the earlier landings convinced the UDT planners that working from boats directly at the target drew too much fire from the enemy and made them too vulnerable a target. The combat uniforms and lifelines were abandoned to give the men more freedom to swim. The wading technique used in earlier operations was abandoned in favor of the men swimming to their target after approaching by fast boat.

As the greater emphasis on swimming continued, the goggles used were increasingly troublesome because of underwater vision distortion and the inability to easily clear them. The goggles were dropped in favor of the now familiar face mask with the single glass plate covering both eyes and nose.

It is important to note that all of the techniques and equipment had to be developed from scratch. There was a small group of spear fishermen working off the shores of California and Hawaii who used the goggles and other primitive diving equipment, but sport diving, as we know it today, was nonexistent. The UDTs were developing the ways and means for performing a task that had never been done before and they were willing to accept ideas from a wide group of sources.

Waterproof watches and compasses now became standard issue to aid in the difficult task of navigation. The buddy system was established at this time during training, with each man having an inseparable "buddy." Each man was responsible for the other's life and duties.

By this time (in early 1944) the new UDTs were receiving all of the graduates from the Fort Pierce CDU school. The men would receive six weeks of advanced UDT training at the Maui facility in Hawaii before being assigned to a UDT unit.

Lieutenant Commander Draper Kauffman, commander of the CDU school, had the school running smoothly and efficiently with a well-qualified training cadre capable of continuing the program. Feeling that his mission at the school was completed, Kauffman requested a transfer to a field unit before the spring of 1944.

Admiral Turner learned of Kauffman's availability and thought that he was just the man to further advance the UDT program. In April of 1944 Turner had Kauffman transferred to the UDT school at Maui to take the advanced UDT course and accept command of UDT-5 in time for the upcoming invasion of Saipan. Admiral Turner wanted the UDT operations at Saipan to be conducted in full daylight to allow the offshore areas to be more fully charted than was possible at night.

Saipan, in the Mariana Islands, was coveted as a forward air base for the newly developed B-29 bomber. Operating out of Saipan, the B-29 would be able to reach mainland Japan with a full bomb load and still be able to return. Saipan had actually been considered Japanese territory since 1920 and operations there would be the first held on prewar Japanese soil, a point not missed by either side.

A little over one hundred miles north-northwest of Guam, Saipan would be the first major Pacific island, rather than atoll, invaded by the U.S. Marines. The charts and available information about the offshore waters surrounding Saipan were very limited, with almost no prewar inhabitants of the island being available for interviews. The waters far offshore of Saipan are among the deepest in the world, with the island itself being one point on the summit of a tremendous underwater mountain.

Thirteen miles long by about five miles wide, Saipan is a rocky island with cliffs overlooking the thin beaches on the east side of the island and wide reefs offshore of the wider beaches on the island's west side. A short channel three miles wide separates Saipan from smaller Tinian Island to the south. Tinian, the other above-water point of the same mountain that makes up Saipan, was also of great strategic importance. The Japanese had built four airfields on Tinian to help support the defense of Saipan.

Several new methods of operation for the UDTs were developed for application at Saipan. The requirement for daylight reconnaissance eliminated the use of on-target rubber boats and the men were expected to swim to their targets. To rapidly insert or evacuate the UDT swimmers from the target area the "casting" technique was developed. This fast method of inserting and recovering swimmers had been developed only a short time before at Fort Pierce by Ensign Wade Theye and Lieutenant Tom Westerlin. The now fa-

miliar casting technique would be first used in the field by
Kauffman's UDT-5.

In the casting technique, landing craft would be used to
deliver the swimmers to the outside edge of the reef, where
the craft would then perform its drop or "splash" run. On
the offshore side of the landing craft was lashed a rubber
boat that flexed with the water. Swimmers would jump into
the rubber boat in pairs from the landing craft and immediately take up position, one behind the other, on the outboard tube of the boat. On signal the pair would roll off the
tube into the water with a second pair of swimmers immediately taking their place on the tube. Each pair would
cast off one hundred yards from the last pair with the landing
craft holding seven pairs and a swimming officer.

The swimming officer, one for each of the four landing
craft used at Saipan, was issued a waterproof walkie-talkie
with which he could send back reports or call for naval
gunfire on a specific target. The new type of hydrographic
survey performed at Saipan required each pair of swimmers
to reel out a line that was marked off at twenty-five-yard
intervals. At each interval a marked sinker line (lead line)
was dropped by one of the swimmers and the depth at that
point was marked on a plastic slate. While one swimmer
was checking the depth his buddy would be marking obstacles with buoys and making note of their location on his
own plastic slate.

Picking up the team would take place after the survey
was completed, with each of the men swimming to a point
determined before the operation started. As the men reached
the predetermined point, they would space out in a line and
wait for the pickup boat. As the landing craft made a run
along the line of swimmers, each man in turn would raise
his left arm above the water. In the rubber boat on the side
of the landing craft the recovery man would lean out over
the water and snag each man's arm with a heavy rubber
loop or "snare" and then lean back into the boat. As the
loop touched the swimmer's arm he would close his arm,
trapping the loop between his arm and body. When the
catcher leaned back the swimmer would be snatched from
the water, over the side, and into the rubber boat, from

which he would scramble into the landing craft to make room for the next swimmer.

This spectacular recovery-and-delivery system allowed the UDT men to be picked up at a rate determined by the speed of the pickup craft. Both the casting technique and the lead-line method of hydrographic survey proved very successful. The techniques first used at Saipan by UDT-5 are taught at BUD/S to this day.

The recon of Saipan was performed on the western beaches and offshore reefs starting at 0900 hours on June 14. The UDTs had to survey a section of beaches 3.5 miles long with offshore reefs that were seven hundred yards wide in places. Wearing knee pads, sneakers, shorts, and gloves for protection from the sharp coral, the swimmers were painted blue to match their deeply tanned skins with the surrounding waters. Horizontal black rings were marked on the swimmers' bodies at one-foot intervals, turning the men into human "measuring rods." This "outfit" was probably the most unique combat uniform in American military history.

The men were covered by a heavy naval bombardment of the island during most of their operation. When the UDTs were nearest the beaches the naval fire was lifted to allow a precise air strike to attack the enemy positions while the UDTs were most vulnerable. The air strike did not arrive on time and the swimmers along with their landing craft came under enemy mortar and small arms fire. Thanks to the excellent work on the part of the pickup boat crews as well as the quality and training of the UDT swimmers they were able to be picked up with relatively few casualties— two men killed, five wounded by enemy fire, and six injured by underwater concussion.

The buddy system also proved worthwhile at the Saipan operations. In one case a man was injured while swimming in to the reef. His partner performed first aid on his injured buddy, completed their assigned sections survey, and returned to tow the wounded man a further mile out to sea and safer waters. The men were both rescued three hours later.

The recon showed the areas of intended operations were

free of man-made obstacles and there was no need for a preinvasion demolition swim. New charts were prepared based on the UDT survey with new routes for the landing craft determined. Later in the day, small craft and swimmers returned to the reefs, where they marked the intended landing craft lanes. During the night of the fourteenth, the Japanese sent men out to plant marker flags between the reef's edge and beach to act as guides for defending machine gun and mortar fire. The next morning, as the invasion forces of Operation Forager moved to the invasion beaches, the UDT officers went along with the first waves to act as guides through the reefs.

After the invasion the UDTs performed demolitions on the wrecked landing craft that were blocking some of the beaches as well as blasting channels through the reefs for the support craft. Four members of the UDT went AWOL on a blasting trip with the invading troops. The risk of such highly trained and valuable specialists in unauthorized activities was seriously discouraged and, as punishment, the four men were assigned to burial details for the rest of the operation.

The captures of Guam and Tinian islands were next on the agenda for Operation Forager. Intelligence regarding the Japanese defenses on Guam was captured during the fighting on Saipan and the invasion of Guam was delayed as a result. Tinian, directly to the south of Saipan, was considered a major target. Of the four airfields on Tinian one was considered superior to the field on Saipan for use by B-29s. The Allied High Command was also concerned about the Japanese using Tinian to launch attacks against Saipan from the airfields or even an amphibious attack across the channel. A bombardment of Tinian was ordered and started on June 13 and continued until the invasion in July.

Twelve miles long, Tinian is a rocky island that is almost completely surrounded by coral cliffs facing the sea, making any amphibious assault very difficult. Only three beaches were available where invasion forces could be landed through the cliffs.

Beaches White 1 and White 2 were directly across the channel from Saipan on the north point of Tinian but were both very small. White 1 was only sixty yards wide, with White 2 being slightly larger at sixty-five yards wide.

On the east side of Tinian was another possible landing site located in Asiga Bay and referred to as Yellow Beach. The most important operations performed by the UDTs at Tinian were the investigation and chartings of the waters off the possible landing sites.

On the night of July 10 a combined force of UDT swimmers and Marines struck out in two ships for an investigation on the beaches on Tinian. Having practiced the operations earlier on beaches at Saipan the combined force was going to operate from rubber boats. The UDT swimmers were outfitted with waterproof flashlights for the first time.

Another first for the UDT was the use of shipboard radar to guide the teams in to their proper beach sites. The radar would keep the small boats on its screen and directions would be sent to the men via their waterproof walkie-talkies.

A strong current was found to be running offshore of White 1 and 2, making the reconnaissance difficult. Little was found in the way of serious obstacles by either the Marines on the beach or the UDT in the water. The team of eight UDT swimmers and twenty Marines who investigated Yellow Beach found quite a different situation. The Japanese, thinking of the beaches at White 1 and 2 as too small to allow an invasion force to land, spent their time and resources strengthening the defenses at Yellow Beach. The Marines found barbed wire entanglements on the beach as well as mines and other obstacles.

On the cliffs facing Yellow Beach they detected gun emplacements and other fortifications as well as troops patrolling the beach itself. Offshore the situation was not found to be much better. The UDTs found large potholes and boulders on the seafloor as well as a large quantity of floating mines anchored just a foot below the water's surface.

On the basis of the information gathered by the UDTs and Marines the invasion was planned for July 24 on White Beaches 1 and 2. A detailed investigation of the waters off White 1 and 2 was conducted by the UDTs before the invasion and a demolition swim was not considered necessary.

As the invasion took place the beach at White 2 was found to be heavily sown with land mines. The preinvasion bombardment of the area had only destroyed about one third of the mines on White 2 and the rest had to be cleared by hand. The men of the UDTs, being trained demolition experts, assisted the engineers and bomb-disposal teams in clearing the beach of mines and booby traps. Due to their combined efforts, the beach was cleared by midafternoon.

Guam was the last and largest of the Marianas to be captured. An American possession before the war, Guam was the first piece of American territory to be captured by the Japanese and its liberation would be a tremendous boost to the civilians back home. Three times the size of Saipan, Guam would be the largest island invaded by the Marines so far. The island was so large that its terrain varied from mountains and cliffs to dense tropical vegetation.

Though a limited number of good maps were available showing the features of the island itself, little was positively known about the coral reefs offshore except that they completely surrounded the island. The American forces had been shelling and bombing Guam occasionally since early June when Operation Forager began.

Admiral Conelly, in charge of Task Force 53 attacking Guam, intended his troops to be able to land on the beaches "standing up" with minimal Japanese resistance, so he ordered the systematic and constant bombardment of Guam starting on July 8 and not ending until the actual invasion took place.

The first recon of Guam's reefs took place at night with the swimmers of UDT-4 finding the situation anything but favorable. The reef itself was found to be dry in places at low tide, with only a shallow amount of water over it at high tide—some of the reef's coral heads were found to have only eighteen inches of water over them at high tide. The reef was about seventy-five feet wide on the average at its shallow spots. Beyond the reef, in the water between the reef's edge and the beach, a new obstruction was found.

The Japanese had built hundreds of coconut log cribs just off of the beach, all of them filled with coral rocks and connected to each other by heavy cables. The cribs and other obstacles prevented the amtracs from being able to land the invasion forces. Though the amphibious tractors could cross the reefs with their treads, they would be held up by the cribs and cables—making them sitting ducks for any Japanese fire. Further UDT reconnaissance in daylight confirmed the type and number of obstacles and indicated a massive demolition effort would be required.

A steel "hedgehog" beach obstacle

A relatively minor incident took place during the night recon that demonstrated the quality of training received by the UDTs. Three men were discovered missing after Japanese machine gun fire forced their group of swimmers to take cover. The men were later discovered at dawn a mile out to sea where they were picked up by a U.S. ship—they had been swimming for over nine hours.

Several UDTs were utilized in the operations off Guam. UDT-4 began its operations at Guam on July 14 and proceeded to perform the largest demolition project attempted by the UDT to date. Both night and day, while under the cover of naval and air bombardment or smoke screens, the two hundred available UDT men planted charges and demolished obstacles.

The demolition was performed using the high explosive tetrytol, a mixture of 75 percent tetryl and 25 percent TNT. The explosive was cast into blocks two inches square by eleven inches long weighing two and a half pounds. Eight blocks were attached lengthwise to a single line of primacord with the blocks being cast eight inches apart. The line of blocks made up the M1 Chain demolition charge, which was then packaged in an olive drab green canvas satchel that measured four by eight by eleven inches and weighed twenty-two pounds. By attaching a flotation bladder to the satchel a swimmer could tow the charge to the target with the charge floating just under the water's surface.

Each UDT man would take two or three demo packs from a rubber raft and cross the reef to plant his charges. There were so many obstacles to be demolished that some of the men crossed the reef three times in a day. The charges were connected to a main line of primacord that would detonate them all at the same instant. A delay fuse was attached to the ends of the main detonating line and ignited at the last moment by a single swimmer after the other swimmers had left the area.

After the primary demolitions were completed the UDT swimmers would return to the reef itself to blast coral heads and open boat channels to the beach. Two hundred men worked the waters off Asan Point and Agat Bay on the west side of Guam for several days, eliminating over one thousand obstacles without taking a casualty.

The night before the invasion several UDT swimmers, camouflaged white to blend with the sand, went ashore on the invasion beaches to check them before the Marines landed the next morning. On the morning of July 21, the Marines landed at two beaches on Guam with few casualties due to obstacles in the water. Mines were encountered by several amtracs off the Agat Bay beaches but this did little to slow the invasion.

The Marines of the First Provisional Brigade, long used to being the first to hit the beaches, learned that their place had been taken by a new group. Greeting the first waves of oncoming Marines was the now famous sign planted by UDTs the night before:

WELCOME MARINES
AGAT USO TWO BLOCKS
COURTESY UDT-4

After the landings, UDT-6 conducted a massive demolition project. In two days thirty-eight tons of tetrytol were fired. One test shot was a charge of nine tons of explosive and the main shot was a twenty-nine-ton charge. The blasts converted seven hundred feet of beach, reef, and coral heads into a landing ramp for heavy equipment.

The "Frogmen" Get Their Feet

Major General William Donovan was the primary moving force behind the Office of Strategic Services—better known by its initials, OSS—a clandestine agency noted for its espionage work. In creating his organization Donovan drew individuals from both military and civilian life. As a result, the OSS formed a repository for some of the highest-trained groups of World War II.

During a discussion with Admiral Chester Nimitz, Commander in Chief of the Pacific Fleet, General Donovan displayed a list of some of the highly trained men and groups he was trying to find assignments for. Among others on the list, Nimitz stated that he could find an immediate use for the OSS Maritime Unit. The men of the Maritime Unit came from Army, Navy, Marine, Coast Guard, and civilian occupations and included lifeguards and professional salvage divers. The OSS training the men received included raiding techniques, demolition, parachuting, reconnaissance, sabotage of all types, unarmed combat, and the use of a wide variety of weapons. The result of all this was a group of men very close in ability to today's SEALs.

The assignment of the OSS men to the UDT started a long tradition of cooperation between the UDT and Intelligence. Starting with the OSS/UDT in World War II, joint missions continued with the successor to the OSS, the CIA, during the Korean and Vietnam wars. Close ties still exist today between the SEALs and the U.S. intelligence community.

Some members of the Maritime Unit were sent to other groups in the Pacific Theater, but the majority were sent to the UDT school at Maui. A group of twenty-one enlisted men and five officers, including Lieutenant Arthur Choat,

C.O. of the Maritime Unit, arrived in Hawaii in June of 1944 and were assigned to a newly formed UDT team. At the same time most of the graduates of NCDU class 6A were sent to Maui to become the nucleus of UDT-10. Arriving in Hawaii on June 19, the group of UDT trainees were joined by the men from the OSS. The entire group, now known as Team 10, were placed under the command of Lieutenant Choat.

One of the first actions performed by Lieutenant Choat was to demonstrate the advantages and proper use of swim fins to the NCDU men. Swim fins had been tried earlier in the NCDU program but were dropped as being ineffective by men unfamiliar with their proper use. The OSS men were very familiar with the use of swim fins and were able to quickly teach all of the men of Team 10 how to use fins efficiently without causing leg cramps.

Commander John Koeler, commanding officer of the UDT school, witnessed the value of the new swim fins and immediately ordered his supply people to obtain sufficient numbers of the fins so that each man could be issued a pair. Swim fins still being something of a novelty, the supply people quickly bought up all the available fins on the U.S. market and still had to put out a priority contract to have a significant number manufactured. Other specialized pieces of equipment were introduced to the UDT by the men of the OSS but none had as enthusiastic a welcome as the new webbed feet for the "frogmen."

The OSS team, which had been in existence since 1942, had other skills they shared with the new UDT. The Maritime Unit had helped develop several new types of breathing equipment as well as weapons (limpet mines) and techniques for attacking ships riding at anchor. These techniques were used by later UDTs and the SEALs. Also developed for use by the Maritime Unit were the waterproof compasses, depth gauges, and watches that had been issued to earlier UDTs. None of these devices and methods had as lasting an impact on the UDT as the swim fin.

Swim fins were not the only item a harried supply department had to come up with for those "half fish, half nuts" as one admiral called the UDTs. Priority was put on any request put forward by the UDTs by direct order of Admiral Turner. Strange requests did arise but the confidential nature of UDT operations prevented any questions from being asked by puzzled supply people.

One supply officer was so alarmed at the quantity of a specialized medical item ordered by the UDTs that he managed to have a meeting with a senior UDT officer to discuss the "problem." The supply man informed the UDT officer that the teams were ordering prophylactic kits at ten times the normal amount issued and did the officer realize his men were some kind of sex maniacs?

In answer to the quartermaster's question the UDT officer took the man to the demolition range where he could see the men loading issue "waterproof" detonators into the rubber condoms, completely sealing them against water and any possibility of a wet misfire. The supply officer returned to his duties and saw to it the UDTs received anything they asked for, in whatever quantity they wished.

Preparations were commencing for the planned invasions of Peleliu and Yap islands by the summer of 1944. Observations indicated underwater obstacles were being installed by the Japanese and a request was put forward by Rear Admiral Paulus Powell for a close-in examination by the UDTs. The request included the suggestion that a submarine be used to deliver the swimmers, a method that had not yet been tried.

Volunteers came forward from Team 10 since many of the OSS men were already familiar with operations using submarines. Chief Howard Roeder, one of the instructors at the UDT school, along with two UDT officers took charge of the five enlisted men who made up the rest of the team and, on July 9, 1944, the submarine *Burrfish* quietly left Pearl Harbor on its mission.

The UDT men had been briefed that this was an especially hazardous mission and that they would be on their own without any friendly cover in the way of a naval barrage or air strike. In the event that they were captured the men were told to tell their captors that all future UDT operations were going to be performed from submarines and that the earlier UDT tactics had been abandoned.

Just a few days from the first target, a valve jammed on the outside of the submarine, shutting down the air-conditioning system. Much to the surprise of the crew, one of the UDT/OSS men was apparently very familiar with the operations of a submarine and claimed to be able to repair the valve. Due to secrecy, none of the crew knew any of the background of the UDT men or the extent of their skills other than that they were swimmers. When the UDT operator went over the side of the sub and corrected the problem it added to the already growing mystique of these web-footed warriors.

The sub was able to continue with the mission and, after avoiding a number of near-fatal encounters with enemy contacts, arrived off the coast of Peleliu. Chief Roeder and three of the enlisted men conducted the reconnaissance with a fifth man to operate the rubber boat the team would use to approach the island. The boat was launched from the submarine by the simple expedient of inflating it on the deck and submerging the ship out from underneath it. The men paddled the boat to within two hundred yards of the shore, where the swimmers then entered the water.

For two hours the men performed a grid pattern examination of the offshore waters and reefs of their assigned area, the first field use of the new swim fins. Returning to the rubber boat, which was being held on station by the fifth man, the team paddled to the *Burrfish* without incident. The result of the recon was not encouraging. The men reported that, just off the beach, there were a large number of log cribs filled with rocks and connected to each other by heavy cables. Before dawn that same night the report of the recon was radioed back to the base in Hawaii.

The *Burrfish* remained off Peleliu for two more weeks, taking photographs through its periscope and attempting to send the swimmers back in for another look. After it became obvious by the increasing amount of enemy activity in the area that the submarine had been detected on radar while surfaced, the *Burrfish* moved off into deeper waters and onward to Yap Island, the next assignment.

Arriving at Yap Island, UDT Lieutenant Massey took a team of four swimmers in to investigate the southern side of the island. Finding a heavy concentration of the same type of obstacles as were found at Peleliu, the men returned to the *Burrfish* without incident and made their report. After two days of dodging Japanese ships the *Burrfish* was able to approach the eastern shore of Yap closely enough to allow a recon swim.

Chief Roeder again led a team of three men in with a fourth man operating the boat. The seas were very rough and one swimmer who had not been UDT trained had to return to the boat aided by a UDT man. He and the operator of the boat would wait for the rest. The UDT swimmer, Robert Black, swam back to where he had left the other swimmers to continue the survey.

The swimmers had not returned to the boat after the prescribed time for their investigation had passed. After waiting as long as he could, the operator of the rubber boat, a chief named Ball, raised anchor and moved along the reef in the direction the swimmers had taken in case they were injured and could not complete the swim. With all his time used up and dawn fast approaching, Chief Ball had to return the boat to the submarine without having found the three missing swimmers.

After picking up the two men in the rubber boat, the submarine moved as close as it could to the reef and patrolled along it on the surface hoping to see some sign of the missing men. With dawn breaking, the threat of discovery forced the craft to submerge and move to deeper waters. After it was fully light, the *Burrfish* returned to the reef and performed a very dangerous patrol along the coral while watching for a sign of the missing men through its periscope. Only after detection by the Japanese and with worsening weather conditions did the commander of the *Burrfish* call off the search and move away from the island.

Records captured from the Japanese several months later showed that the UDT men had been captured and only revealed to their interrogators what they had been told to say. The men were listed as having been sent to a prison camp in the Philippines, where all record of them disappeared. Chief Howard Roeder, John MacMahon, and Robert

Black were posthumously awarded the Silver Star; the survivors of the *Burrfish* expedition also received this honor.

Peleliu was invaded by the U.S. Marines on September 15, 1944, after a successful demolition of offshore obstacles by UDT swimmers. It was decided that Yap would be too difficult and costly to take for its level of importance and it was bypassed until the end of the war.

By the fall of 1944, UDT missions were becoming standardized in their manner of execution subject to the specific conditions at the target. The primary mission role of the UDT became the reconnaissance of the assault beach landing area from the high-water mark out to the three-and-a-half-fathom line (where the water was three and a half fathoms [twenty-one feet] deep). After, or sometimes during, reconnaissance, the UDTs would clear all obstacles and obstructions that would block or otherwise hinder the landing craft.

The recon swim was usually performed during the morning or evening of D-4, four days before the invasion (D day). In the Navy, D day was also referred to as L day or Love day—L for "landing." After debriefing and after the gathered intelligence was analyzed, a demolition swim, if needed, would be performed either on D-1, the day before the invasion, or on the morning of D day itself. The reconnaissance would be performed by the "splash-run" system, with the required number of LCP/Rs (landing craft personnel/reconnaissance) each carrying one or two squads of swimmers.

On the demolition swim the same technique of the splash-run would be used to insert the swimmers. While the men would be entering the water on the offshore side of the LCP/R, crewmen would be tossing the heavy equipment, explosive packs, or marking buoys, over the shore-facing side of the craft. The men would swim to their equipment, secure it, and then continue with their mission.

The methods of placing and detonating charges had also become somewhat standardized. The system used was primarily the same as that pioneered by the NCDUs at Normandy Beach. Each swimmer would apply packaged charges of a known strength to his assigned targets as determined by the earlier reconnaissance swim.

After placing their charges, the swimmers would gather the trailing leads of primacord leading to each charge and move shoreward with them. While the men were placing their charges flank swimmers would be moving across the front (shoreward) side of the target area, moving in from the outside end.

Each flank swimmer, instead of explosive charges, would be carrying large reels of primacord, which they would unwind behind them as they moved along. As flank swimmers would meet they would tie the ends of their primacords together so that when they were finished, a long length of primacord would stretch in an unbroken line across the entire front of the target area parallel to the line of obstacles. Each swimmer would attach his charge leads by a simple knot to the main primacord line, the master line, and then swim out to the recovery point.

Individual swimmers, known as "fuse pullers," would have been laying out a line of primacord from the seaward side of the target line in to where they would attach it to the master line. The fuse pullers would attach their line at a right angle to the master line and then move back to their starting point at the seaward side of the target. The fuse pullers would wait until all of the other swimmers had been picked up and then, as their own pickup boat was moving toward them, pull the waterproof igniters on delay fuses attached to the end of the primacord line, starting the explosive train.

The delay to detonation would have been carefully calculated, giving the fuse pullers time to be safely picked up while not leaving excess time to spare. Each additional moment's delay would increase the chances of the primacord line's being broken at some point by a stray enemy shell, leaving unexploded charges attached to intact obstacles. Missed obstacles would require a return demolition swim to an area where the visibility would be poor in the stirred-up water and the enemy more than just alert.

Thanks in no small part to the expertise of the UDT

swimmers and their extensive training, a follow-up swim would rarely be needed. As the teams would be returning to their transports they would often see the waters behind them, which they had just left, erupt with a massive concussion into towering columns of white spray dotted with the remains of demolished obstacles.

Underwater Demolition Teams themselves reached a regulation size and organization with a team generally being made up of thirteen officers and one hundred enlisted men. The team would be organized into four operational platoons with a small headquarters platoon. Each operational platoon would be further broken down into three squads of eight men each, four pairs of buddies, led by an officer. The headquarters platoon would be the commanding officer along with several enlisted men. UDTs were each numbered, with several teams making up a unit and several units in turn making up a squadron. By the end of World War II there were thirty-four operational UDT teams consisting of about 3,500 personnel.

To assist in transporting this large number of men and their equipment, destroyer escorts were converted to carry a full UDT team along with its necessary supplies. The converted ships, known as Attack Personnel Destroyers (APDs), would also carry four of the LCP/R craft for inserting the team.

At Lingayen Gulf on Luzon in the Philippines the full force of a new weapon was felt by both the U.S. Navy and the UDTs. The first waves of many kamikaze attacks by Japanese suicide planes took place on January 4, 1945, with the light carrier *Ommany Bay* being struck and damaged by a single plane. The UDTs, not being directly part of the APD ships' crews, had no battle stations and could only watch as the kamikazes made their attacks.

Though the reconnaissance by the UDTs on January 7 at Luzon was made difficult due to heavy surf and murky water at the target, the UDTs completed their missions. No obstacles or mines were found and the invasion at Lingayen Gulf was able to go ahead on January 9.

Another type of suicide attack was encountered during

the Lingayen Gulf operations. The weapon was an eighteen-foot plywood speedboat that could be operated by one man and loaded with two 260-pound depth charges fused for impact and armed with a light machine gun. The damage inflicted by the speedboats was relatively light, but all craft of the American fleet stayed on station to help defend the invasion beaches from the kamikazes.

The men of UDT-9 on board the APD *Belknap* encountered several teams of Japanese swimmers who were quickly dispatched when they attempted to throw hand grenades into the UDTs' approaching small boats.

On January 12, the *Belknap* was attacked and hit by a kamikaze plane, resulting in eleven UDT swimmers' being killed and thirteen wounded, the worst loss sustained by the UDTs since Normandy.

The Final Islands

The U.S. General Staff desperately wanted Iwo Jima as an air base for B-29 operations against Japan, and its invasion was planned for mid-February. Four teams, UDTs 12, 13, 14, and 15, were placed under the command of Commander Kauffman, who was to direct their actions during Operation Detachment, the invasion of Iwo Jima.

Iwo itself is a rather small volcanic island, four and a half miles long by two and a half miles wide, shaped roughly like a pear. Mount Suribachi, an extinct volcano, is located at the southern-pointing "stem" end of Iwo.

The UDTs were to explore and clear an area of beach on the southeast side of the island extending for two miles from Mount Suribachi to East Boat Basin. The beaches started with Green, nearest Mount Suribachi, and extended north with Red 1, Red 2, Yellow 1, Yellow 2, Blue 1, and finally, Blue 2.

The APDs *Bates*, *Barr*, *Bull*, and *Blessman* put their UDTs into the water on the morning of February 17 to begin the preinvasion reconnaissance. The few man-made obstacles discovered by the UDTs consisted of underwater mines, which were quickly disabled. UDT-12, operating off Red 1, discovered several large sunken rocks off a point known as Futatsu Rock and placed buoys to mark the underwater boulders. They also put a seaward-facing flashing light on Futatsu Rock itself. The major obstruction to the landings found by the UDTs consisted of a heavy six-foot surf found to be running just offshore.

The concentration of APDs, Landing Craft, Infantry gunboats, and destroyers, all providing close-in covering fire for the UDTs, caused the Japanese to think that the LCP/Rs transporting the UDT swimmers were the invading force and the Japanese opened fire from their camouflaged gun positions.

The swimmers suffered few casualties, but the supporting craft received a severe battering and heavy losses. The gunboat Kauffman was using to direct operations received a direct hit from an eight-inch shell, killing the radio operator standing next to Kauffman but leaving the commander untouched.

The very cold waters surrounding Iwo caused cramps in many of the UDT swimmers but they continued their reconnaissance. Several of the men moved onto the beach itself to gather samples of the black volcanic sand for analysis back in the fleet. While gathering the sand, several swimmers placed yet another of the UDTs' famous signs, this one reading:

WELCOME TO IWO JIMA

The casualties among the UDTs during their operations at Iwo were low in spite of the heavy enemy fire. One man was wounded at Futatsu Rock and one man was missing and presumed lost. The missing man, Carpenters Mate 1st Class Edward M. Anderson, was last seen swimming near the base of Mount Suribachi bracketed by enemy mortar fire. Through excellent planning and extensive training, the UDTs seemed to lead charmed lives while in the water. The heaviest loss was yet to come.

On the evening of February 18, the day before the invasion was scheduled, the men of UDT-15 aboard the APD *Blessman* were relaxing, playing cards, and writing letters in the messroom below decks. Around 22.30 P.M. a single kamikaze plane approached the fleet and managed to drop two hundred-pound bombs before being shot down. One of the bombs struck the *Blessman*, penetrating down into the ship before detonating in the ship's mess. The blast killed eighteen UDT men and wounded twenty-three others as well as wounding eleven of the ship's crew members. The *Blessman* immediately caught fire, but most of the ship's fire-fighting pumps had been damaged in the blast.

Commander Kauffman, aboard the *Gilmer*, was close by the *Blessman* when the attack took place. Ignoring the fact that the burning *Blessman*'s magazines were full of tons of the explosive tetrytol, which could explode at any moment, the *Gilmer* moved in to help fight the fire with her pumps and personnel. Commander Kauffman led a boarding party onto the *Blessman* to aid the wounded and help put out the fire. The heroic actions of both ships' crews, and the UDT men, saved the *Blessman*. Forty percent of UDT-15's men were casualties of the attack, making the loss the greatest suffered by any single UDT during the war.

Operation Iceberg, the invasion of Okinawa, was next on the agenda for the U.S. Pacific Fleet. Over 500,000 men would land on the island on April 1 with 1,000 men from ten UDTs having first cleared the way. This was to be the largest amphibious operation in the Pacific and second only to the Normandy landings for all of World War II.

The UDTs for Iceberg were organized into two groups, Group Able and Group Baker. Group Able was assigned to a separate attack group that was to take the Kerama Retto, a small group of islands fifteen miles west of Okinawa, before the main landings took place.

On March 25 three UDTs started their operations among the Kerama Retto islands. The waters were extremely cold at that time of year and the swimmers coated themselves with silver axle grease to protect them from some of the cold and camouflage them from Japanese snipers.

One platoon from UDT-19 actually landed on what they thought was an uninhabited islet. One of the UDT swimmers had a pistol and the rest of the team were armed only with their knives. The Japanese who were hidden on the islet opened fire, wounding one man. The wounded man was carried back to the team's rubber boat while a single man, Ensign Bob Killough, held off the enemy with the pistol. Killough quickly followed the rest of the platoon offshore after he had run out of ammunition. The platoon was reprimanded, after their safe return to their APD, for having left the water.

The beaches of the Kerama Retto group were cleared by the twenty-sixth of March and landings began immediately on six islands of the group. On the next day, five more landings completed the capture of the Kerama Retto. Besides being an excellent base to refit and resupply ships from the Okinawa invasion fleet, another advantage to the islands' capture was discovered after the invasions.

Over three hundred of the explosives-filled kamikaze speedboats were discovered hidden throughout the islands of the Kerama Retto group. If the boats had been able to attack the main fleet they could have caused untold damage to the massed ships.

Off the beaches of Okinawa the first major operation planned by the new UDT Operations Staff was commencing. The majority of the staff's officers were not UDT qualified but were experienced coordinators and strategists. Through careful planning, combined with the experience gathered from earlier operations, the UDT flotilla performed in an outstanding manner, clearing literally thousands of obstacles from the twenty-one intended landing beaches.

Beaches Red 1, Blue 1, and Blue 2, north of the town of Hagushi, were found to contain 2,900 obstacles consisting of foot-thick logs driven into the seafloor and tied to one another with an interlacing network of barbed wire. Each obstacle had to be individually charged for destruction.

One team, UDT-11, in two solid days of operations, cleared 1,300 yards of beach of almost 1,400 obstacles. To perform the demolition the men prepared their own charges the night before the operations. Each individual charge consisted of a single two-and-one-half-pound block of tetrytol wrapped with a piece of primacord tied in a special demolition knot and having a two-and-a-half–foot trailer end for tying the charge into the master primacord trunk line. Each block, in addition to the primacord, was wrapped with a length of soft wire, with the dangling ends being used to secure the charge to an obstacle.

Four prepared charges were inserted into a fabric pouch attached to a flotation bladder and referred to as a Schantz Pack. Each swimmer would take five Schantz Packs, fifty pounds of explosives, with him on his operation.

The operations began with the reconnaissance swims on March 29 and the subsequent demolition swims on March 30 and 31. On April 1, 1945, the invasion of Okinawa itself took place with many of the UDT men guiding the first waves in to the beaches through the opened channels. Afterward, back on their APDs, the men of the UDTs helped man machine guns around the clock, defending the fleet from the almost one thousand kamikaze planes sent by the Japanese.

Further operations by Allied forces and the UDTs took place in Borneo during June and July. The intent was to further cut Japan off from supplies of oil and rubber, weakening her ability to fight. At the time of the Borneo operations the invasion of mainland Japan herself was considered necessary to finally finish the war.

Operations against the Japanese mainland were planned to take up to a year and a half, until the winter of 1946, to prepare, and that would give plenty of time for the further operations in Indonesia needed to eliminate isolated pockets of Japanese. To give the British fleet a safe haven from which to operate in the area, Brunei Bay in Malaysia, on the north side of Borneo, was to be captured. A combined force of the 9th Australian Division, backed by Task Force 6 of the U.S. Seventh Fleet, would perform the invasion on the tenth of June. On the north side of the mouth of Brunei Bay is the small island of Labuan.

While conducting a beach recon of Labuan prior to its intended capture, the UDT swimmers were bombed by planes from the U.S. 13th Air Force who mistook them for Japanese forces. The incident, which took place on June 10, resulted in one swimmer's being killed and six injured. The invasion itself took place the same day with no further losses to the UDTs.

In late June, UDTs 18 and 21 performed an in-depth recon and preinvasion obstacle demolition off a beach on the south side of Borneo. The heavy concentration of obstacles, as well as the twelve-foot surf, compounded to make the job of the UDTs particularly difficult.

The UDTs developed 150-pound packs of explosives that floated just below the surface of the water and could be pushed by a single swimmer. In spite of the heavy mortar and sniper fire from the shore, the UDTs conducted the complete demolition job with only a single casualty, a man injured by the concussion of an exploding mortar round. A postdemolition swim of the demolished obstacles was performed and the entire operation critiqued before the UDTs moved on to the actual invasion site at Balikpapan.

Though the volume of fire was much greater at the actual invasion site, the reconnaissance swim and subsequent demolition swim went off without a hitch. As a final point, the UDTs guided the first ten waves of invasion troops through the openings blasted in the obstacle barrier during the landings on July 1.

Borneo proved to be the last major amphibious operation of the war, as the Japanese surrendered after the atomic bombings in early August.

As the occupational forces from the United States moved into Japan proper, the UDTs conducted their normal beach recon prior to the troops' landing. While on Japanese soil the UDT platoon accepted the formal surrender of a small Japanese fort and received the fort commander's sword. As the Marines hit the beach they ran into the last of the now famous UDT beach signs:

WELCOME MARINES!

From the CO

The following letters were recently discovered in a desk on the island of San Clemente. They give a great deal of insight into the attitudes and problems facing the UDT teams during that war.

UNDERWATER DEMOLITION TEAM NO. 6
1 July 1944

From: The Commanding Officer
To: The Officers and Men of U.D.T. No. 6.
Subject: Forager Operation—Performance of Team Personnel.

1. Inasmuch as the end of the subject operation is near enough to permit a preliminary review of its performance, I wish to take this opportunity to thank the officers and men of U.D.T. No. 6 for the manner in which they have performed their duties.

2. In every military operation it falls to the lot of certain units to be held in reserve. The selection of the reserve units is seldom based on any conception of inferiority of those units, but rather on the military necessity that forces must be held ready for use when-

ever and wherever they may be needed. The task of adequately preparing for such a varied assignment requires a greater degree of application than is required of those performing definitely assigned duties. Furthermore, the inactivity and uncertainty necessarily arising from the reserve status imposes a severe strain on the morale and efficiency of any organization. You have borne that strain very well.

3. You have grumbled and occasionally felt left out; you have thought that the parts played by all of the teams in general and by this team in particular have been of no military value; and you have often said to yourselves that you want to get into an outfit which sees real service. To all of these complaints there are very obvious answers. The first is that it's a fighting man's privilege to grumble and gripe; his officers are always wrong, his outfit is "no good," and he's in the wrong branch of the service. If he doesn't feel that way at times he's ready for the doctors. The second is that if the work of these teams were of no military value the Commander in Chief of the Pacific area would very quickly disband the teams; and the commanders of these large task forces would hardly waste so much of the forces' naval strength in supporting the work of the teams if that work did not markedly further the successful performance of the operation. And the third answer is that if you want to get a better view of what the service thinks of your work, talk to men in other parts of the task force.

4. In spite of the difficulties under which you have worked you have done a good job on everything that this team has been directed to do. You have shown courage, skill and obedience in the face of the enemy. You have proved what I felt from the outset—that ours is the best team in the outfit. Let's keep it so.

5. This war is not yet over. There is still much unfinished business before us. In many respects our ability to do our work can be improved. It is hoped that certain changes can be made in our organization

and equipment, but we must recommend those changes to the proper authorities. You are the ones who can best discover how we can improve our team. If you have any suggestions I would like for you to discuss them with me so that proper action can be taken on them.

6. There are greater operations ahead of us; operations that before too many months will put an end to Tojo's fantastic dreams of empire and will permit us all to return to our homes and loved ones in a victorious America. I sincerely hope that it will be my privilege to be your Commanding Officer in those operations.

D. M. LOGSDON

UNDERWATER DEMOLITION TEAM NO. 6
1 August 1944

From: The Commanding Officer.
To: The Officers and Men of U.D.T. No. 6.
Subject: Commendation.

1. This team has now completed its part in the Saipan-Guam-Tinian Operation. As you know, this operation has consisted of three distinct but interrelated phases. Although the military operations of two of these phases are still underway there is no room for doubt that their outcome will be a complete victory for the American forces. When this operation is concluded a tremendously important link will have been forged in the United States' chain that is being inexorably wound around the Japanese Empire.

2. The part that you men have played in the progress of that operation should have cleared your minds of any thoughts that Naval Combat Demolition can serve no useful purpose in furthering our ultimate victory. The organization of which you are a part was born out of the blood and misery of Tarawa. Without your work and that of the personnel of the other teams that have participated in this operation many more of our forces would have died on the beaches of

Saipan, Guam and Tinian than died in trying to land at Tarawa. If that work had not been done many would also have been needlessly slaughtered because of the inability to get vital equipment ashore when and where it was needed.

3. A high ranking Marine Officer has stated that without the work done by these teams the attempted landings on Guam would have been disastrous failures. In consideration of the bravery which you have shown and of the skillful manner in which you have done your work, the commander of the Southern Attack Force has recommended that each officer and man of the teams participating in the Guam operation be awarded the Bronze Star. Such recognition of the work performed by each man in an organization is a very rare thing.

4. In the forenoon of 27 July 1944 this team was ordered to blast ramps for tank landing craft over an area of at least 700 feet on the reef off Dadi Beach on the southwest coast of Guam. This work was required to be completed before 1400 the following day. A predemolition reconnaissance of the reef indicated a very irregular reef front with numerous fissures and a large number of coral heads. Lieutenant (jg) Y. F. Carr was directed to take two platoons and make a test loading of about 200 feet of the reef. This work was begun at about 1400 and the charge was fired at about 1800. About nine tons of tetratol were used in this charge. A hurried check the next morning showed that the test shot had produced an excellent ramp with a clear approach; at about 0730 on 28 July 1944 Lieut. (jg) Carr resumed operations with the entire team, less certain personnel left aboard the *Clemson* to handle explosives. By 1230 an additional 550 feet of reef and off-lying heads had been loaded with twenty-nine tons of tetratol. This shot was fired at 1245. Due to the departure of the *Clemson* from the area that afternoon it was impossible to test the ramp that was blasted, but it was probably as good as that of the previous day. It is believed that this is a record

for U.D.T. reef loading and blasting and has been reported as such to the base of Maui.

5. While this work was going on Lieutenant (jg) F. M. Methvin organized a detail of U.D.T. No. 6, aided by personnel generously furnished by the *Clemson*, and transferred all unexpended U.D.T. explosives from the ship to the beach as well as loading all boats returning for tetratol. A total of twenty-two tons of various types of explosives were removed from storage space and sent to the beach and seventeen tons of tetratol were sent out to the reef.

6. As a result of the excellent job of organizing done by Lieutenants (jg) Methvin and Carr and by the other officers of the team and of the careful and diligent work done by the men of U.D.T. No. 6 the team accomplished what had seemed an impossible task.

7. My heartiest congratulations on a tough job well done.

D. M. LOGSDON

UNDERWATER DEMOLITION TEAM NO. 6
22 October 1944

From: The Commanding Officer.
To: The Officers and Men of U.D.T. No. 6.
Subject: Palau and Leyte Island Operations—Performance of Team Personnel.

1. Upon completion of the underwater demolition work required in connection with the retaking of Guam, this team was ordered to join the task force which was then being assembled for the attack on Palau. Pending departure from the staging area the team was reorganized, additional personnel were obtained and a full outfit of battle equipment was procured.

2. Military intelligence indicated that the Peleliu phase of the Palau operation would entail difficult and dangerous work for the team, but it was not until the reconnaissance data was assembled that the real

character of the work became known. The three beaches and the LST landing area which were assigned to this team were found to be littered with large coral boulders which would prevent the passage of tanks, DUKW's and vehicular equipment. Furthermore, the enemy had erected lines of heavily braced posts near the shore abreast these beaches. The reconnaissance showed that passages had to be blasted through these boulders and obstacles before landings could be made, and it showed how effectively the enemy had emplaced its heavy machine guns covering those beaches.

3. The attack plan assigned two of the beaches to this team and the third beach and the LST area to another team. An operational casualty in the early morning of the day on which the work was to begin, however, made the employment of that other team impossible and necessitated the assignment of all the work of both teams to Team No. 6.

4. The reconnaissance, made three days before the assault, was accomplished under heavy machine gun and sniper fire. On the two following days the operating platoons were engaged in blasting boulders on the reef where all hands were exposed to constant enemy fire. On the second night before the assault eight demolition groups from this team proceeded across the reef under cover of darkness and placed over a thousand demolition charges within fifty yards of the enemy machine guns and rifle pits; these charges cleared the obstacles to the beaches. A happy combination of good fire support, coolness and battle-wisdom on your part and rare good luck enabled you to accomplish these dangerous tasks without a casualty.

5. On the twelfth day of the battle for Peleliu when the marines had driven the enemy to the northern end of that island, this team and Team No. 8 were directed to conduct a daylight reconnaissance of the narrow strait between Peleliu and Ngesebus Islands.

The reconnaissance parties were required to swim a total distance of three miles; over a great part of this distance they were under constant mortar, machine gun and sniper fire from both shores.

6. The excellent work that you did in that operation, under conditions which were worse than those ever before experienced by an underwater demolition team, aroused the unstinted praise of all fair-minded observers. The commander of the demolition group, in his action report on the Peleliu operation, commended this team for its "outstanding performance in action requiring extraordinary courage and endurance while working with high explosives on an exposed reef without natural cover, while under enemy machine gun and sniper fire, for daylight reconnaissance under fire on 12 September 1944 and 26 September 1944 and night demolition work close to enemy-held beaches."

7. Upon completion of the Ngesebus reconnaissance the team was ordered to join the task force which was then assembling for the long awaited attack on the Philippine Islands. In this campaign, however, the conditions were far different from those to which you had become accustomed. The attacking force had such a wide choice of islands and beaches that the enemy was unable to prepare adequate beach defenses. Your task was therefore far easier than it had ever been in the earlier operations. Since there were no man-made obstacles nor coral to be removed, your only task consisted of reconnoitering the assault beaches and searching for mines. The enemy was able to give you a moderately warm reception with its mortars, machine guns and sniper fire but you did your job quickly and well.

8. This war will go on for many months more, but the extent to which beach reconnaissance and underwater demolition work will be necessary in those future theaters of action remains to be seen. Of this, however, you can be fairly sure—no team will ever

be required to do a more difficult and dangerous job than this team did at Peleliu, nor will it be able to do it better.

9. You can now look back on four successful operations, operations in which you carried out your dangerous missions with superb courage and skill. You have won the respect and admiration of those fighting men for whom this work was done.

10. In congratulating you for what you have already done I feel sure that in the performance of those duties that lie ahead you will show the same courage and competence that you have in the past.

D. M. LOGSDON

The UDT Gets Gills

The Postwar Years

During World War II, thirty-four UDTs had been commissioned. By the end of the war thirty of these teams were in the field and four teams were in training. The last UDT to see official "action" against the Japanese was UDT-26. During October 1945, UDT-26 performed beach-clearing operations at several locations on the Japanese mainland. The operations were to remove mines and beach obstacles to allow the landing craft of the U.S. 8th Army occupying forces to land safely. After this rather tame operation, UDT-26 was moved to Coronado, California, for demobilization.

By February of 1946 the last of the wartime UDTs had been demobilized and their equipment put into storage or sold as surplus. Since the end of the war the UDTs had been performing "cleanup" operations, clearing areas of obstacles, eliminating mines, and assisting in the destruction of hundreds of tons of Japanese ordnance. With these jobs completed, the teams were disbanded and many of the men returned to civilian life.

Some of the UDT swimmers who stayed in the Navy after

the war returned to fleet duties in their original specialties. Out of the 3,500 UDT men of the war years, only a few hundred were retained in postwar teams. Four new UDTs were commissioned in 1946, with the first, UDT-1, receiving its commission on May 21. Two of the new UDTs, 1 and 3, remained in Coronado, where they were attached to the Pacific Fleet (ComPhibPac). In June of 1946, UDTs 2 and 4 transferred to their permanent assignment with the Atlantic Fleet (ComPhibLant) and were stationed at Little Creek, Virginia.

A few members of the new UDTs became closely involved with the new era of atomic warfare when they were assigned to Operation Crossroads. In July of 1946, the Navy exploded two atomic bombs to measure their effect on ships. The UDT men assisted in the preparation and measuring of the beaches of the Bikini Lagoon where the blasts would take place. Test Able was an above-water detonation of a twenty-kiloton air-dropped bomb on July 1. The same work was done by the UDT to prepare for Test Baker, the shallow underwater blast of another twenty-kiloton device fired on July 25, 1946. Almost no information is available on the extent of UDT involvement with the development of the atomic Navy. It is known that the UDT men were considered instrumental in the pre- and postblast surveys conducted at Bikini in 1946.

In the postwar era of "push-button" warfare the mission of the UDTs was considered obsolete. The massed invasion armadas of World War II could not be gathered in one place safely given the existence of atomic weapons. The general opinion was that the swimmer/demolitionist could no longer operate effectively and that the UDTs' greatest weapon, surprise, was now gone.

A new project was undertaken by the UDTs to try to increase their capabilities. The quest was for a method to allow the swimmers to remain underwater for more than the thirty to sixty seconds a man could hold his breath and continue to work. During the war an underwater combat team, using the then new Lambertson Amphibious Respiratory Unit (rebreather), was formed by the OSS. This OSS team later became part of the Maritime Unit that worked closely with the UDT.

The wartime mission of the UDT did not call for extended underwater swimming, and the complex rebreathers were not called into general use. Postwar experimentation proved the usefulness of the rebreather but a way had to be found around the limitations of the system. Pure oxygen becomes toxic at a pressure equivalent to a depth of thirty feet in salt water and poisonous at a pressure of sixty feet. The rebreather, however, does not release any bubbles into the water to betray a swimmer's position.

A fully automatic, high-pressure-air breathing system had been developed in France in 1943 by J. Y. Cousteau, then a French naval officer and diver, and Emile Gagnan, an engineer. The device had been smuggled out of France and kept out of German hands during the war. It was referred to by its inventors as the *Scaphandre-autonome*, but we now know this important device as the aqualung or scuba (self-contained underwater breathing apparatus).

The introduction of the aqualung allowed a swimmer complete freedom while underwater for a period of up to several hours and to a depth past 140 feet. The use of this system allowed the UDTs to develop new techniques underwater without the danger of oxygen poisoning. The aqualung is, however, an open-circuit design and releases bubbles into the water. These bubbles could easily give away a swimmer's position in wartime.

The open-circuit designation for the aqualung means that the swimmer uses the breathing mixture, usually air, only once and then exhausts it into the water. The heart of the system is the demand pressure regulator pioneered by Cousteau and Gagnan. The regulator releases air, automatically adjusted to the pressure of the water, when the user sucks on the intake. The air is carried in steel or aluminum tanks, where it is held at a pressure of several thousand pounds per square inch. This type of system is relatively easy to use and was first obtained by the UDTs in 1947.

The closed-circuit system, such as the Lambertson rebreather does not release any bubbles into the water and the swimmer breathes the same gas over and over. As the swimmer exhales, the gases enter a flexible breathing bag. Before the gases can inflate the bag they must first pass through a canister where the carbon dioxide breathed out by the swimmer is chemically absorbed. Extra oxygen, replacing that amount used by the swimmer, is added to the gases in the breathing bag before being "rebreathed." The system is complex and has a great number of dangers inherent in its use. But a swimmer with a closed-circuit rebreather is very difficult to locate from the surface. The rebreather also tends to have a much longer underwater staying time, up to six hours, than a conventional open-circuit system.

With the variety of open- and closed-circuit systems used by the UDTs and the SEALs, any system is either known by its specific name, such as Mark IV, or by the collective term UBA (underwater breathing apparatus).

Besides the problem of suppyling breathing gases underwater the problem of heat loss by the swimmer to the surrounding water was a severe one. The UDT operations off Okinawa were made more difficult because of the cold temperature of the water. In relatively cold (60°F) water the average man can survive for about two hours. In cold (42°F) water, that same man will be helpless inside of thirty minutes and probably dead after an hour. To allow the UDT swimmer to function in very cold water the dry suit was developed shortly after the war. In the dry suit the swimmer would wear a set of normal long underwear to create a layer of trapped air. To trap the air and keep the water out the swimmer would wear a suit made of thin rubber over the underwear. The rubber suit would be sealed at the face, hands, and feet to keep the swimmer's body dry. While wearing the dry suit the UDT swimmer could operate in very frigid waters for a reasonable length of time. The greatest failing of the dry suit was that it was relatively fragile and any holes in it would allow water to leak in, destroying its insulating properties.

In 1947 UDT-1 used the dry suit while involved in the Point Barrow Alaska Resupply Expedition. This was the first of many operations for the UDT in arctic waters. A detachment of men from UDT-1 worked with Marine reconnaissance personnel during joint maneuvers against Kodiak Island near Alaska. The combined UDT/Marine unit conducted its operations from the submarine *Perch* (APSS 313) during the maneuvers.

By 1948, the UDTs had reached their lowest numbers in terms of personnel. Each UDT retained only a skeleton complement of seven officers and forty-five enlisted men. Still, development of new capabilities continued. The UDTs perfected lockout techniques that allowed them to operate from a submarine while it was submerged. The technique would work with either open- or closed-circuit UBAs. The swimmers would leave or enter the submerged submarine through its forward escape trunk, preferably while the ship was stopped, but the operation could also be done while the vessel was under way.

Proved safe during fleet maneuvers near Florida, the new lockout techniques allowed a few UDT swimmers to leave their submarine undetected in simulated wartime conditions. These same UDT men successfully attacked a large fighting ship while it was under alert. The men attached limpet mines to strategic sections of the ship and officially "sank" her. Though the UDT swimmers would have been able to get back to their own ship safely, they surfaced and were "captured" in order to inform the captain of the major ship that he had been "sunk"!

Even though it was peacetime the men of the UDTs were at risk. The equipment and techniques they were developing were still experimental and not all the hazards were known. Though using air with the open-circuit UBAs eliminated the chance of oxygen poisoning, a new difficulty had to be overcome. Past a depth of about 100 feet in saltwater the nitrogen normally found in air starts to become toxic. Nitrogen narcosis becomes a serious problem past about 180 feet and deadly much past 300 feet. While intoxicated from nitrogen a diver can easily make a mistake that could cost him his life.

With training a man can overcome many of the effects of nitrogen narcosis, and the UDTs train very hard. The use of other gases, such as helium, prevents nitrogen narcosis and offers the possibility of deeper dives with relative safety. In 1949, a UDT volunteer, Boatswains Mate Harold Weinsbraud, was taken to an equivalent depth of 561 feet using a helium/oxygen mixture while in a simulated dive in a pressure tank.

Bullfrog of the Pond*

Master chief Boatswain's Mate Rudy Boesch has spent the last 42 years on active duty with the U.S. Navy and he looks it, with his close-cropped silver hair and his tanned face, well-weathered by wind, sun and sea. Boesch says he has wrung more saltwater out of his socks than most sailors have ever sailed on. Although he has served in the Navy just eight years short of a halfcentury, Boesch still doesn't quite fit the image of an "old salt." Even if he has spent the last 35 years in Navy special warfare (specifically in UDTs and SEALs), Boesch, 59, is no dowdy, bewhiskered, sea-going sexagenarian, but a fit, active, hard-working sailor.

Boesch needs to stay fit, since he is presently the enlisted ramrod of SEAL Team Two, based at Little Creek, Va. He is also the only Team Two plankowner still on active duty and holds the distinction of being the senior enlisted man within the special warfare community. "I'm what the SEALs call the 'bullfrog,'" said the Rochester, N.Y., native. "That means I'm the senior guy in terms of length of

*As published in the official Naval publication and reprinted from *All Hands* magazine, December 1987.

service in special warfare." In recognition of this honor, a replica of a large bullfrog sits in the showcase at SEAL Team Two headquarters. "That frog is mine until I retire," said Boesch. "Then I turn it over to the next guy with the longest time in."

But retirement is not on this SEAL's agenda at the moment. "With any luck, when I leave, it'll be because I died on the quarterdeck," Boesch said. "I don't even want to think of retirement. Even though the Navy can pay three seamen for what they pay me, by letting me go they would lose all I know," he said. "Maybe the policy is to put out anyone who has been over 30 years . . . but they haven't said anything about those with over 40 years," he said with a smile.

Boesch first enlisted in the Navy in 1945, just before the end of World War II. Although the war in Europe ended while Boesch was in recruit training, Japan was still undefeated in the Pacific when he completed boot camp.

Boesch recalls that, one day shortly after graduation from boot camp, his company was lined up and the company commander asked if anybody wanted to volunteer for duty with a special outfit. Boesch was the only one to raise his hand. At that moment, his long association with Navy special warfare began, for Boesch had just volunteered to serve with the UDTs, otherwise known as the Scouts and Raiders.

Sent to Fort Pierce, Fla., then home of the UDTs, Boesch became part of one of the most illustrious special warfare units to come out of World War II and one that would become the nucleus of the present-day SEALs.

Boesch said that the UDTs at Fort Pierce learned demolition, small boat handling, combat swimming and small arms, and were taught how to help organize guerrillas in Japanese-occupied China. These guerrilla units would have supported the planned Allied invasion of Japan had the war not ended in August 1945.

With the war over, the Scouts and Raiders were soon disbanded. Boesch recalled, "We had to tear our base down at Fort Pierce. We did it overnight. It wasn't very difficult, since we were living in tents."

Following the decommissioning of the Scouts and Raiders in 1945, Boesch was assigned duties with, as he put it, "the regular fleet." For the next six years, the former commando served both at sea and ashore at duty stations ranging from Shanghai, China, to Grosvenor Square and the American Embassy in London, before rejoining the UDTs and the special warfare community in 1951. He hasn't left since.

Boesch remained a combat swimmer with the UDTs for 11 years until 1962 when the mission of special warfare was expanded and the UDTs took on a new name and role. They became known as "SEALs" because they would operate in the three environments of Sea, Air and Land and would be called upon to conduct unconventional warfare at sea and in coastal and river areas. The initial muster role was made up of men already in the old UDT organization. Initially, two SEAL teams were established; Boesch was one of the first members of SEAL Team Two, formed at Little Creek, Va. That was a long time ago.

Boesch joked, "I have more time at Little Creek than some of the barbers do in the barbershop there. Military barbers are like permanent fixtures at some bases—they never seem to leave. But I've seen a lot of them come and go at Little Creek, which gives you an indication how long I've been there with special warfare."

According to Boesch, it takes a very special person to be a SEAL. It requires excellent physical conditioning, motivation and determination. Parachuting from fixed-wing aircraft or helicopters, swimming or rafting long distances to shore from a ship or submarine, exposure to arctic water, jungle swamps and survival in enemy-controlled areas are all a part of being a SEAL. Just thinking about such demands makes some men shudder. But for those in the SEAL teams, like Boesch, these challenges are the spice of life.

Boesch, who served with the SEALs in the Mekong Delta and Cam Ranh Bay during the Vietnam War, says, "being a SEAL is one of the best things in the Navy. I obviously like what I'm doing or I wouldn't have stayed in so long. If I got out I couldn't duplicate what I've got now. It's an exciting life. When you get up in the morning, you don't know whether you'll soon be finding yourself 30 feet underwater or 10,000 feet in the air. That's what I like about it. There's something different every day.''

The men who work closely with Boesch in Team Two accord him the highest respect with their genuine praise. ''Rudy Boesch is one heck of an individual,'' said one team member. ''He sets a good example for all of us. He's a real morale builder.''

Another member in the training cadre said that, thanks to Boesch and his extensive experience, there is a lot of continuity in the team. He said, ''Nothing changes with Rudy. For example, on Tuesdays, he always looks for haircuts. If you don't have a haircut, you stand duty. There is no question with anybody in the team—if it's Tuesday and your hair is getting long, Rudy's going to tap you on the shoulder and you will have the duty.''

The member also added, ''Rudy sets the standard. When he says 'complete uniform,' it's complete uniform with brass polished and shoes shined. Nothing changes from one year to the next. You always know where you're supposed to be, when you're supposed to be there and how you're supposed to look when you arrive.''

Boesch's rank, experience, and seniority allow him considerable latitude in his duties with the team. ''He really does it all,'' as one member put it. During training exercises, Boesch may do all the administrative chores so that the training cadre can devote their full energy to training SEAL teams in the field. On the other hand, he may decide to assign the administrative details to others and take personal charge of the team, leading the men in a regimen of PT, running and swimming that would make the most fanatic fitness freak cringe in terror.

Boesch has seen a lot of changes in the Navy over the years, but he is impressed by what he sees today. ''The Navy is in good shape right now and we are getting some real high-caliber people, especially in the SEALs,'' he said. ''We have men in this outfit who can do anything. They're intelligent, they learn quickly and can think for themselves.''

Boesch admits that if he had it all to do over again, he wouldn't change a thing. "In the SEALs there is always something new and different to see and do all the time," he said. "It's an exciting life."

Rudy Boesch, a satisfied bullfrog, summed up his career with a smile. "Just being with the SEALs has been one good, long experience."

The UDT in Korea

The peacetime operations of the UDT came to an end on the morning of June 25, 1950. On that date the North Korean Peoples Army (NKPA) crossed the 38th parallel and invaded South Korea in force. President Harry Truman immediately ordered his Far East Commander, General Douglas MacArthur, to support the South Koreans with ammunition and equipment. After seeing the situation in Korea and reporting to Truman, MacArthur was authorized to use naval and air forces against the NKPA.

A detachment of ten men from UDT-3 was in Japan when the North Korean invasion took place. Under the command of Lieutenant (j.g.) George Atcheson, the detachment was in Japan to train with the American 8th Army. Training was suddenly cut short and the UDT men ordered to Rear Admiral James H. Doyle's flagship, the U.S.S. *Mount McKinley*.

The UDT team learned of the situation in Korea upon their arrival on the *McKinley*. Admiral Doyle was the commander of the 1st Amphibious Force and had been ordered by MacArthur to break the Communists' line of supply from the north. Due to the rocky terrain of most of Korea, especially the shores, and the technical inadequacies of naval radar at the time, the Navy's guns could not sight on the NKPA supply trains, which were moving south at night. The answer to stopping some of the trains was thought to lie with the UDTs.

The UDTs had been receiving training in land operations, night reconnaissance, small unit tactics, and weapons since the end of World War II. Commander John T. Koehler had been the commander of the advanced UDT training base at Maui during the latter part of World War II. Having won a Silver Star while commanding UDT-1 during the Roi-Namur operation, Koehler had a good grasp of the potentials of the UDTs. Koehler saw the UDTs as having to move inland to continue their primary mission of reconnaissance. Training for land combat would increase the UDTs' chances of survival and Koehler saw to it that the necessary skills were incorporated into the UDT training schedule.

Commander Koehler's training program was continued after the war and was incorporated into the UDTs' mission profile. Koehler's vision of the possibilities of the UDTs included inland demolition raids, intelligence gathering, and the infiltration/exfiltration of guerrillas or intelligence agents. The image of the UDT put forward by Commander Koehler almost exactly correlates with the missions and capabilities of today's SEALs.

Lieutenant Atcheson learned that the mission given to his UDT group was not to scout a beach for a possible landing. The men were to demolish a railroad bridge at Yosu, forty-five miles behind the enemy lines!

The team was quickly moved to the APD *Diachenko*, which would act as their base of operations. Late in the evening on August 5, the *Diachenko* arrived in the target area. Two LCP/Rs, each towing an Inflatable Boat, Small moved away from the *Diachenko* toward the beach. In the first IBS was Lieutenant Atcheson and Boatswain's Mate Warren G. Foley, along with their chosen weapons and equipment. In the second IBS was Lieutenant Bill Thede, along with a landing party of UDTs. Thede's men would transport the explosives aboard their IBS and then move them inland to the target, acting as a "powder train."

Atcheson was concerned that the bright, full moon was a sign of bad luck, as it clearly illuminated the target area. After being towed to within one thousand yards of their target, Atcheson and Foley cast off from the LCP/R and began paddling their IBS toward shore. The primary target turned out to be inaccessible to the men if they landed on the beach so they paddled to a secondary target, a railroad bridge and tunnel, nearby.

Atcheson and Foley paddled five hundred yards closer to their target before entering the water for a quiet swimming insertion. Not having brought flotation equipment for their two heavy Thompson submachine guns irritated Atcheson, who decided that they would leave the guns behind. Taking three hand grenades and a .45-caliber pistol for himself, Atcheson entered the water. Foley armed himself with several grenades and his K-Bar combat knife and quickly followed his lieutenant.

The two men swam for five hundred yards against a surprisingly strong current before they reached the beach. The swim took the men thirty minutes and left them strained on the shore. UDT training took over and Atcheson and Foley got up and continued their mission. Moving inland the two men almost immediately found their way blocked by a twenty-foot-high seawall. Finding a way around the seawall, the two scouts moved to the intended target for a fast recon. Signaling with their penlights for the other IBS to come to shore, Foley backtracked to the beach in order to lead the powder train to the target.

While waiting at the target for the powder train, Atcheson suddenly found himself facing a railroad handcar with ten North Korean soldiers aboard. The Koreans stopped after leaving a tunnel, probably startled at seeing the rubber boats, LCP/Rs, and APD all lying out before them lit up by the full moon. Atcheson quickly recovered and took cover under the railroad bridge. Foley heard the arrival of the North Koreans and rushed back to where he had left Atcheson, bringing a Thompson submachine gun with him. As Foley ran along the seawall, both the North Koreans and Atcheson, not identifying the armed figure running toward him, opened fire. Foley fell off the seawall, out of sight onto the rocky beach.

Realizing the situation was more than a single UDT should probably face, Atcheson made ready for a run to the beach. Throwing his grenades at the Koreans, Atcheson "retired from the target area." The startled Koreans took cover from the explosions and probably thought the APD was shelling them. Atcheson stopped to look over the seawall on his run back to the beach and almost had his naval career cut short as an alert sailor on the beach, expecting an armed Korean soldier, shot at the lieutenant's head as it appeared over the wall. Atcheson soon convinced the sailor just who he was shooting at and the group quickly returned to the *Diachenko*.

Foley, who had been picked up on the beach, was wounded in his hand and thigh besides having smashed his kneecap in the fall. The injuries resulted in Foley's being the first official Navy casualty of the Korean War. Atcheson was very relieved to learn of Foley's survival, and even more relieved when he learned that Foley's wounds had been caused by rifle-caliber bullets and not by heavy-caliber slugs such as those fired by a certain Navy-issue .45 pistol.

As the *Diachenko* was returning to Japan, the APD *Horace Bass* (APD 124) was arriving at Camp McGill, twenty miles outside of Yosuka, Japan. Aboard the *Bass* was UDT-1 with a half-strength complement of fifty men under the command of Lieutenant Commander David F. "Kelly" Welsh. Also aboard the *Bass* were two platoons of the Marine 1st Amphibious Reconnaissance Company under the command of Lieutenants Dana Cashion and Phil Shutler. After returning to Japan and debriefing, Lieutenant Atcheson's UDT detachment was attached to UDT-1. The UDT-and-Marine unit was combined into the first Special Operations Group (SOG).

Marine Corps Major Edward P. Dupras, a decorated veteran of World War II, was put in charge of the two Marine platoons of the SOG. Intense training followed for both the UDT and Recon personnel. Lessons taught by Atcheson's unsuccessful raid and the experiences of the many combat veterans in both the UDT and Recon Marines were combined for a Standard Operating Procedure (SOP) for the unit.

The SOG was to perform reconnaissance and demolition raids along the Korean coastline, well behind the enemy lines. The primary mission for the SOG was to "disrupt enemy logistics" by "destroying tunnels and bridges of coastal railroads and highways." To complete this mission the SOG developed the following SOP:

1. Personnel would be transported to within striking range (two or three miles) of an objective aboard the *Bass*.
2. The *Bass* would launch her LCP/Rs, which would tow IBSs carrying the raiding party of UDTs and Marines. The LCP/Rs would move to within one thousand yards of the objective before releasing the IBSs. *Note*: Since the LCP/Rs had special mufflers attached to their engine exhausts, they made little noise to possibly alert enemy guards.
3. The lead UDT IBS would paddle to within five hundred yards of the shore before at least two scout swimmers would leave the boat for the final swim in to shore. Other UDT men aboard the IBS would use the new infrared "snooper scope" and binoculars to examine the target area as best they could.
4. The scout swimmers would perform a brief, fifteen-to-thirty-minute, advance recon of the objective area before calling in the rest of the raiding force. The call-in would be by a prearranged signal, usually a penlight.
5. The Marines of the raiding force would quickly establish a security perimeter around the objective. With the perimeter secured, the UDT would move to the target and "load" it with explosives. The explosives would be connected by primacord with an additional primacord line laid out to the perimeter edge. The end of the primacord line would be attached to a thirty-minute-delay detonator system.
6. All personnel would return to the LCP/Rs using the IBSs except for the fuse pullers. After confirming everyone else was away, the fuse pullers would initiate the delay

system and then quickly join the rest of the raiding team. Returning to the APD, the team would witness the explosion and report for debriefing.

The SOP worked well and the Special Operations Group conducted several successful missions using it. North Korean supply lines were constantly being disrupted, due in no small part to the SOG's successful targeting of tunnels and bridges. On one such operation the scout swimmers of a twenty-five man raiding party located their target fifty feet above the beach and more than 150 yards from the water.

The target was a small railroad bridge between two tunnel mouths. When the scouts approached the target they found two sleeping North Koreans in an unarmed machine gun nest near one of the tunnels. Instructed to immobilize the captured "guards," the UDT scouts tied them up with the closest available material—primacord. The two Koreans probably never realized they had on the deadliest "handcuffs" ever used.

Calling forward the balance of the team, the raiders quickly loaded the tunnel mouths and bridge with explosives. As the raiders were returning to their APD they had the "pleasure" of seeing a loaded supply train sweep through the target area ten minutes before the charges went up. The *Bass* returned to Japan to restock with explosives for further missions.

When the North Koreans invaded the South they found that the South Korean army was able to offer little in the way of effective resistance. The actions of the SOG from August 12 through 25, combined with U.S. air strikes and other missions, served to slow down the North Koreans' advance by limiting their supplies.

The U.S. and UN forces found themselves driven south until they reached Pusan on the southeast coast of Korea. Combining with the few remaining units of the South Korean army, the UN forces dug in to a line of positions around the city. This line of fortifications and foxholes came to be known as the Pusan Perimeter.

Reinforcements arrived from the United States and Great

Britain to assist the beleaguered defenders at Pusan. In early September a final offensive by the NKPA was thrown against the Pusan Perimeter and the line held. Disrupted and confused, the NKPA began a withdrawal from the UN forces. To complete the destruction of the NKPA an amphibious landing was suggested by MacArthur to split up the NKPA forces.

Rear Admiral Doyle and 1st Marine Division C.O. General O. P. Smith were convinced that MacArthur's preferred location for an invasion, Inchon, would be too difficult and that an alternate location should be found. The SOG was ordered to suspend demolition raids and concentrate on hydrographic surveys of possible landing sites. Major Dupras was given a list of alternate sites and told to develop the techniques needed to survey them.

The earlier SOP for insertion procedures was used with changes to meet the new problems. Since the invasion beaches were in enemy hands any advanced warning given to the Communist forces had to be avoided and this ruled out traditional recon techniques in daylight. Nighttime survey methods had to be created and perfected. Landings would be done as before with the Marines establishing a secure perimeter around the target area after an initial survey by scout swimmers.

Pairs of UDT swimmers would work together using "flutterboard" lines and lead lines to survey one thousand yards of beach frontage. One man of a pair would remain ashore, securing one end of the flutterboard line and controlling two range lights. The range lights would be two poles, one three feet tall and the other five feet tall, with flashlights attached. As one UDT swimmer would swim out from the beach with the flutterboard line he could look back at the beach and keep his direction. When one range light was directly above the other the swimmer would know he was traveling out at ninety degrees from the beach. As the swimmer moved out from the beach he would stop at regular intervals, marked on the flutterboard line, and measure the water's depth with his lead line, making notes on his swimmer's slate. When the swimmer had reached a point where the water was twenty-one feet deep, the twenty-one-foot curve, he and his partner on shore would move fifty feet along the beach. After the two men had moved along the shore and aligned the flutterboard line with the range lights, the swimmer would move in toward shore. As the swimmer moved in he would again take depth soundings at regular intervals in from the twenty-one-foot curve to the beach.

On August 21, the *Bass* arrived at the first of the alternate landing sites, the head of a small bay sixty miles south of Inchon. With a full moon illuminating the operation, the SOG survey was completed without problems. A sandbar near the landing site almost grounded the *Bass* on the way in to the target. Besides depicting the sandbar that almost captured the *Bass*, the report from the UDT survey indicated the beach was not a suitable landing site.

Another alternate landing site was next surveyed by the SOG. The site was a beach south of Inchon near the Kunsan airfield. The team timed their insertion to just before high tide so that they would be able to leave on the ebb tide. Major Dupras himself led the Marine security detachment to the beach after the preliminary investigation by the scout swimmers. Dupras held an ill feeling about the operation's being conducted while a full moon shone over the beach area.

As the UDTs started their survey, Major Dupras moved up and down the beach, staying in constant contact with the UDTs and Marines by radio. As luck would have it, the beach chosen for the initial survey was between two North Korean strong points. A permanent machine gun nest was located at one end of the beach and a troop barracks was at the beach's other end.

A short time into the survey, Marine sentries reported that armed soldiers were approaching the survey party. Koreans in the machine gun nest had seen movement on the beach and had called for troops from the barracks to investigate. As soon as the Korean troops approached and recognized the survey team they opened fire. The machine gun nest started firing when the soldiers did, catching the survey party in a withering crossfire.

Major Dupras's staff sergeant was hit in the opening bursts and knocked to the ground. Ordering the UDTs and Marines to immediately withdraw, Major Dupras, with the help of his two radiomen, moved the wounded sergeant to an IBS.

Hearing the gunfire, Kelly Welsh moved his LCP/R closer to the beach to give the men a shorter distance to travel to the boat. Both the Marines and the UDTs were heading out to the LCP/Rs as fast as they could paddle their IBSs. Still clearly illuminated by the full moon, the slow-moving IBSs were good targets for the North Koreans, who sent bullets splashing all around the rubber boats. Some UDTs left the IBSs to take their chances as smaller targets swimming in the water.

After the LCP/Rs had picked up the men and returned to the *Bass* a muster was held and it was found that nine of the Marine detachment were still missing. Lieutenant (j.g.) Ted Fielding immediately volunteered to lead a rescue party ashore to find the Marines. Welsh, along with two Marines, took their LCP/R back to the beach towing an IBS. Aboard the IBS were Lieutenant Fielding; Fred Morrison, the only black man in the UDTs at the time; Lieutenant George Atcheson, Lieutenant Phil Shutler, and UDT swimmer E. P. Smith.

Fielding worked the IBS in close to shore while rifle and machine gun bullets flew about them. Five of the missing Marines were quickly found and picked up by the IBS as they waded out from shore. After putting the Marines aboard the LCP/R, Fielding and his crew went back to the beach to locate the final four missing Marines. The Marines were soon located and picked up, including two of their number who had been wounded.

All of the Marines had kept their wits about them during their time on the beach and had fought a successful holding action against the Koreans. All of the SOG personnel had been told that no one would be left behind in enemy territory, and the Marines had calmly waited for their pickup.

After returning to the *Bass* it was found that one of the UDT swimmers was missing. Within a short time the call

"Ahoy the *Bass*" was heard from the waters near the APD. UDT swimmer Mack Boynton, the missing man, had swum out from the beach, a distance of over two miles.

The *Bass* rendezvoused with a small aircraft carrier the next day and the wounded were transferred to the larger ship for more medical attention. Returning to Japan, the men of the SOG reported to Rear Admiral Doyle that the alternate sites were unfit for landings; Inchon was it. This was to prove to be the last mission of the SOG.

For its two weeks of demolition raids and surveys, the Special Operations Group was awarded the Navy Unit Commendation. For his selfless acts in leading the Marine rescue party, Lieutenant (j.g.) Fielding was awarded the Silver Star. The example of excellence shown by this first SOG would be repeated many years later in the jungles and swamps of Vietnam. These later exploits would be conducted by the group known as the MAC-V SOG.

The SOG broke up, with the lieutenants taking their platoons to join up with the 1st Marine Brigade at Pusan. Major Dupras was attached to the staff of Amphibious Group One to assist in the planning for the upcoming landings at Inchon. UDT-1 moved out in the *Bass* to recon the beaches for the Inchon landings.

At Inchon, UDT-1 conducted a series of recons and surveys. The harbor was charted and buoys attached to underwater obstacles. So few man-made obstacles were found (most of the marked obstacles were boulders) that it was decided that a demolition swim would be unnecessary and would attract too much attention for the little good it would do. Enemy emplacements were also scouted and some of these missions resulted in close-quarter combat for the UDTs with the North Koreans. With Inchon having extensive mud flats that were exposed when the tide went out, the reconnaissance by the UDTs was even more important than usual.

Operation Chromite, the landings at Inchon, took place on the morning of September 15. To be sure that the landing craft would safely navigate the treacherous waters of Inchon Bay, members of UDT-1 served as Assault Wave Guides on the first ships in.

After the difficult invasion was over, UDT-1 assisted in the mop-up operations. The UDT helped salvage equipment, demolished hazardous wrecks, set buoys to mark safe channels, and conducted mine-and bomb-disposal operations.

The landings at Inchon split the Communist forces and began their long retreat north. The supply lines of the UN troops now became stretched and new ports were deemed necessary to complete the defeat of North Korea. The ports of Wonsan, on the east coast, and Chinnampo, on the west coast, were decided to be the best locations for amphibious landings.

Wonsan itself was in UN hands when the troops were ready to land at the harbor. The North Koreans still held some islands in the bay and were able to hamper mine-removal efforts with cannon fire. The city had been in North Korean hands since the end of World War II and the Communists had heavily mined all the water approaches. On October 11, the *Diachenko* arrived at Wonsan to lend the men of UDT-3 to the task of clearing mines.

On their first day of operations the "utes," as the UDTs were called in Korea, found and marked fifty mines for later disposal. Operating from their shallow-draft LCP/Rs, the UDTs realized that if they struck a mine before seeing it, they would never even hear the mine's 250 pounds of explosives go off.

The minesweeper *Pirate* struck one of the mines in the late morning of October 12 and quickly sank. Later that afternoon, the minesweeper *Pledge* struck a mine. Many of the sailors aboard the *Pledge* were injured from the massive blast. The destroyer *Endicott*, ignoring the threat of the mines, rushed to rescue the men of the stricken *Pledge*.

LCP/Rs full of UDTs pulled up to the sinking *Pledge* and the UDT swimmers piled aboard the ship to rescue the wounded. Just before the *Pledge* went under the UDTs abandoned ship. The result of the efforts of the men of UDT-3 was that only six men were lost when the *Pledge* went down and over fifty of her wounded survivors were saved.

For several more days UDT-3 helped clear mines. The

Diachenko was at Wonsan for a time and the men of UDT-1 joined the men of UDT-3 in clearing mines. The techniques learned, the men of UDT-1 moved out to Chinnampo to clear the mines there. Before moving out, UDT-1 conducted a recon of the landing beaches at Iwon, near Wonsan, for the use of UN troops.

On October 29, the sweep of Chinnampo's mines began. The men of UDT-1 went ahead of the minesweepers, spotting the mines from their LCP/Rs and from a helicopter. Lieutenant Commander Kelly Welsh was aboard the helicopter, which would fly in front of the LCP/Rs and spot mines that were moored just a few feet below the surface of the water. Hovering over a mine, Welsh would call over an LCP/R, whose UDTs would go over the side and deal with the mine. The swimmers would either place a timed destructor charge on the mine or cut it loose so that it could be destroyed on the surface by rifle fire.

Lieutenant Ted Fielding, team EOD officer "Jungle Jim" Lyon, and other UDTs were using these methods when they came across a new type of mine. It was a Soviet M26 inertia-type mine, and this was the first time one had been found in Korea. The mine was safely disarmed, raised, disassembled, and shipped back to the States for study.

The Chinnampo clearing operations ran from November 2 to December 1, 1950. By November 17, UDT-1 had assisted in clearing over two hundred miles of channels. Now UDT-1 was able to make its final reconnaissance of the Chinnampo docks before the UN forces landed. During the minesweeping operations the new dry suits were used extensively and UBAs also saw field use. The suits had made possible the long hours spent in the cold waters by the UDTs.

While the major portion of UDT-1 was either mopping up after Inchon or performing minesweeping operations, a new international SOG was put together. A detachment of UDTs from UDT-1 was attached to a group of men from the 41st Royal Marine Commandos of Great Britain. During the night of October 7, the combined unit of UDTs and 120 Royal Commandos attacked and destroyed railroad bridges and tunnels at two locations. The first set of bridges and tunnels were located sixteen miles south of Kyong Song and the other group was four miles south of Songjin, both locations in North Korea, well behind enemy lines.

On November 27, 1951, all actions by the UN forces changed. On that date the Chinese Communists sent over 200,000 troops across the Yalu River, North Korea's boundary with China. The rapid influx of the Chinese caused a major redistribution of the UN forces and a need for the amphibious removal of UN troops.

UDT-1 was deployed on the *Bass* to recon likely extraction beaches on a ''rush'' basis. Following normal SOP, Lieutenant Fielding and UDT Gordon Tribble were paddling with an IBS crew to investigate a beach in full daylight. Time was so short that the team was unable to wait for the tide. Fielding and Tribble ended up wading through several hundred yards of mud to get to the beach. When they reached the shore, the men found that the cliffs overlooking the beach were filled with enemy emplacements, some of them newly excavated.

But for all of the fortifications Fielding and Tribble saw there were no North Koreans. However, the North Koreans could return as easily as they had left, and the beach was written off as a possible extraction site. Successful extraction of the UN troops was later made at another location.

CIA Operations with the UDT

During the Korean War the UDTs continued their close ties with the U.S. intelligence community started with the OSS in World War II. The CIA, then a very new organization, requested that an officer qualified with rubber boats be sent to Japan for temporary duty. It being just a few days after the Inchon invasion, Lieutenant George Atcheson suddenly found himself being directed to Japan for training duty. Arriving at Camp Drake, north of Tokyo, Lieutenant Atcheson was put in with a mixed group of Air Force, Army, and Navy officers along with a hundred Koreans. The Koreans were part of a unit raised by ROK (Republic of Korea) Army Captain Han Chul-min.

The CIA's plan was to develop a network of positions across North Korea, manned by trained guerrillas, to help rescue downed airmen. A number of islands off the east and west coasts of Korea would be the pickup points the airmen would be moved to. Once the airmen were on the islands, the Navy could rescue them via submarine. This was to be the E&E (escape and evasion) network used by the United States during the Korean War.

Atcheson found himself not a rubber boat trainer but instead a military trainer to a guerrilla force. Atcheson helped teach the Koreans map reading, compass use, marksmanship, and other skills he was not particularly prepared to teach. On occasion, Atcheson would take groups to an old artillery range near Maebushi for combat firing, target practice, and grenade throwing. After a month of training the Koreans, Atcheson was told to take the guerrillas to Seoul. In Seoul Atcheson was to turn over his men to an Air Force intelligence officer and at that point his assignment would be over.

Atcheson returned to UDT-3 for other duties, and another officer, Lieutenant (j.g.) Dave Gleckler, was chosen to replace Atcheson as the rubber boat trainer for the CIA operation. Marine Corps Major Vincent "Dutch" Kramer was the operations chief for the CIA program and directed the training Gleckler was responsible for. Beside teaching IBS skills, Gleckler, along with some other UDTs assigned to the program, taught the guerrillas demolitions and basic reconnaissance. Major Kramer and others taught the guerrillas how to handle heavy weapons, such as mortars and recoilless rifles, as well as survival and clandestine communications.

Lieutenant Gleckler was also put in charge of several missions to insert the trained guerrillas to man E&E positions. The unit was operating from the APD *Begor* and was also manned with several operators from UDT-3. Arriving at the first target area, Gleckler followed SOP and sent in a pair of scout swimmers to recon the area. Waiting for the signal from shore to send in the six loaded IBSs full of guerrillas, Gleckler decided something had happened to the original pair of swimmers. Unknown to Gleckler, the two swimmers had missed the target beach and were still looking for the proper landing site.

The lieutenant decided to go in to the beach himself and examine the situation. At around 0230 hours, Gleckler moved out with another UDT and swam to the correct beach. The beach checked out to be all clear but when Gleckler asked his partner for the light to signal the "go-ahead" to the waiting boats, he didn't have it. The signal light had been lost during the swim in, so Gleckler and the UDT swam back out to the *Begor*. Gleckler picked up another UDT swimmer and returned to the beach. The area still checked out clear and the guerrillas were signaled to come in.

The guerrillas finally arrived on the beach and organized for their trip inland. Disguised as ChiComs, Chinese Communists, the guerrillas set off into the nearby hills. All during the operation dogs had been barking at a village down the coast. Getting out undetected, Gleckler considered himself very lucky as he returned to the APD. The whole dog-and-pony show had been going on for over two hours since the *Begor* had arrived at the target. Things had worked out and even the lost recon team made it back to the boat.

Other operations for the CIA did not always turn out as well as Gleckler's adventure. Lieutenant Atcheson returned for further duties with the E&E program later in 1951 and experienced several of the less favorable missions.

The first operation for Atcheson was to train a small team of guerrillas and infiltrate them into a mountainous area on the east coast of Korea, between the cities of Hungnam, to the south, and Chongjin, to the north. The area was reported to be something of a refuge for dissidents in North Korea, with a number of monasteries that disagreed with the Communist government. If the reports were true, the area would be an excellent location for an E&E position. A preliminary recon would have to be made of the area to confirm the reports. During the recon an attempt would be made to contact one of the monasteries.

Atcheson was assigned six of Captain Han's guerrillas to

train for the operation. For four weeks, Atcheson drilled the men in the use of the IBS and spent countless hours with them practicing in the harbor at Pusan.

The plan was to take the Korean guerrillas in by boat and leave them on the target beach. The guerrillas would examine the area and try to contact any monasteries that would be friendly to their mission. One week from the date of drop-off, the boats would return to the same beach to pick up the team.

The insertion went according to plan. Atcheson swam to the chosen beach, a small rocky strip backed by steep but climbable cliffs, and okayed it as clear of the enemy. The guerrillas were signaled to come in and then Atcheson returned to the *Begor*. The pickup went considerably differently than had the rather smooth drop-off.

The guerrilla group had done their recon of the area and had almost missed reaching the rendezvous point on schedule. Arriving at the beach after sunset, the guerrillas had to climb down the cliffs in the dark. Having been chased by an enemy patrol earlier in the day, the men were concerned about being caught on the beach, trapped between the cliffs and the sea.

Atcheson violated his own security rules and tried to signal the guerrillas from the ship when he thought they were on shore. The team did not realize how late they were and thought Atcheson's signal was a trap by the North Koreans. Eventually, Atcheson managed to get his seasick interpreter to call out to the guerrillas and convince them to come out to the ship.

Though the system for infiltration and exfiltration of the guerrillas was proved out by the mission, it failed in other respects. No monastery was contacted or dissidents found. The area was not used as part of the E&E network.

Another type of mission where the UDTs worked closely with the CIA was demolition raids deep behind enemy lines. In these raids, the UDTs performed the scouting and insertion work and the actual demolitions were done by ROK guerrillas. Atcheson led a force of ROK guerrillas on a number of these raids, not all of them successful.

In one operation, the target beach was in the same area of the first successful UDT demolition raid. Reconnaissance showed the area to be clear of enemy activity, but, in fact, North Koreans were hiding nearby, waiting to ambush the raiders.

The UDT scout swimmers approached the area and saw no sign of the enemy. Considering the area clear, the scouts called in the main raiding force.

As the raiders landed, the North Koreans charged them, hoping to capture the raiders and the boats intact. A firefight started, with the raiders trying to make it back to the sea. Lieutenant Atcheson moved his LCP/R as close as he dared to the shore to try to pick up the raiders. One raider was rescued by Atcheson's boat and several others were picked up by the other LCP/Rs.

All in all, there were about nine men lost in the aborted raid. Atcheson later realized how close he had come to becoming a casualty. Not only was the lieutenant's interpreter aboard the LCP/R killed by a shell fragment, grenade fragments were later found imbedded in the LCP/R's plywood hull.

UN Cooperation

The contribution of the UDTs to the UN effort was considered a very important one. During the early part of the war a new team, UDT-5, was commissioned to help support the UDTs' mission in Korea. UDT-5 was assigned to the Pacific Fleet and operated out of Coronado along with UDTs 1 and 3.

The earlier missions where the UDTs worked with the Royal Commandos had been considered successful enough to warrant further joint operations. The value of the UDT was recognized by the British, who held in high regard their abilities. In one operation, a UDT detachment was assigned to the Royal Navy to assist in a river reconnaissance.

A recently promoted Lieutenant Ted Fielding led the UDT detachment from UDT-1 in their recon of the Han River estuary. The reconnaissance was to determine if a British destroyer could operate and maneuver in the restricted waters of the river. The APD *Bass* would act as the destroyer and explore the river while the UDTs ran a hydrographic survey and reconned the beaches.

The *Bass* was able to penetrate far enough inland that it was thought the destroyer would be able to do the same. Having gone as far as they could with the *Bass*. Lieutenant Fielding took his UDTs ashore to scout the area. While collecting information, Fielding noticed a pair of children from a nearby village beckoning from a field near the men. Fielding ordered his men to continue their work and not pay any attention to the children.

The kids were still waving at the Americans when one of the UDTs noticed something strange about the haystack the children were standing next to. As the man shouted "Hey, that haystack just moved!" Fielding ordered his men to drop to the ground. Just then the machine gun nest in the haystack opened fire.

While the UDTs were under cover they could not be hit by fire coming from the haystack. Neither could they move away from the beach they were on. Using his radio, Lieutenant Fielding called for gunfire support from the *Bass*'s five-inch guns. The first arriving salvo obliterated the machine gun nest and the UDTs left the area. Only a few minor injuries were suffered in the ambush.

Near the end of his tour of duty in Korea, Lieutenant Fielding volunteered for duty with the 41st Royal Marine Commandos. Fielding was to serve as a reconnaissance scout on a series of demo raids to be conducted behind enemy lines. Three raids were planned along the east coast of Korea, targeting railroad facilities north of Hamhung.

On December 2, 1951, Fielding was climbing into the front seat of a commando kayak to perform his part in the first operation. In the rear seat was Sergeant Major Dodds, holder of the European twenty-four-hour kayak distance-paddling record. Feeling himself in good hands, Fielding moved out with the sergeant major.

When they were about seven hundred yards offshore, Fielding entered the water for his recon swim. Without the rubber dry suit he had on, Fielding probably could have never completed the swim. After studying the targets, Fielding returned to the kayak and back to the command LCP/R. The report by Fielding indicated that earlier intelligence about the target was wrong and that the targets were much higher, thirty feet, above sea level than they were originally stated to be.

The commanding officer of the commandos, Lieutenant Colonel Grant, decided to go ahead with the operation. As the commandos were reaching the target a group of ChiComs appeared from the mouth of a nearby railroad tunnel. The Chinese were riding a railroad handcar armed with machine guns. From their higher position the ChiComs were able to direct fire all around the commandos' position. Grant ordered his men to withdraw under fire and the commandos returned to their boats.

Possibly expecting a trap, the ChiComs also ceased firing. Whatever the reason, the commandos were able to leave the area with only a few casualties.

On the next evening, the planned target was up the coast from the one of the previous night. Following their standard procedure, Fielding and Dodds again performed a preraid recon and found the area clear. It may have been that the Chinese were alerted by the previous night's mission, but whatever the reason, the Chinese were waiting in ambush by the railroad bridge that was the commandos' target. A heavy firefight resulted and the commandos received 50 percent casualties before they were able to withdraw.

The aborted raid left half a ton of C3 explosives unused aboard the command LCP/R. Conceiving of a good use for some of the explosives, Fielding received permission to attack a bridge just one thousand yards down the beach from the first target. Figuring the ChiComs would never be ready for such an audacious attack, Fielding prepared several sixty-pound charges for fast use. Priming the charges with a sixty-second delay detonator, Fielding had the LCP/R move out toward the target.

Set to take off the moment the boat's bow ramp hit the ground, Fielding braced himself in the front of the LCP/R, the explosives cradled in his arms. As the LCP/R struck the sand, Fielding launched himself through the opening and plowed face-first into deep water. The LCP/R had not reached the beach but had struck a sandbar some distance from shore. Weighted down with the heavy explosive charges, Fielding almost drowned, but someone dragged him back aboard the LCP/R.

Checking his charges, Fielding was preparing to try again when the LCP/R struck another sandbar. The jar knocked one of the demolition charges over the side—with the fuse activated! Fielding immediately jumped after the charge, knowing that if it went off it could sink the LCP/R or at least warn the ChiComs.

Under the water, Fielding retrieved and disarmed the pack in time. While showing his UDT style and flipping aboard the LCP/R, Fielding sprained his ankle striking the bottom of the boat.

While lying on the deck of the LCP/R, Fielding was offered a drink and was asked if he wanted to continue. Accepting his drink Fielding replied, "No, I promised my wife I'd never take any unnecessary chances."

Fielding was later awarded both the U.S. Navy Cross and the British Distinguished Service Cross. Both medals were awarded for his actions during the missions he performed with the commandos.

Operation Fish

As the Korean War dragged on, the conflict became stalemated and turned into a war of attrition. A great deal of the Koreans' diet was made up of fish they netted from the sea. Since China was in an era of near famine, they had no food stocks to send to their soldiers in Korea. The Korean fishermen had to support both the Korean people and the army from the north.

The UDTs were given orders to remove or destroy all North Korean fishing nets they came across. While moving along the coast on recon or demolition raids, the UDTs made note of the location of nets for Operation Fish. When they could, the UDTs would go over the side and destroy or confiscate the nets. Those nets taken tended to be given to South Korean fishermen. The mission was just another strange aspect of a very unusual war.

The End of the War

With the signing of the armistice on July 27, 1953, the Korean War ended. The UDTs had assisted in sixty-one assault landings, using much smaller units than they had in World War II.

Having proved their abilities both in and out of the water, the UDTs had entered into a new form of warfare where they could find themselves fighting on dry land. All of the teams had performed countless missions in support of the UN forces in Korea. UDT-1 alone conducted 125 reconnaissance missions, twelve demolition raids, and an uncounted number of special missions.

The Fifties

After the Korean War, the UDTs returned to the United States and continued their prewar projects and training. A major change in the history of the UDTs took place on February 8, 1954. On that date all of the UDTs were redesignated, apparently to prevent confusion with earlier units in World War II. West Coast UDTs 1, 3, and 5 became UDTs 11, 12, and 13, respectively. In Virginia, East Coast UDTs 2 and 4 became UDTs 21 and 22, respectively.

After the end of the Korean War and their redesignation by the Navy, the UDTs further developed their new missions that had come about during the Korean conflict. The primary mission of the UDT remained reconnaissance, but a number of new secondary missions were now considered a standard part of the UDT repertoire. These missions included:

1. Demolition of obstacles.
2. Clearance of harbors or channels.
3. Penetration of bays, harbors, or rivers for the purpose of limpeteering (attacking ships at anchor), net cutting, and demolition strikes.
4. Mine clearance.
5. Dissemination of intelligence.

 6. Guidance of assault waves.
 7. Acting as lifeguards during military maneuvers.
 8. Inland penetrations for reconnaissance and/or demo-
    lition.
 9. Landing, supplying, or evacuation of raiders, sabo-
    teurs, or guerrillas.
10. Improvement or marking of channels and harbors.
11. Destruction of port facilities during withdrawal.

These secondary missions are not listed in any particular order and any one of them is considered reason enough for a UDT operation. To insure the success of their operations, the UDTs constantly practiced all of the skills necessary for any of their missions.

During the summer months of 1954, the reconnaissance aspect of the UDTs was practiced during exercises. Since the UDTs almost never do things the easy way, a simple practice beach recon was made much more interesting by staging it in the cold waters of Dutch Harbor and Kodiak Island in Alaska.

A strategic decision was made by the Nationalist Chinese to evacuate their troops from the Tachen Islands near mainland China in February of 1955. As the U.S. was bound by treaty to assist the Nationalist Chinese, the U.S. Seventh Fleet was dispatched to Tachen to aid in the move.

UDT-11 was tasked with charting a safe passage for the amphibious transport group that was being escorted by the Seventh Fleet. After the Nationalist troops had left the islands and were safely away, the UDT conducted a massive demolition project on Tachen. Fortifications and munition stockpiles were destroyed to keep them from falling into Communist hands.

A peaceful, but considerably more difficult, mission was also undertaken by the UDTs during 1955. The Distant Early Warning system (DEW line) was being built by the United States across the northern areas of Alaska and Canada. The UDTs conducted extensive underwater surveys and demolitions in the extremely cold waters of the Arctic Ocean. The water was so cold (27°F) that if it had not been salty it would have frozen solid.

In such cold waters a man can survive for only a few minutes before lapsing into a coma and dying. The DEW line mission gave the UDT an opportunity to develop and test new cold-water-protection systems. The dry suit was used but still had the problem of being relatively fragile. If the integrity of the dry suit was broken, the water would quickly flood in, soaking the diver's long underwear and exposing him to the direct cold of the water.

A new suit was first used in the cold Arctic operations. The suit was made of quarter-inch-thick foam rubber and was first worn underneath the dry suit in place of the normal woolen underwear. If the outer dry suit leaked, the foam rubber would continue to insulate the diver. The UDTs quickly discovered that the foam rubber suit could be worn by itself as a "wet" suit. The wet suit would allow only a small amount of water in, which would be quickly warmed by the diver's body heat. This new style of suit has become the most popular cold-water protection for all divers today, both civilian and military.

UDT swimmers accompanied the first nuclear submarines when they traveled under the Arctic ice. UDT Lieutenant Commander Robert Terry swam over a quarter mile underneath the Arctic ice cap. Terry described the ice as having a beautiful diamond-blue color when observed from underneath.

Not all of the Arctic explorations went smoothly for the UDTs. Two UDTs were swimming on their own when they noticed an Eskimo village nearby. Thinking to visit the Eskimos, the UDTs moved out of the water and began sliding across the smaller ice floes to get nearer to the villagers. Until the DEW line and the UDTs, the average Eskimo had never seen a man swimming. In the world of the Eskimos to enter the water not in a kayak is to court a quick death from the cold waters.

When faced with two black-suited figures sliding across the ice with their large webbed feet, the Eskimo villagers reacted in a manner they found most natural. The two UDT swimmers became very concerned when the first bullets from the village bounced off the ice near the two odd-looking "seals." Seals never acted like those two UDT swimmers when they started jumping about, waving their arms and yelling.

The cutbacks of a peacetime Navy took their toll of the UDTs as well as the rest of the services. UDT-22 on the East Coast was decommissioned in June of 1956 due to personnel shortages. The men who had been in UDT-22 were reassigned to UDT-21. On the West Coast the same action took place, with UDT-13 being decommissioned and its men being split up into UDTs 11 and 12.

There may have been thoughts among the higher officers in the Navy that the UDT had outlived its usefulness and should be abolished altogether. Training actions by the UDTs helped lay those thoughts to rest. In November of 1956 a combined detachment from UDTs 11 and 12 conducted an attack against the Panama Canal. Though all of the details about the attack are still classified, it is known that the operation was conducted as a sneak attack against the canal itself and was considered a success.

The UDTs became known for performing difficult tasks in unusual, but effective, ways. Men on board ships during training exercises had to be especially alert when the UDTs were around. Resourceful UDT men tried to sneak aboard one such target ship by pretending to be from another ship and wanting to exchange movies with the target ship. The guards did not accept the UDTs' story and the men were sent away from their victim.

But that same group of guards took no special notice of the group of sailors in dirty fatigue uniforms who came aboard lugging their dented trash cans. After they had gone below decks, the UDT operators took their dummy explosive charges out of their "transport" containers and prepared to sink the ship.

Finding the ship's captain asleep in his quarters, the UDT men "borrowed" the captain's keys. Using the captain's keys, the UDTs were able to unlock the cabinet where the gunnery officer's keys were kept. With the gunnery keys, the UDTs were able to unlock the ship's powder and ammunition magazines and plant their timed charges. Returning all of the keys to their proper places, the UDTs once more took up their trash can "passports" and calmly left the ship.

Told by the exercise's umpires that his ship had been "sunk," the angry captain ordered an immediate search for the explosives. Not finding any charges, the captain accused the UDT men of cheating and challenged them to prove their "kill." The UDTs returned to the target ship and, borrowing the necessary keys, opened the secured magazines and displayed their handiwork.

Other ships and bases had their security checked by the men of the UDTs. Most of the time, the UDTs were successful in their penetrations but most of the reports remain classified. It was quickly learned by the rest of the Navy that if there was a weakness in security, the UDTs would soon find and exploit it.

Other actions continued in the later 1950s to keep the UDTs occupied. As in the earlier tests at Bikini, the UDTs were asked to examine underwater bomb damage during the hydrogen bomb tests. Other water-oriented nuclear testing also used the UDTs' abilities to fully measure damage. During the latter part of 1956, members of UDT-11 were performing coral demolition off Midway Island to improve beach facilities. At the same time these members of the team were in the warm waters of the Pacific, other members of UDT-11 were working in the frigid waters of the Arctic conducting DEW line resupply operations.

Not all of the operations performed by the UDTs during the late 1950s were as peaceful as simple training exercises. Though no reports are available about their possible actions, the UDTs were in a state of alert during the Lebanon crisis in the summer of 1958. No sooner was the Lebanon crisis over than action was again seen by the UDTs off the coast of China.

The Nationalist Chinese had been staging actions against the mainland from a number of islands off the coast of Communist China. In 1958, the Communists began shelling the Nationalist Chinese complexes on the islands of Kinmen (Quemoy) and Matsu. The United States took immediate action by sending the Seventh Fleet into the area. A UDT detachment was with the Seventh Fleet during its deployment. The UDTs conducted beach surveys and hydrographic recons in case an evacuation of the islands proved necessary. It was the presence of the Seventh Fleet that is credited with preventing the Communist Chinese from having captured Matsu and Kinmen that year.

Besides their military operations, the UDTs were busy with several scientific experiments during the late 1950s. UDT volunteers spent long and dangerous hours in pressure tanks helping to develop mixed-gas deep-diving systems. The mixed-gas decompression tables used today owe much to those early UDT volunteers.

Probably the most unusual experiments involving the UDTs took place in the 1950s. UDT men were known to be among the physically toughest men available in the U.S. military, as well as being the most fit. These aspects of the UDTs, combined with their underwater experience, qualified them as candidates for "G"-force and weightlessness testing for America's new space program.

Twelve UDT men reported to Johnsville, Pennsylvania, for a series of grueling tests conducted by the Aero Medical Personnel. The men were placed in centrifuges to determine their resistance to G-forces. With their abilities to withstand physical and mental stress a known factor, the UDTs were used to prove an unknown factor. Could man stand the stresses of launching, weightlessness, and reentry?

The UDTs first entered a centrifuge to simulate the G-force equivalent to being launched into space. After the "launch" the volunteers were immediately submerged in a tank of water to simulate weightlessness. After eighteen hours of "weightlessness," the UDTs were placed back in the centrifuge to experience the stress of reentry. The results established that men could withstand the stresses connected with space travel but that at least one other problem should be faced. Eighteen hours in a pool was almost too long for the active men of the UDTs—they were bored stiff!

Another test was conducted for space research at the Naval Air Station in Norfolk, Virginia, during April 1959.

Five UDT volunteers were tested for reactions to long periods of weightlessness. The men spent forty-eight hours continuously underwater during the experiment. Food was available to the men through tubes, also testing a possible method of feeding orbiting astronauts. A TV set was visible to the volunteers and waterproof reading material had been made available to help pass the time. The UDTs discovered for themselves that an ordinary newspaper could be read underwater, but you had to be very careful turning the pages.

After the experiments, the UDTs were barely able to stand up out of the water. Within a few hours though, the men had recovered completely. The UDTs had helped to establish that long hours of weightlessness could be coped with by the human body. It was through experiments such as these that the first men could go into space with the best possible chance of returning safely to Earth.

Vietnam: The Early Years

When John F. Kennedy took the oath of office in 1961, he became the youngest president in the history of the United States. President Kennedy's military background in the Navy as the commander of a PT boat during World War II was well known. This background enabled Kennedy to have firsthand knowledge of how small groups of well-trained men can have an effect far out of proportion to their numbers.

President Kennedy recognized the need for the U.S. forces to successfully fight a guerrilla-style war as well as conventional war in this age of nuclear weapons. As commander in chief of the U.S. military, President Kennedy ordered all of the services to increase their capabilities in the field of unconventional warfare. Early in 1961, President Kennedy further stressed that the U.S. military should have the ability to train foreign forces in guerrilla warfare.

The Navy started preparations to comply with the president's directive during the late summer and early fall of 1961. Design of shallow-draft boats for operations in a riverine-type environment were pushed forward. Studies had been done to establish the best Navy unit to perform guerrilla warfare. The UDT was easily determined to be the most suitable unit for the assignment, but the primary task of the UDT, reconnaissance, was still considered a vital one.

Since early March, the Unconventional Activities Committee had been considering several ideas to give the Navy a unit with a specialized guerrilla warfare capability and still leave the UDTs to perform their primary mission. Among other recommendations, the committee suggested the creation of two new units, one each for the Pacific and Atlantic Amphibious Commands.

These new units would become the center focus of the Navy's guerrilla warfare program. Originally referred to as Special Operations Teams (SOTS), the new organizations would be attached to the UDTs to help cover their existence to outside observers. The units would be code-named after the acronym SEAL, a contraction of "sea, air, and land," indicating their capacity to operate in any environment. Each SEAL unit would initially consist of twenty to twenty-five officers and fifty to seventy-five enlisted men. The assigned mission of the SEALs would have three parts:

1. To develop a specialized Navy capability in guerrilla/counterguerrilla operations to include training of selected personnel in a wide variety of skills.
2. Development of doctrinal tactics.
3. Development of special support equipment.

These suggestions became the basis around which the Office of the Chief of Naval Operations (CNO) built the Navy plan for the future creation of the SEALs.

The advent of the Berlin crisis in the fall of 1961 curtailed the development of new special military units. While the specter of an armed confrontation in Europe loomed, emphasis was placed on the increase in conventional ground forces.

The Navy encouraged officers and commanders to "enhance and augment present Naval support capabilities within the Underwater Demolition Teams for demolition, sabotage, and other clandestine activities in order to complement the inherent unconventional warfare capabilities of Marine

Pathfinder and Reconnaissance Units'' (CNO letter serial # 0087P43, 27 Oct 61).

Specialized guerrilla warfare training was completely lacking for naval personnel during the fall of 1961. By October 1961, only four naval officers, including two officers from UDT-21, had attended or were attending courses at the U.S. Army's Special Warfare Center. Developments in South Vietnam would greatly increase the speed of the Navy's guerrilla warfare program.

By late September in South Vietnam, the progress toward a stable government had ground to a halt. The State Department estimated that the number of Viet Cong operating in South Vietnam had increased from 7,000 men at the beginning of 1961 to 17,000 by the end of September. Increasing flows of men and supplies from North Vietnam were allowing the Viet Cong to go more and more on the offensive. Many of these supplies were making their way south by water and entering South Vietnam through the Mekong Delta and the Rung Sat Special Zone.

The response of the Kennedy administration was to increase the emphasis on unconventional warfare capabilities for U.S. forces. The Navy answered by accelerating its guerrilla warfare program. The specialized SEAL units would be established along with the administrative organizations needed to support them.

The Vietnamese themselves felt a need for a naval unit with some of the capabilities of the U.S. UDT. When U.S. advisors initially recommended against the idea, the Vietnamese turned to Taiwan and the Nationalist Chinese for training. The Nationalist Chinese ran a course of training that the UDTs had helped to establish during the 1950s. A single Vietnamese officer and seven men completed the course in 1960.

By July of 1961 the Lien Doc Nquoi Nhia (LDNN), literally "soldiers who fight under the sea," had been established by the South Vietnamese government. The LDNN was authorized forty-eight officers and men for the task of removing underwater obstacles, protecting military ports, and conducting special operations in waterways.

The final paperwork resulting in the creation of the SEALs took place in the last months of 1961. The Chief of Naval Operations had a letter written outlining the size and organization of the two proposed SEAL units (CNO letter serial # 02158P10, 13 Nov 1961).

The two SEAL teams were to be initially made up of sixty men each, ten officers and fifty enlisted men. Team 1 would be stationed at the Coronado Naval Amphibious Base (NAB) near San Diego and attached to the Pacific Amphibious Command. Team 2 would be based at the Little Creek NAB near Norfolk, Virginia, and attached to the Atlantic Amphibious Command.

Final authorization of the SEALs came from the CNO, Admiral George W. Anderson, Jr., in CNO speedletter number 697P30, dated December 11, 1961. Also contained in the document was the intended mission of the SEALs and other specifics pertaining to their organization, command, and logistical support.

On January 1, 1962, SEAL Team 1 was commissioned by presidential order. A week later, on January 8, SEAL Team 2 received its commission from President Kennedy. Both teams were commissioned as Navy fleet tactical units tasked with conducting naval special warfare.

Lieutenant David Del Giudice, USNR, was put in command of SEAL Team 1 at its commissioning. The initial personnel complement for Team 1 consisted of five officers and fifty enlisted men. The personnel were volunteers from UDTs 11 and 12.

SEAL Team 2 was assigned Lieutenant John F. Callahan, Jr., as its first commanding officer. The volunteers who made up the initial complement of personnel for Team 2 almost all came out of UDT-21. Team 2 started out with ten officers and fifty enlisted men.

Recognizing the very real possibility of a great increase in U.S. naval activity in Vietnam, CINCPAC (Commander in Chief, Pacific Fleet) authorized a beach survey of the South Vietnamese coast to be conducted early in 1962. The APD *Cook* was assigned the task of examining beaches in the vicinity of Quang Tri, Da Nang, Nha Trang, Cam Ranh Bay, Vung Tou, and Qui Nhon.

The mission began on January 4, 1962, with a UDT detachment conducting most of the surveys. The investigation of beach configurations, gradients, underwater obstacles, and tides of the assigned areas was completed without incident by January 27. This ended the first field operation by the UDTs in Vietnam.

During the early months of 1962, the new SEAL personnel were undergoing a high-priority training program. The SEALs were to be ready to send detachments to Southeast Asia within eight to ten weeks of their date of commissioning. Two officers from SEAL Team 1 spent part of January and February in South Vietnam. The mission of the officers was to help determine the specific requirements of the South Vietnamese and how the SEALs could best satisfy those needs.

The other SEALs who had volunteered to go to Southeast Asia were attending several Army schools to prepare them for their mission. The SEALs received training in special forces techniques, evasion and escape, jungle warfare, unconventional warfare equipment use, and how to conduct operations in rivers and restricted waters.

By March the plans to send SEAL detachments to Vietnam had been finalized. On March 10, two instructors from Team 1 arrived in Saigon for a six-month tour of duty. During their tour, the two SEAL instructors would be teaching South Vietnamese personnel how to conduct clandestine maritime operations.

During April 1962, the first of many SEAL Mobile Training Teams (MTTs) left for Vietnam. Under the command of Lieutenant (j.g.) Philip P. Holtz of SEAL Team 1 MTT 10-62 consisted of nine enlisted men, seven from Team 1 and two from Team 2. The mission of MTT 10-62 was to train a group of Vietnamese Coastal Force personnel in reconnaissance, sabotage, and guerrilla warfare.

The intent was to have the Vietnamese graduates of the SEAL-taught course become a cadre of instructors for a Vietnamese-run training course. The Vietnamese instructors would be able to maintain a high state of training and operational readiness of the new Vietnamese Biet Hai (Junk Force Commando Platoons). The SEALs of MTT 10-62 were also to act as advisors in developing tactics, equipment, and operating procedures for the Biet Hai. By October, sixty-two men had completed the SEALs' grueling course of training.

MTT 4-63 relieved MTT 10-62 in October 1962. MTT 4-63 was made up of one officer and seven enlisted men from SEAL Team 2 and was placed under the control of Lieutenant (j.g.) Alan C. Routh of SEAL Team 1.

Coordinating their training through Lieutenant (j.g.) Ninh of the Vietnamese navy, the men of MTT 4-63 continued the program begun by the SEALs of MTT 10-62. Emphasis was now on teaching the Vietnamese graduates of the earlier class land navigation, further guerrilla warfare techniques, ambush and counterambush, and raiding techniques.

These MTT detachments and the training they were performing caught the unwelcome interest of news reporters in Saigon. Articles like the following ran in several U.S. newspapers:

A tough American-trained team of Republic of Vietnam frogmen-commandos will be ready soon for underwater missions against communist coastal bases, a highly informed source has reported. Eight U.S. Navy instructors [MTT 4-63] at the coastal town of Da Nang are putting about 65 Vietnamese frogmen through courses in underwater demolition, long distance swimming, and commando combat. The sixteen-week course will be finished in about two months. . . . Men assigned to the Junk fleet, including the frogmen, have the motto "SAT CONG" tattooed on their chests. It means "kill communists." Presumably, any prisoner taken would be dealt with similarly.

Though the above press release is representative of only those that ran in the U.S. papers, it is interesting to wonder what the reporters would have thought if they knew that the "Eight U.S. Navy instructors" were members of America's newest, most secret, military elite.

While the MTTs were conducting training in Vietnam,

other SEAL Team detachments were working with NATO forces in Europe. Primarily from SEAL Team 2, the detachments' operations were conducted with NATO forces in Norway, Greece, and Turkey. As the SEALs were still developing their capabilities, the operations were, in part, to determine if the SEALs would be able to carry out their primary missions of maritime sabotage and the training of indigenous personnel.

In Norway, the SEAL detachment (four officers and twenty enlisted men) spent fifteen days at the Norwegian Froskenenn (frogman) school in Bergen. After the school training, the SEALs took part in a joint exercise where they had to penetrate twenty-four miles of enemy-held territory in order to reach a friendly base. During the exercise, members of the Norwegian Naval Home Guard, backed up by aircraft from the Royal Norwegian Air Force, acted the part of the "enemy." The SEALs completed their mission and the Norwegians were suitably impressed with this new U.S. unit's capabilities.

In Greece, a SEAL detachment (two officers and fifteen enlisted men) trained selected Greek forces in maritime sabotage techniques. The techniques taught included the use of closed-circuit scuba, demolitions, small arms, and hand-to-hand combat. The detachment parachuted into the area, conducted the training, and then participated in a combined attack on a fuel pier, radio station, harbormaster facility, and bridge, all in the Volos Harbor area.

The SEAL detachment in Turkey (one officer and five enlisted men) conducted a submarine exfiltration of a Turkish guerrilla unit. The knowledge and experience gathered by the SEALs on these operations were considered invaluable by the planners back in the United States.

By the end of the SEALs' first year, enough information and experience had been gathered on the probable activities of the SEALs that it was thought their mission could be more accurately stated. At the end of December 1962, Rear Admiral Allen L. Reed, Assistant Chief of Naval Operations (Fleet Operations and Readiness), issued Naval Warfare Information Publication (NWIP) 29-1.

The SEAL's primary mission was stated in NWIP 29-1, "SEAL Teams in Naval Special Warfare," and was made up of several parts. As the specific text of NWIP 29-1 still remains classified, the SEAL mission assignments are condensed as follows:

1. To develop a specialized capability for sabotage, demolition, and other clandestine activities conducted in and from restricted waters, rivers, and canals. Specifically to be able to destroy enemy shipping, harbor facilities, bridges, railway lines, and other installations in maritime areas and riverine environments. Also to protect friendly supply lines, installations, and assets in maritime and riverine environments from similar attack.
2. To infiltrate and/or exfiltrate agents, guerrillas, evaders, and escapees.
3. To conduct reconnaissance, surveillance, and other intelligence-gathering activities.
4. To accomplish limited counterinsurgency civic action tasks that are normally incidental to counterguerrilla operations. Possibilities include medical aid, elementary civil engineering activities, boat operations and maintenance, and the basic education of the indigenous population.
5. To organize, train, assist, and advise the United States, Allied, and other friendly military or paramilitary forces in the conduct of any of the above tasks.
6. To develop doctrine and tactics for such operations.
7. To develop support equipment, including special craft.

These are the general mission outlines that are still followed by the SEALs today. Since 1983 the SEALs have also been given the responsibilities for reconnaissance once conducted by the UDTs.

A SEAL MTT detachment of two officers and ten enlisted men from SEAL Team 1 was based at Da Nang from January to December 1963. The detachment continued the training program for selected South Vietnamese military personnel started earlier at Saigon. The Vietnamese received training in small boat operations, sabotage, amphibious landing techniques, and other related skills. The SEALs had by now established themselves in Vietnam and there would be a constant SEAL presence in Southeast Asia until the U.S. withdrawal in 1973.

In 1963, SEAL Team 1 concentrated its efforts on the SEAL MTTs in Vietnam as well as how the SEALs could best support the U.S. commitment in the area. SEAL Team 2 took responsibility for SEAL actions in Central and South America as well as in Europe.

MTTs made up of SEAL Team 2 personnel continued operations in Turkey to establish a Turkish-run UDT/SEAL-type operation and training program. It was during their deployment to Turkey that the SEALs suffered their first loss.

On May 21, 1963, Lieutenant (j.g.) Painter was reported to have been lost and presumed drowned in the Bosphorus as the result of a diving accident. At the time of the accident, Turkish students were practicing buoyant ascents under the observation of their SEAL instructors. Lieutenant Painter put on an aqualung to observe the students underwater. Lieutenant Painter was seen to surface from his first dive; he dove a second time, and was never seen again. Extensive searches of the area were conducted for several days but his body was never recovered.

Other SEAL detachments performed operations with Italian forces during Operation Springtime in Sardinia. In the fall of 1963 SEALs also took part in Operation Sea Ruler in Greece and Corsica. For operations with the Greek forces the SEALs were based out of Crete. During part of their operations, the SEALs used a Greek fishing boat and played the part of Greek fishermen in order to infiltrate into the target area.

By the fall of 1963 the number of SEALs and other Navy units involved with unconventional warfare in Southeast Asia and elsewhere in the world was increasing. It was decided to centralize control and administrative support for all of the Naval Special Operations forces. On October 10, 1963, the Naval Operations Support Groups were estab-

lished in the Pacific and Atlantic fleets. The groups took
over the administrative control of all of the fleets' SEAL
teams, UDTs, beach-jumper units, and PT boat units. Later,
during the Vietnam War, the Operations Support Groups
would be renamed Naval Special Warfare Groups 1 and 2.

The UDTs also conducted operations in Vietnam early in
1963. The APD *Weiss* was to conduct a survey of possible
landing sites along the shore near Cape Vung Tau, Qui
Nhon, Da Nang, and Bac Liew. On February 21, UDT-
12's Detachment Bravo, along with a team from the 3rd
Marine Reconnaissance Battalion, began their site survey.
The Marines would conduct a survey past the high-tide line
into the jungle, and the UDTs would survey the beach and
waters.

Three days after they started, the Marine recon party came
under sniper fire. No casualties were taken by the Marines
and the *Weiss* continued her operations. The Marines once
again came under attack, by an estimated twelve to fifteen
Viet Cong, on March 12. Again withdrawing without casualties, the Marines returned to the *Weiss*. The *Weiss* was
recalled to Subic Bay in the Philippines along with her
detachments without further incident on March 14.

On November 7, 1963, President Kennedy wrote a memo
to the Chief of Naval Operations, Admiral David L.
McDonald, and the new Secretary of the Navy, Paul H.
Nitze. In what was to prove his last memo to these men,
President Kennedy said:

> When I was in Norfolk in 1962 I noted particularly
> the members of the SEAL Teams. I was impressed
> by them as individuals and with the capability they
> possess as a group. As missiles assume more and
> more of the nuclear deterrent role and as your
> limited warfare mission grows, the need for special
> warfare in the navy and marine corps will in-
> crease.

During 1964 both SEAL teams continued to conduct training to increase their capabilities. SEAL Team 2 performed

advanced training in scuba and submersible techniques while operating out of Saint Thomas in the Virgin Islands. Extensive training in swimming, deep diving, closed-circuit swimming, compass accuracy, and submarine operations was conducted. Further training was also done in parachute jumping, demolitions, SPU (swimmer propulsion unit) operation, and inland penetrations.

Further operations were conducted with the Greek and Turkish forces. The Turkish UDT school conducted its first all-Turkish UDT class during 1964. In December, a joint operation with UDT-22 and the U.S.M.C. Second Force Reconnaissance Company was conducted by SEAL Team 2 in Puerto Rico. Emphasis was placed on training in underwater reconnaissance and swimmer lock-out and recovery techniques.

More training was conducted by SEAL Team 2 in the Virgin Islands during the winter months of 1965. The SEALs conducted refresher training as well as instructed a Special Forces team in scuba techniques. SEALs also worked with a small team of Royal Canadian Navy Clearance Divers. The two groups of divers were able to exchange valuable ideas about diving apparatus and procedures.

An extended program with the Special Forces team was conducted in the area of Salt and West cays, to the west of Saint Thomas. The training with the Special Forces personnel was to prove useful much sooner than any of the SEALs suspected.

On April 30, a small detachment of SEAL Team 2 personnel reported aboard the U.S.S. *La Salle* for deployment to the Dominican Republic. The detachment consisted of one officer, Lieutenant (j.g.) Doran, and five enlisted men. On May 16, a second detachment from Team 2 was ordered to Santo Domingo to conduct reconnaissance work with members of the 7th Special Forces Group. The recon was to be done of Samona Bay on the northeastern tip of the Dominican Republic.

The SEAL detachment consisted of three officers and ten enlisted men, all under the command of Lieutenant Kochey. Suspicious small boat traffic had drawn the military's attention to the Samona Bay area. It was suspected that rebels might be using caves in the bay area to hide arms and ammunition caches. The whole country was considered a hot spot and the SEALs were facing the real possibility of armed combat.

Since an obvious search by military personnel would cause the rebels simply to remove any supply caches, the SEALs decided to do their search in a covert manner. The SEALs conducted their reconnaissance and searches while dressed in civilian clothes and carrying props. To any casual observer the SEALs were simply a group of tourists on a fishing trip.

This time the fishermen came up dry. The caves were thoroughly searched but no rebel materials were found. However, members of the SEAL detachment did find themselves involved in several firefights with rebels in the streets of the capital, Santo Domingo. None of the SEALs were wounded and both detachments returned to Little Creek on May 28.

In the fall of 1965, the whole of Seal Team 2 participated in Operation Sand Crab, conducted at Long Island, New York. The SEALs also joined with the Italians for Exercise Aquila Bianca in Italy. During Aquila Bianca, the SEALs worked with the Italian Seventh Air Commando Squadron and worked out of the U.S. submarine *Sea Owl*. The Italians and the SEALs each felt a great deal of mutual benefit was derived for both units during the exercise.

Vietnam: 1966

It was during 1966 that the SEALs' presence in Vietnam began to be actively felt by the Viet Cong. In February, SEAL Team 1 sent Detachment Golf, a pilot group of three officers and fifteen enlisted men, to Vietnam for active combat duty. Placed under the command of the Commander Naval Forces Vietnam (COMNAVFORV), the SEALs of Detachment Golf were to conduct field actions in the Rung Sat Special Zone (RSSZ).

The Rung Sat Special Zone was of particular strategic importance since it covered all of the major water approaches to Saigon from the South China Sea. Running between the Long Tau and Soi Rap rivers, the RSSZ is a thirty-by-thirty-five-kilometer area of mangrove swamp containing thousands of meandering tributaries and streams located on the northeastern edge of the Mekong Delta. Ships trying to reach Saigon would first pass Vung Tau, a town on a peninsula that juts into the South China Sea to the northeast of the Rung Sat. Once Vung Tau was passed, ships would have to navigate forty-six miles of bending river before they could reach Saigon.

Physically, the RSSZ was a foreboding area to anyone who entered it. The more than one-thousand-square-

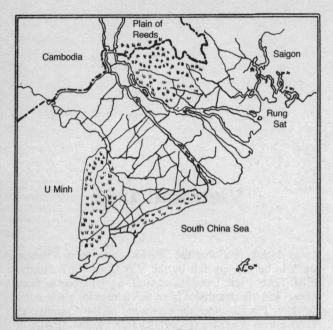

Mekong Delta

kilometer area of the Rung Sat (four hundred plus square miles) contained some of the most difficult terrain in Vietnam. The vegetation of the RSSZ consisted of tropical lowland plants, mainly mangrove with an impenetrable barrier of twisted roots, and tightly growing packs of nipa palm. From the riverbanks in, and for some distance beyond, the plants grew low to the ground. In the somewhat drier areas, the Rung Sat had a double canopy of trees that easily hid activity from aerial searches.

As a river delta area, the Rung Sat had tides that ran at speeds of four knots and raised the water level by an average of eight feet. When the tide was out, the mud left behind was a thick river silt that could often be chest-deep on a wading man. The heavy vegetation of the mangrove swamp was home to numerous mammals, insects, and reptiles.

Jungle cats, pythons, crocodiles, and venomous snakes all found a home in the RSSZ. Besides the billions of mosquitoes, numerous large spiders and scorpions, and bloodsucking leeches, the Rung Sat also housed millions of a particular species of large, stinging ants.

Referred to by the Vietnamese as the Forest of Assassins, the Rung Sat area had for centuries been a haven for Southeast Asian pirates, bandits, and smugglers. By 1964 the area

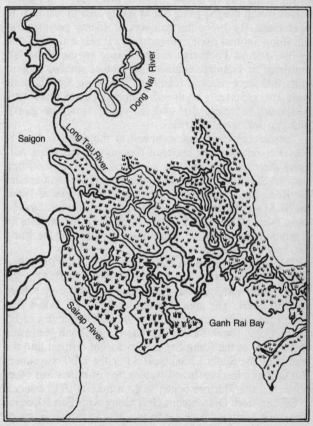

Rung Sat Special Zone

had also become a haven for the Viet Cong.

There were about sixteen thousand civilians living in and around the Rung Sat in 1966. There were few isolated houses, and the majority of inhabitants were spread out among nine villages that were further subdivided into twenty hamlets. Almost all of the civilians lived either by rice farming, woodcutting, or fishing the rich waters.

An estimated two hundred Viet Cong had taken refuge in the Rung Sat by 1964. Other neighboring Communist forces would use the Rung Sat as a safe area to rest in after operations. By 1966, the numbers of enemy personnel in the Rung Sat had risen tremendously. It was estimated that by the end of February, enemy forces in the Rung Sat consisted of infantry, engineer, and other smaller support units including medical facilities. The Rung Sat VC units were also reportedly equipped with small arms, automatic weapons (including .50- and .51-caliber machine guns), mortars, and recoilless rifles.

Detachment Golf was stationed at the naval facility at Nha Be, on the river between Saigon and the Rung Sat. From their location near the northwest corner of the Rung Sat, the SEALs were able to conduct operations throughout the Rung Sat. During late March and early April of 1966, the SEALs of Detachment Golf operated with combat swimmers from UDT-11 and troops from the Fifth Marines in Operation Jackstay, the amphibious invasion of the Rung Sat Special Zone.

The landings began on the morning of March 26 with a beach reconnaissance by swimmers from UDT-11. The UDTs were working from the APD *Weiss* and went ashore at 0330 hours. The area checked by the UDT, called Red Beach for landing purposes, was on the southernmost tip of the Long Thanh Peninsula. The Long Thanh Peninsula is the point of the Rung Sat that sticks out farthest into the waters of the South China Sea. After the UDT swimmers had declared the beach and waters free of mines and other obstacles, the Marines began to go ashore at 0715 hours.

SEALs from Detachment Golf along with Force Reconnaissance Marines made up twenty-one four-man teams to detect VC movements. The small teams moved deeper into the Rung Sat than the rest of the units and set up surveillance points to watch for VC activity. Setting up late in the afternoon on March 26, the surveillance teams maintained watch throughout the night. During the night, some teams reported that the VC had moved so close to where the men lay concealed that the Americans "could hear the VC breathing."

The teams were extracted by boat the next morning. Though the men were not normally to engage the enemy during observation duty, the SEALs and Marines had accounted for four VC killed during the night. Those VC were the first confirmed enemy casualties of Operation Jackstay.

Operation Jackstay ended on April 7, 1966. The operation had been very successful in routing the VC from their large emplacements in the Rung Sat. Large bunkers and munitions factories had been located during the operation and the SEALs and UDT personnel had been kept busy using their demolition skills to destroy the emplacements. VC attacks had not resulted in any casualties among either the SEALs or the UDTs. The routine of the VC operating in the Rung Sat had been permanently disrupted by Jackstay. No longer would the VC be inviolate inside their former sanctuary. The SEALs had arrived, and a new era in amphibious warfare had begun.

During the first field operations by the SEALs in Vietnam, the men had little or no practical experience in combat. SEAL fire teams of seven, or smaller units of three men, conducted missions in all parts of the Rung Sat, determining Areas of Operations (AOs) and developing Standard Operation Procedures (SOPs). Supposedly limited to intelligence gathering and reconnaissance patrols, the SEALs had great leeway in completing their missions. The result of this situation was that the ambush became the primary SEAL field operation. Though somewhat inexperienced, the SEALs were technically proficient and superbly trained— as well as being fast learners.

A lack of firsthand intelligence had hampered actions during Operation Jackstay. The SEALs were determined not to allow that situation to develop again. Valuable intelligence on enemy troop and supply movements in the Rung Sat was gathered by the SEALs in their new field operations. The SEALs' value to the Vietnam effort was soon recognized by higher command, and Detachment Golf was authorized to increase in size.

By the summer of 1966, Detachment Golf had grown to five officers and twenty enlisted men divided into two operational platoons and a command element. SEAL operations also grew to include, but were not limited to, harassment of the enemy, intelligence collection, and the limiting of enemy movement by using ambush/counterambush tactics.

Patrols were difficult and the SEALs were constantly learning and refining methods of operating in the field. Lieutenant Bell was one of the SEAL officers assigned to Detachment Golf in Vietnam and acted as the Detachments Executive Officer (XO). Between July 13 and October 26, Lieutenant Bell led his fire team on more than thirty combat operations in addition to carrying out his duties as Detachment XO. These combat operations included patrols, ambushes, and observations of enemy movements. On August 7, Lieutenant Bell's fire team ambushed a VC convoy consisting of a junk and two motorized sampans.

During the ambush, Lieutenant Bell and his team had to expose themselves to enemy fire by standing in hip-deep mud and water in order to have a clear field of fire. The ambush was successful, resulting in seven enemy dead with no losses by the SEALs. A number of enemy documents containing valuable intelligence were also captured. This ambush was just one of many conducted by Detachment Golf as they increased their operations in the Rung Sat.

The increase in SEAL operations was not without a price. On August 19, 1966, SEAL Team 1 suffered their first combat casualty. Petty Officer Billy W. Machen was killed while part of a patrol conducting operations in the Rung Sat. Lieutenant (j.g.) Truxell was leading an eight-man patrol on a recon mission deep in the RSSZ. The day before, on August 18, the patrol had discovered two buildings hidden in the swamp and containing a supply cache of an estimated 306,000 pounds of rice. The loss of the rice cache was greatly felt by the VC operating in the Rung Sat.

The patrol was moving through the jungle on August 19 in search of hidden sampans reported by friendly forces. The patrol had reached a clearing and stopped when suddenly the point man, PO Machen, fired on hidden enemy forces, initiating a Viet Cong ambush before the rest of the patrol had entered the killing zone. Due in part to the leadership of Lieutenant (j.g.) Truxell and the Assistant Fire Team Leader, Petty Officer Moscone, the patrol was able to suppress the enemy fire from the estimated thirty to forty Viet Cong of the ambush force and recover Machen's body. Petty Officer Moscone carried the body of his fallen comrade through five hundred meters of heavy jungle swampland before the patrol was able to be exfiltrated. Machen was posthumously awarded the Silver Star for his gallant actions that prevented further losses from his patrol teammates.

On October 7, SEAL Team 1 suffered its greatest number of casualties in a single engagement. An armed LCM (Landing Craft, Mechanized) was ambushed on the Long Tau River when it came across a group of Viet Cong conducting a surprise water crossing. With the SEALs and other Navy units making travel on the Rung Sat waterways hazardous, the VC had taken to traveling overland and crossing waterways when they had to.

In the ambush, the LCM was taking heavy fire from the large number of VC on either side of the river. The VC were firing small arms, automatic weapons, light machine guns, and mortars at the SEAL craft. If the LCM had not been converted into a fighting boat, it would not have lasted a moment in the heavy fire. The sides of the LCM had been covered with armor, and weapons had been fitted to it. The LCM was armed with a 20-mm cannon, two .50-caliber machine guns, four .30-caliber machine guns, and a 60-mm mortar, and the nineteen SEALs aboard had their personal weapons. The open hull section of the LCM gave the SEALs a good area from which to fight but was vulnerable to overhead attack. During the ambush, the inevitable happened.

An enemy mortar round made a direct hit on the open section of the boat. Sixteen of the nineteen men on board the LCM were wounded by the blast.

Lieutenant Truxell was one of the SEALs on board the LCM when it was hit. In spite of the personal danger to himself, Truxell continued firing his weapon, passing ammunition and helping to care for the wounded throughout the ambush. Seaman Penn was manning a .50-caliber machine gun on the LCM and continued to pour accurate and deadly fire into the enemy positions around him. Penn was felled by wounds to his back and head when the mortar round detonated just aft of his position.

Another SEAL, Petty Officer Pearson, was manning the LCM's other .50-caliber gun during the ambush. In spite of wounds in his head and right hand from the mortar round, Pearson continued to man his gun, driving the enemy back with his constant firing.

One SEAL, Chief Petty Officer Churchill, was later awarded the Silver Star for his actions on board the LCM during the ambush. When the VC opened fire on the LCM, CPO Churchill quickly manned a .30-caliber machine gun and began returning fire. When the machine gun jammed, Churchill worked feverishly to try to clear his weapon. While Churchill was struggling with his weapon, the enemy mortar round struck the LCM about six feet from his position.

Although seriously wounded and only semiconscious, Churchill noticed smoke coming from the boat's mortar position. Moving to the mortar, Churchill found that a hot fragment from the exploded mortar round was igniting the wooden boxes holding the LCM's 60-mm mortar ammunition. Realizing that if the mortar ammunition exploded, the LCM would be destroyed, Churchill acted immediately. Disregarding the pain from the severe burns he had suffered, Churchill picked up the hot fragment and threw it overboard.

CPO Churchill then noticed that one of the .50-caliber guns was no longer firing. Moving to the weapon's position, Churchill saw that the gunner was slumped down unconscious. Though he had to expose himself to enemy fire to move to the position, Churchill went over to where the gunner, Seaman Penn, lay stricken. Pulling the unconscious gunner from his weapon, Churchill then attempted to man the gun himself. The senior officer present moved to Churchill's position and took over manning the .50-caliber gun. CPO Churchill then began caring for the seriously injured SEALs around him, further exposing himself to enemy fire.

After the ambush was over, intelligence reports indicated that the SEALs had accounted for forty enemy dead from the ambush force. Three of the SEALs aboard the LCM who had been wounded in the ambush—Lieutenant (j.g.) Pechacek, Petty Officer First Class Henry, and Petty Officer Third Class Penn—retired from naval service due to the disabling wounds they had received.

On December 3 and 4, 1966, SEALs from Detachment Golf volunteered to conduct reconnaissance patrols in support of U.S. Army units during Operation Charleston in the RSSZ. Using intelligence sources developed by the SEALs, a six-man SEAL patrol captured a large VC arms cache. A 57-mm recoilless rifle, two 7.92-mm German World War II machine guns, two U.S. M1 carbines, one U.S. M3A1 submachine gun, and 10,000 rounds of assorted ammunition were recovered in the cache. The particular recoilless rifle captured by the SEALs in Operation Charleston is now part of a Vietnam display at the Navy Museum in the Washington Navy Yard in Washington, D.C.

Intelligence gathered by the SEALs helped guide Army units to the locations of other VC arms-and-supply caches. On December 15 and 16, the SEALs were asked to conduct additional patrols in support of Operation Charleston. On December 21, one of the SEAL patrols discovered an extensive Viet Cong base camp. Finding the camp usable but unoccupied, the SEALs radioed for quantities of explosives to be airlifted to their position. Using their demolition skills, the SEALs obliterated the VC camp. Many enemy documents and other items of intelligence value were collected by the SEALs during Operation Charleston.

Although they do not show the quality of the intelligence

gathered, the following figures do show the results of SEAL operations conducted in Vietnam during 1966:

VC KIA	86
VC KIA (probable)	15
Sampans destroyed	21
Junks destroyed	2
Huts/bunkers destroyed	33
Rice captured or destroyed	521,600 pounds

Numerous enemy documents, diaries, and papers were also retrieved.*

Besides actions by Detachment Golf in Vietnam, the other platoons of SEAL Team 1 were conducting operations in the United States, including the operational evaluation of the Aerial Recovery System Skyhook.

In Skyhook, an inflated hydrogen balloon carries aloft a cable attached to a harness. A specially equipped plane can grab the cable from the air and winch it into the craft. On the ground, an individual wearing the cable's harness is jerked high into the air to be drawn into the plane. During the evaluation, SEAL Team 1 personnel made several live, two-man pickups using the Skyhook system. Tests were conducted both during the day and at night. An S2F-type aircraft was used, flying at speeds of 110 knots.

SEAL Team 2 was also busy during 1966 but saw no action in Vietnam. From February 25 to March 1, the entire complement of SEAL Team 2 participated in Operation White Geese. The operation was an extensive penetration problem conducted against the Coast Guard facilities at Cape Hatteras, North Carolina. The SEALs were divided into seven assault teams and each team was assigned a specific target. Further training was conducted during 1966 with other U.S. military and NATO units.

In August, SEAL Team 2 was told to prepare an operational detachment for duties in Vietnam. Later in the year, members of the team were told it would be expanded and

*Figures derived from *Command and Control Histories*, U.S. Navy Seals, 1962-1973.

have a new organizational layout. The team would now have ten operational platoons of two officers and twelve enlisted men each.

The detachment that would be going to Vietnam would at first be made up of two of the old organizational platoons along with an officer in command (OIC). Five officers and twenty enlisted men would make up the two platoons and OIC for the Vietnam detachment. On September 26, the Vietnam unit, known as Detachment Alpha, began conducting extensive training to prepare for their deployment to Southeast Asia. Detachment Alpha arrived for duty in Vietnam early in 1967.

One very unusual action took place during 1966 involving the UDTs in Vietnam. A detachment from UDT-11 was conducting beach reconnaissance in South Vietnam. Working from the submarine U.S.S. *Perch*, the UDTs were operating in support of Operation Deckhouse III. The objective of the UDT operation was a detailed examination of the beach area north of Qui Nhon in II Corps. The area was a notorious VC stronghold and landings were going to be conducted to clear the VC out. Unknown to the UDTs, the VC had learned of the *Perch*'s planned visit to their area.

On the night of August 20, a UDT party conducting beach reconnaissance came under fire from a Viet Cong unit that had been waiting in ambush. Though the fire from the VC positions was inaccurate, a group of the UDT swimmers became lost in the confusion while trying to return to the submarine. The *Perch* launched a UDT search team to try to locate the missing swimmers.

While the search party was out, the lost swimmers made it back to the sub. A team of three UDT men took out an IBS to help locate the search party after its men had missed their return time. Taking a known risk, the UDT lieutenant in the IBS ignited a signal flare when the IBS was midway between the shore and the submarine. Immediately the lost men were heard shouting to the boats, and the Viet Cong opened fire. The *Perch* which had moved in closer to shore, opened up with her .50-caliber machine guns to cover the return of all the UDT men.

The next day the *Perch* again engaged enemy units onshore. This time the *Perch*'s gun crews opened up with all of the boat's weapons, her .50-calibers and her 40-mm cannon. The heavy gunfire from the submarine helped defeat the Viet Cong, who had pinned down a supporting ARVN unit on shore. Later that afternoon the *Perch* again used all her weapons to help defeat the Viet Cong, who were attacking the UDT men and ARVN (Army of the Republic of Vietnam) soldiers staging a small invasion of their own against the Viet Cong positions.

The results of the *Perch*'s operations proved successful without the loss of a single man. This also proved the end of the last surface actions that would be performed by a U.S. Navy submarine.

The combat capabilities of the UDTs were not ignored during 1966. UDT-11 received new weapons during the year to replace older models they still had in use. Smith & Wesson 9-mm automatics replaced the S&W K-38 .38 Special revolvers the UDTs had been using. UDT-11 also received fifty twelve-gauge shotguns, four M79 40-mm grenade launchers, and one hundred M16 rifles.

Vietnam: 1967

SEAL Team 1 began 1967 with twenty-five officers and ninety-seven enlisted men divided into ten operational platoons. The ten platoons were designated alphabetically Alfa through Kilo; India was omitted to prevent communications confusion with the number 1. With SEAL Team 1's increasing commitment in Vietnam and the Mekong Delta, an eleventh platoon, Lima, was added in March of 1967. March also saw the expansion of the number of men in a SEALs platoon. The ten (later eleven) platoons each had two officers, a platoon leader and his assistant, and ten enlisted men to start and were expanded in March to twelve enlisted men each. By March, SEAL Team 1 had twenty-seven officers and one hundred and thirteen enlisted men on board.

Platoons were further broken down into two squads of seven men each, six enlisted men and an officer. The size of the squads had been determined to be the most suitable number for many of the clandestine operations the SEALs conducted in Vietnam.

The increasing demands on the SEAL team personnel resulted in a severe shortage of qualified men. The shortages resulted in a draft being placed on new BUD/S graduates to enter the SEAL teams. The January class of 1967 was the first such class to be subject to the draft. By September, the drafting of graduates was threatening to seriously deplete the UDTs of all their experienced personnel. Since that time, a portion of each BUD/S class has been considered for direct training and duties in the SEAL teams.

Platoon training was the primary occupation of those SEALs from SEAL Team 1 who were in the continental United States (CONUS). Each platoon underwent an extensive series of exercises based on the probable future operations that would be conducted in Vietnam. Exercises included field operations on land in ambush/counterambush techniques. The exercises were conducted along the Alamo River in Southern California. Other training included submarine operations conducted in the nearby Pacific Ocean.

Extensive weapons firing and familiarization was also conducted. Weapons used included the M16 series, 9-mm Smith & Wesson pistols, .50- and .30-caliber machine guns (M2HB, M1919A4, and M60), M79 and XM148 40-mm grenade launchers, the 57-mm M18A1 recoilless rifle, M19 60-mm and M29 81-mm mortars, and the .45-caliber M3A1 and 9-mm Smith & Wesson M76 submachine guns. Parachute jumps, both day and night, were practiced from helicopters and fixed-wing aircraft. Deploying platoons to Vietnam were stressing helicopter operations. Particular attention was being placed on insertion by rappelling from a hovering helicopter and extraction using the McGuire rig or Jacob's ladder.

The McGuire rig was adopted from the Army Special Forces and consisted of a number of ropes and harnesses that would be attached to the pickup helicopter. The rig would be dropped from both sides of the helicopter while the aircraft hovered fifty or more feet above the ground. Each man would sit in one of the three webbing harnesses on each rope and secure himself. The helicopter would then fly off with the men suspended underneath the craft. When the helicopter had reached a secure area it would land and the suspended team would board normally and continue the flight.

The Jacob's ladder was an even simpler but less secure system. The men being exfiltrated would step into loops on a dangling rope attached to the pickup helicopter; a rope ladder with solid rungs could also be used with the men stepping on a rung and standing to the side of the ladder. By having their feet in the loops or on a rung and hanging on to the suspension rope, the SEAL squad could be quickly evacuated from an area. The drawback with the Jacob's ladder system was that it could not be easily used with a severely injured or unconscious man.

Communications training was also conducted by the platoons. Besides Radio Telephone Operator procedures, the SEALs were given a thorough indoctrination in the operation of several types of communications equipment. Particular concentration was given to operating the AN/PRC-25, AN/PRC-47, and Motorola hand radios, as these were the primary systems the SEALs were using in Vietnam.

Further training was given in all types of booby traps, explosives use, diving gear, swimmer delivery vehicles, and surface and underwater electronics (fathometer, hand-held sonar, Burdette acoustic equipment). The use and operation of foreign weapons was also taught to the SEALs. Particular emphasis was placed on those weapons the SEALs might encounter in Vietnam, such as the AK-47 and its variants, the SKS carbine, and other weapons.

During 1967, about 20 percent of the SEALs in CONUS at any one time were attending outside civilian or military schools. Schools and students were chosen with the intention of increasing the operational knowledge available within the team. Military schools included Ranger, Pathfinder, and Jungle Warfare courses. Civilian-run courses attended by SEALs included gunsmithing, Stoner weapons system school, and locksmithing, among others. Twenty-nine SEALs attended language schools during 1967. Languages studied included French, Thai, and Vietnamese.

Detachment Golf was conducting extensive operations in the RSSZ by the beginning of 1967. Activities included prisoner abductions, listening-post operations, diving operations, and reconnaissance patrols. The first translations of documents captured by the SEALs during Operation Charleston became available early in January. The documents indicated that the Viet Cong were dependent on a number of freshwater wells located in the southern section of the Rung Sat near the village of Thanh Thoi.

Aerial reconnaissance of the suspected area showed numerous trails leading from the jungle to the locations of several of the wells. To put a stop to this valuable source of resupply to the VC, the SEALs decided to systematically destroy the wells.

On January 12, two six-man fire teams, Teams 9 and 5, were inserted by helicopter into the Rung Sat near the village of Thanh Thoi. The SEALs were going on a demolition raid and were carrying quantities of high explosives. The two fire teams located and destroyed eight wells without incident. The raids were considered completely successful.

About two months after the well-destruction raids, the SEALs received a report on the extent of their success. A U.S. Army advisor was located in the village of Can Gio in the RSSZ, about two and a half miles from the Thanh Thoi village. The advisor informed the SEALs that the Viet Cong units in his area were forced to travel long distances to other villages in order to obtain fresh water. This was very good news to the SEALs, as the Viet Cong entering a strange village would be easily recognized and thereby vulnerable.

The SEALs realized that water sources were a very worthwhile target in their operations against the VC. During subsequent operations in the RSSZ, freshwater wells were considered prime targets of opportunity, but the opportunity was not always acted on. A report filed by Fire Team 6 of Detachment Golf illustrates this.

Over the period of May 4-5, 1967, Fire Team 6 was on a patrol in the RSSZ. During the patrol, the team came across thirteen freshwater wells as well as a number of bunkers and some booby traps. Though the bunkers were destroyed, the wells were left alone as it was known to the SEALs that they were very important to the local civilian population and were used by area farmers (Report # 195).

On January 20 the SEALs were working on an operation as part of Operation Game Warden. Moving with other units from Control Task Force 116, the SEALs were helping to support an Army unit conducting a sweep of a portion of the RSSZ. The SEALs were using their armed LCM-3 and an LCPL Mk 4 to block the Viet Cong possibly escaping from a river island while the Army unit swept the area.

As the LCM-3 approached a village, hidden Viet Cong forces launched an ambush against the SEAL craft. Heavy automatic weapons fire, combined with B-40 antitank rockets, poured into the LCM. In spite of the fact that three SEALs were wounded and an ARVN officer was killed, the LCM withstood the enemy assault. The SEALs aboard put out a heavy fire of their own, using all of their personal weapons as well as the mounted guns of the LCM. Gaining fire superiority, the SEALs defeated and drove off their Viet Cong ambushers.

The entire operation was later termed a total success by the U.S. Army commander in charge. Four Viet Cong were killed during the action, and large caches of food, ammunition, demolitions, clothing, and documents were captured. All the participating units in the operation and each of the SEAL personnel received a letter of appreciation from the Army commander.

During April, while again providing support for other units during a joint operation, the SEALs' LCM-3 again came under fire. While traveling along the Vam Sat River, the SEAL LCM was attacked by heavy fire coming from hidden Viet Cong bunkers along the shore. Aboard the LCM were Fire Teams 3 and 4 (Kilo platoon), along with some South Vietnamese naval personnel undergoing field training. During the firefight, the SEALs were holding their own against the fortified VC when there was a sudden explosion directly over the boat.

The airburst explosion was later believed to have been caused by a large-caliber VC mortar round with a proximity fuse. The blast and fragmentation caused serious casualties throughout the SEAL boat. Twelve SEALs were wounded and two SEALs were killed outright from the blast. Two of the Vietnamese personnel on board were also wounded and one of the SEALs later died of his wounds.

In spite of the large number of casualties, the LCM managed to fight its way free of the ambush. The LCM quickly moved to an area where its wounded could be evacuated by helicopter. With a skeleton complement on board, the LCM was able to return to the SEALs base at Nha Be under its own power.

Most of the SEALs on board the LCM during the attack had only been in-country for three days, Kilo platoon having arrived in Vietnam on April 4. Killed in the action were SEAL Lieutenant (j.g.) D. Mann, IC3 Boston, and RM3 Neal. Some of the wounded SEALs were sent Stateside for hospitalization. After being released from the hospital, most of the injured SEALs reenlisted and requested immediate return to Vietnam duty.

The SEALs also learned by the above actions to no longer use their larger craft for simple support operations. The SEALs' LCM and other craft would be primarily used for insertions and extractions, communications, and logistic support. Using the SEALs for general duty, though important and of an aggressive nature, only resulted in large numbers of casualties among the few available SEALs.

New methods for using the craft assigned to them were constantly being devised by the SEALs in the field. One such development was a new insertion technique used by Detachment Golf during March. On March 19-20, Fire Team 9 was inserted into the Rung Sat to conduct a night ambush/capture patrol. All week the SEALs had been using PBRs for insertions. The PBR would run as close as possible to the bank with its engines running at 1,500 rpm. The SEALs would jump from the stern of the craft and swim in to shore. The Patrol Boat River would neither change speed nor direction and the sound of the engines would cover any noise the SEALs might make.

For the ambush/capture operations, the SEALs would go in very lightly equipped. No web gear would be worn that could interfere with the swimming insertion. For the same reason no radio would be taken with the patrol. The SEALs would take only their weapons, two magazines of ammunition, a flare, and a flashlight with a red lens. Though Fire Team 9 inserted three ambush teams along the shore of the Soi Rap, the hunters had no luck that night and the team came up empty.

A third SEAL platoon arrived in April to increase the SEALs' presence in the RSSZ. Detachment Golf was now made up of three platoons from SEAL Team 1, with a complement of seven officers and thirty enlisted men.

The increase in the available number of SEALs made a new type of operation more feasible. From April 3 to 10 a new listening-post operation, with an extended time on station, was tried out in the Rung Sat by Detachment Golf. Continuous surveillance of specific waterways was needed by higher command to establish a pattern, if any, to Viet Cong supply efforts. To this end, one SEAL platoon activated a number of listening-post (LP) sites for a four-day time in place. Three LPs were manned for an even longer period—seven days without relief. The major point of military significance proved by the operations was that the SEALs were able to effectively conduct reconnaissance missions over extended lengths of time. The SEALs could man their positions without outside resupply, which could compromise their location.

The extended-time patrol was used for other purposes than just listening posts. Combined LP/ambush operations were also started during April, May, and June. At times SEAL units had to wait quietly for up to four days in insect- and reptile-infested jungle before successfully completing their mission. While gathering intelligence, the SEALs would often find themselves in very close proximity to the enemy. Sometimes only a few yards would separate the SEALs and the Viet Cong. Hidden SEALs could hear VC troops talking quietly among themselves, not even suspecting the nearby SEALs.

If a SEAL unit on LP duty was ever detected by a larger enemy force, it would be almost impossible for outside assistance to reach the SEALs in time to rescue them. Though the SEALs were superbly able, they were still human and subject to mistakes. During one ambush operation, the SEALs had been quietly holding position for hours, waiting for an enemy force to use the nearby stream. Just as a sampan was approaching, one of the SEALs coughed. The approaching sampan quickly turned about and scurried away. If the sampan had been the first boat of an armed VC convoy, the story for the SEALs could have turned out to have had a much worse ending than simple disappointment.

During one operation, a team of SEALs under the command of Lieutenant Michael Troy were working deep inside enemy-controlled territory. Lieutenant Troy, a 1960 Olympic gold medal winner in the 200-meter butterfly, was leading his SEALs on an ambush mission. Before the SEALs were able to spring their ambush, a large force of some sixty Viet Cong approached their shore position.

The SEALs quickly took cover in the dark waters of the river. With only their camouflaged faces exposed above water, the SEALs waited motionless for twelve hours until the Viet Cong left the area. The VC searched the area for the Americans that they suspected were there but found nothing. Lieutenant Troy later remembered, "One VC came so close to me I could have reached out and touched him." The area the SEALs had been operating in was thick jungle down to the water's edge with visibility limited to only twelve feet during daylight. At night, when the incident took place, there was effectively no visibility at all.

The number of operations conducted by the SEALs during June slacked off due to the arrival of the monsoon season. New techniques for insertions and extractions using PBRs were practiced and perfected by the SEALs during this time. The PBRs were used very successfully by the SEALs, who liked the small boat's quietness, speed, and ample fire support.

During the last week of June, Admiral Veth held a SEAL symposium. The symposium was to determine who could best use the SEALs' capabilities. It was generally agreed that the SEALs' operations in the RSSZ were very valuable and should continue uninterrupted. It was also thought that combining the SEALs' capabilities with those of the Mobile

Riverine Force (CTF 117) would result in a very potent fighting force for use against the VC in other areas of Vietnam.

During the first week of July, the SEALs worked with a combined force in what was to prove a very successful operation. Juliet and Kilo platoons from Detachment Golf joined forces with units of the 2/7 First Air Cavalry, the Navy destroyer U.S.S. *Brush*, and the U.S. Coast Guard cutter *Point White* in Operation Shallow Draft 11-A on July 2. The target of the SEALs raiding force was a Viet Cong stronghold in the Hon Heo Secret Zone northeast of Nha Trang in II Corps area. The stronghold was suspected to have several leaders of the local VC infrastructure inside it, and the SEALs intended to abduct them.

The raid was launched from the U.S.S. *Brush* and marked the first utilization of a destroyer in direct support of a SEAL Team 1 combat mission. In addition to acting as the raid's launch platform, the *Brush* remained on station for three days to provide radio relay service. The *Brush* also fired 162 rounds of five-inch ammunition in support of the SEALs' operation.

The SEALs moved to within range of the shore in IBSs. Swimmer/scouts then entered the water to swim in for a beach recon. Their recon completed and the beach found clear, the scouts signaled in the boats. The team moved inland to their first rally point and stopped to establish radio communications with the *Brush* and the *Point White*. The team then moved west to the Nui Binh Whon hill. Climbing the hill, the SEALs established an observation point and settled in for the night.

The next day the team observed the Twin Lakes region throughout the day. Just before last light, the six-man abduction patrol moved out to their target. Later, a four-man unit of VC were seen to leave the treeline and move to a well the SEALs had under observation. The abduction team was notified and the *Brush* was put on alert. The *Brush* had a preplanned concentration of fire they would launch when signaled.

The four Vietnamese, two men and two women, approached the well and were hailed by the abduction team's interpreter. The four took off running but were stopped by the SEALs. One of the women was killed by a gunshot during the chase. One of the male VC received a slight flesh wound, but it was not considered serious.

Extraction helicopters and gunships were called in from Phan Thiet. Naval gunfire from the *Brush* impacted in the woods near the SEALs. The first round from the *Brush* was on the way within four minutes of the capture. The SEALs exfiltrated with their prisoners by helicopter without mishap.

The dead woman turned out to be the head of a VC women's organization. The two male prisoners were VC cell leaders. Papers found on the prisoners turned out to be valuable intelligence, with a list of VC cell members among the information captured.

The results of the operation were considered very worthwhile. More of the same type of combined operations was suggested. The key to the success of the operation was, according to the SEALs, the availability of current, accurate intelligence on the target as well as effective on-call support.

Though the CTF 117 combined operation was the most spectacular success performed by the SEALs during July, the rest of Detachment Golf was also conducting actions against the enemy. In a period of fourteen days in July, Kilo platoon conducted a number of extended ambushes in the RSSZ. Kilo made enemy contact three times, killing several VC and capturing a number of documents. Other Detachment Golf SEALs on reconnaissance or ambush patrols in the RSSZ made direct contact with the enemy on nine occasions during July.

In the first weeks of August, Detachment Golf had new demands placed on it for SEAL personnel. The Army's 199th Brigade was performing operations in the Rung Sat with the SEALs acting as advance scouts and intelligence-gathering units. Forty-eight-hour extended ambushes were still performed by the SEALs on the major waterways of the Rung Sat in August. During one of these ambushes, Echo platoon took out a VC courier who was carrying ten pounds of the most valuable documents yet captured in the RSSZ.

Throughout September and October the weather continued to clear as the monsoon season came to an end. To take advantage of the good weather, the schedule of patrols and ambushes conducted by Detachment Golf was increased to good effect. One ambush took place on September 21, and it proved very worthwhile.

Alfa platoon successfully ambushed a Viet Cong sapper squad before the VC could emplace their weapons. The VC sappers had been preparing to mine the Long Tau River with a number of command-detonated mines. In the ambush, seven VC were either killed or wounded and a quantity of mine-detonating equipment was captured.

September and October also saw the introduction of high-speed Boston Whalers to SEAL operations in the RSSZ. The Whalers were intended for the quick recovery of ambushed sampans before the craft had a chance to sink. Using this tactic increased the amount of intelligence captured by the SEALs while conducting ambushes. The Boston Whalers proved so successful and versatile that the SEAL teams continue to use them to this day.

With the increasingly favorable weather during November and December, a greater emphasis was placed on Detachment Golf's conducting ambushes rather than patrols. This emphasis, combined with the new equipment and techniques, resulted in the SEALs' capturing an increasing amount of valuable intelligence. Eight successful ambushes were conducted by the SEALs during November and December.

On December 9, Bravo platoon relieved Echo platoon at Detachment Golf. The heavy stresses SEAL duty forced on the men was part of the reason the SEAL platoons had only a six-month tour of duty. However, the small number of available SEAL platoons often resulted in a relieved platoon's going to another detachment and relieving a platoon there. This is called a "port and starboard" rotation in the Navy.

Bravo platoon was taken under heavy enemy fire on December 23 while patrolling deep inside the T-10 VC Regimental Headquarters area. During the firefight one SEAL, the point man, SN F. G. Antone, was killed along with a

South Vietnamese scout. Three SEAL riflemen were also wounded in the exchange. In spite of the casualties, the SEALs suppressed the enemy fire long enough to stage a helicopter extraction. It was later learned that the platoon had walked into the outer perimeter of a VC base camp.

Detachment Golf's actions in the RSSZ were considered very successful during 1967. The patrol and ambush operations conducted by Golf placed a substantial psychological burden on VC units operating in the RSSZ. The Viet Cong could not be sure where or when in the RSSZ a supposedly safe shoreline would suddenly erupt in a devastating ambush. The "men in green faces," the name the VC gave to the SEALs, could rise up from the ground at any time and suddenly snatch people away. This situation resulted in an increased number of VC defectors entering the Chieu Hoi program.

Not all of the operations by Detachment Golf could strike fear in the hearts of the Vietnamese people. SEAL team members also organized a program in CONUS for collecting clothing and other needed items to be sent to villages in the field. One SEAL, Warrant Officer Wayne Boles, was particularly helpful to an orphanage in Vinh Long. When Boles received a package of cookies from a ten-year-old Burbank Girl Scout, he also received a note asking what else could be sent to the American military men. Boles wrote back to the girl, Patty Basso, and told her about a local orphanage and what it needed. After a number of other people became involved, a 1,600-pound package of badly needed supplies arrived for the local Vietnamese civilians. The SEALs personally delivered fifty pounds of diapers to the seventy-five orphans at the Vinh Long orphanage.

Presidential Unit Citation—Seal Team 1

Perhaps the best introduction to the SEALs' actions in Vietnam is the following official document:

The President of the United States takes pleasure in
presenting
THE PRESIDENTIAL UNIT CITATION to
SEAL TEAM ONE
as set forth in the following
CITATION:

For exceptionally meritorious and heroic service from
16 July 1966 to 31 August 1967, in the conduct of naval
unconventional warfare operations against the Viet
Cong in the Republic of Vietnam. Although often required to carry out their operations in treacherous and
almost impenetrable mangrove swamps against overwhelming odds, SEAL TEAM ONE personnel maintained
an aggressive operating schedule and were highly successful in gathering intelligence data and interdicting
Viet Cong operations. On one occasion, a six-man fire
team ambushed one junk and two sampans, accounting
for seven Viet Cong dead and the capture of valuable
intelligence data. During this daring ambush, all members of the fire team remained in exposed, waist-deep
mud and water in order to obtain clear fields of fire. As
a result of their constant alertness and skillful reading
of Viet Cong trail markers, patrols of SEAL TEAM ONE
succeeded in discovering numerous wellconcealed Viet
Cong base camps and supply caches, capturing or destroying over 228 tons of Viet Cong rice, as well as numerous river craft, weapons, buildings, and documents.
The outstanding esprit de corps of the men of this unit
was evidenced on 7 October 1966 when a direct hit by
an enemy mortar round wounded sixteen of the nineteen
men aboard the detachment's armed LCM, and again on
7 April 1967 when three members of the SEAL TEAM
ONE LCM were killed and eleven were wounded in a
firefight with Viet Cong positioned along the banks of a
narrow stream. On both occasions, SEAL TEAM ONE
men who were able, even though seriously wounded,
returned to their positions and continued to fire their
weapons until the boat was out of danger, thereby helping to save the lives of their comrades. The heroic
achievements of SEAL TEAM ONE reflect the outstanding professionalism, valor, teamwork, and selfless dedication of the unit's officers and men. Their performance
was in keeping with the highest traditions of the United
States Naval Service.

Richard Nixon

> "I would like to have a
> thousand more like them."
>
> General William C. Westmoreland
> Commander MAC-V, after being
> asked his opinion of the Navy
> SEALs actions during 1967.

Vietnam: 1968

In 1968 SEAL Team 1 was still continuing to grow. A total allowance of 33 officers and 195 enlisted men had been authorized for Team 1 by the CNO on January 22, 1968. By July, SEAL Team 1 had 29 officers and 182 enlisted men on board organized into twelve platoons. Platoons were designated Alfa to Mike, India being omitted, and not all of the platoons were completely up to strength.

SEAL Team 1's Vietnam commitment was now five operational platoons divided among three detachments. Detachment Golf, stationed at Nha Be, consisted of three SEAL platoons and an OIC. Golf still operated primarily in the RSSZ but extended its operations into the Mekong Delta area during the year.

Detachment Bravo was under the operational control of the Commander MAC-V and worked in support of the Phoenix Program. One platoon from SEAL Team 1 and a partial platoon from SEAL Team 2 made up the personnel for this unit.

The third unit in Vietnam manned by SEAL Team 1 personnel was Detachment Echo. Detachment Echo was also under the operational control of the Commander MAC-V and was stationed at the Naval Advisory Detachment at Da Nang. The smallest Vietnam detachment supported by the SEALs, Detachment Echo had one officer and five enlisted men. Acting as advisors, the men of Detachment Echo were continuing an operation the SEALs had begun in 1962 with MTT 10-62, the instruction of Vietnamese personnel in how to conduct special warfare in a counterinsurgency environment.

Detachment Golf performed the majority of the actions that were recorded by SEAL Team 1 in its official history. Occasionally, SEALs would be assigned to duties with the Special Operations Group of the Military Assistance Command (MAC-V SOG). Specific operations that the SEALs were involved in were rarely reported in unclassified form and are generally unavailable for publication. Though the SEALs will not officially talk about it, unofficial sources say there were a number of men who had operated in the waters of North Vietnam.

There are many rumors concerning the activities of the SEALs in Vietnam. If there were as many SEALs in Vietnam as individuals claim to have been, General Westmoreland would have had his "thousand just like them." It is reasonable to believe, however, that there were SEALs "intimately familiar with the waters of Haiphong Harbor." Other stories have the SEALs stealing a SAM-7 missile launcher from a Russian cargo ship while it lay at anchor in North Vietnamese waters. Still more stories tell of SEALs sinking Russian ships in Haiphong Harbor or destroying strategic targets, such as bridges, on North Vietnamese waterways.

These stories, though interesting, are almost impossible to confirm. The reality of SEAL operations is reflected in the long hours on patrol or waiting in ambush along the waterways of the Rung Sat or Mekong Delta. But even in these areas, the actions of the SEALs, and the part those few played, are an almost unbelievable story in itself.

The first SEAL operations for 1968 took place as combined operations with units from the riverine forces. On January 2, a SEAL squad from Bravo platoon of Detachment Golf left Nha Be to stage an operation from Binh Thuy, a riverine base just west of Can Tho in the Mekong Delta. The squad was working with the riverine forces of CTF 116 as part of Operation Game Warden. On January 11 WO1 Casey, Bravo's assistant platoon leader, led a patrol that engaged the VC.

The squad was approaching a known VC bunker when it suddenly came under fire. Unknown to the SEALs, a five-man VC rocket squad was in the bunker as the SEALs moved in. A single Viet Cong ran from the bunker, firing his AK-47 at the approaching SEALs. The opening burst of fire mortally wounded Seaman Keith, who thus became the first SEAL killed in action in 1968.

Reacting quickly, the squad eliminated the entire VC team. Four Viet Cong bodies were found, and a fifth man, who escaped, was thought to have been badly wounded. One RPG-type rocket launcher, three rockets, and three AK-47s were captured.

Bravo platoon also conducted a combined operation with SEAL Team 2 personnel in January. The SEALs cleared a canal blockage that was preventing the PBRs of CTF 116 from using the canal. On January 22, the SEALs used three hundred pounds of explosives and cleared three hundred meters of canal for boat traffic.

The Australians were one of the foreign forces operating in Vietnam in cooperation with the United States. The Australian *Special Air Service (SAS)* operated primarily in the Phuoc Tuy province east of Saigon but it also joined in operations in the Mekong Delta area. Preferring the U.S. unconventional forces to what the Australians would politely refer to as the ''ponderous'' U.S. regulars, the Australians would readily operate with the SEALs.

On the night of January 22 and the early morning of January 23, a team of five Australian SAS joined the second squad from Alfa platoon (Alfa 2) in conducting an overnight ambush in the RSSZ. The team inserted by helicopter, using rope ladders to descend. The terrain was mangrove swamp, the weather was clear, and the moon was in its last quarter. Inserting at 1830 hours, the team prepared their ambush site and settled in to wait for their target.

Eleven hours after insertion, at 0530 hours, the SEALs heard the approach of several boats. Three sampans, holding eight to twelve VC, came out of the mouth of a small stream about three hundred meters north of the ambush site. But they were moving away from the ambush site. Rather than let their quarry escape, the combined team quickly moved up and initiated an ambush.

The SEALs called in fire support in the form of 81-mm mortar illumination rounds from an armed LCM waiting close by to pick up the team. All of the mortar rounds fired by the LCM were duds and the SEALs had to illuminate the ambush site with hand-fired parachute flares.

Two VC were killed and a sampan, a number of grenades, and the personal gear of the two dead enemy soldiers were taken. Examination of the soldiers' uniforms indicated that they were North Vietnamese army regulars rather than Viet Cong.

The LCM took the two escaping sampans under fire when they entered the Thai-Vai River, where the LCM had been waiting. At 0600 hours the LCM extracted the ambush team.

It was the opinion of the SEALs that there was a large VC base camp near where the ambush site had been. The camp was suspected to be at the head of the stream from which the sampans had first come. Due to a lack of friendly Vietnamese civilians in the immediate area, a large number of VC were able to use the base camp undetected.

On January 28, Delta platoon arrived at Nha Be and relieved Foxtrot platoon. In February, Delta platoon began conducting field operations in the RSSZ. To become familiar with the terrain, Delta's first operations were performed while working with elements from Alfa platoon.

Delta's first operation was a twenty-four-hour patrol/ambush. Squads Alfa 1 and Delta 1 were on the operation, backed by Seawolf attack helicopters. Inserting by LCM, the team was moving in an area of dry ground with sections of nipa palm. Nothing of note was encountered during the day's patrol.

By 2225 hours, the moon was up and shining in its first quarter in the warm night air. After hearing two sampans moving on the nearby Rach Tram River, the SEALs prepared to initiate their ambush. When the two sampans entered the killing zone the SEALs opened fire.

The ambush resulted in two VC KIA and two VC missing. A rifle and ammunition were captured along with the two sampans. The area was considered an excellent training site to break in new platoons and Delta demonstrated its capabilities.

Delta platoon left Nha Be on March 1 and moved to Binh Thuy to conduct operations as part of CTF 116 and Operation Game Warden. Bravo platoon returned to Nha Be and continued operations in the RSSZ with Mike platoon. The two SEAL platoons conducted several successful ambushes and bunker demolitions during March.

Special operations were increasing in the SEAL platoons and often showed spectacular results. Two such operations were performed by Delta platoon on March 29. Delta 1 (first squad) along with the Seventh platoon from Detachment Alfa, went on a mission to capture an arms cache and destroy a reported weapons factory in the upper Mekong Delta.

The SEALs worked the mission with the assistance of riverine PBRs and Seawolf helicopters. Inserting by PBR, the SEALs worked their way inland through cane fields interspersed with banana and coconut groves. Starting their patrol at 0430 hours, the SEALs were being led to the caches by the Hoi Chanh. The moon was in its last quarter in a partly cloudy sky, making the area very dark and the SEALs dependent on their VC defector (Hoi Chanh).

Arriving at the target area, the SEALs established a security perimeter around the small village. Four targeted huts were pointed out by the Hoi Chanh as being used by the VC. Before the SEALs could start their sweep of the objective, two Viet Cong walked into the security element holding the perimeter.

Both of the enemy soldiers were killed in hand-to-hand combat before they could give the alarm. Lieutenant (j.g.) Freedley, the only SEAL casualty of the operation, suffered a knife wound in his left leg.

After securing the village, the SEALs killed two more Viet Cong who were trying to escape. The Hoi Chanh located the well-camouflaged cache that was hidden inside one of the huts. The cache contained a complete hand grenade factory. This was the only cache that the Hoi Chanh knew of, but he suspected that more was hidden in the village.

Interrogation of one of the villagers revealed the existence of a second cache, containing heavy weapons and ammunitions, in an underground storeroom nearby.

The SEALs loaded the supporting PBRs to their maximum limit with the captured materials. Due to the weight limitations of the PBRs, and the fact that the tide was going out, the SEALs were forced to destroy at least half of the material by blowing it in place.

The operation resulted in four Viet Cong killed and the following equipment either captured or destroyed:

Twenty-eight Claymore mines (locally produced)
Five eight-pound water mines
Twenty-five fifteen-pound water mines
Two MP-40 submachine guns
Two M1 carbines
Two 75-mm recoilless rifles with mounts
Five 120-mm locally produced high-quality rockets
   with launcher
Twenty-five Chinese Communist grenades
Nineteen CS grenades
One box of medical supplies
Fifty electric blasting caps
Seven boxes of Viet Cong grenades
Eight cases of Chinese Communist ammunition
One Chinese Communist carbine
Numerous fuses, primers, and caps
An assortment of gunsmithing tools
One complete grenade workshop with dies, molds, and
   components

The twenty pounds of ordnance documents found in the cache were of intelligence value. Several of the molds, grenade castings, and other items captured by the SEALs in the operation are presently on display in the Vietnam section of the Navy Museum at the Navy Yard in Washington, D.C.

On March 29, Delta 2, Delta platoon's second squad, also conducted an unusual operation—a "quick kill" operation, or quick reaction sweep of a high-value target of opportunity. The squad was inserted and later extracted by PBR. The area was a dry section of the north central Mekong Delta and was covered with varying lengths of grass.

While looking for a reported VC concentration of men, the SEALs came across five armed VC in a hootch (small hut). Taking them under fire, the SEALs eliminated the Cong without suffering any losses themselves. As the SEALs examined the area, they found the bunkers and trenches of an old VC base camp.

While they were examining the camp the SEALs came under fire from a number of automatic and semiautomatic weapons. Two of the SEALs located the source of the incoming fire and moved to engage the enemy. As the SEALs were maneuvering and returning fire, they heard whistles being blown in the jungle nearby and noticed changes in the pattern of the incoming fire.

The Viet Cong had apparently been using reconnaissance by fire, an unusual tactic for them, to draw the SEALs' fire. As the SEALs were returning fire, the VC were using signal whistles to help maneuver their men to encircle the SEALs and cut them off from escape. The SEALs realized that they were facing a large enemy force, estimated later at two Viet Cong infantry platoons.

Seeing the danger, the SEALs radioed for their pickup PBR to come in for an immediate extraction. After the SEALs had safely left the area, they called in a Seawolf air strike. A Light Helicopter Fire Team (LHFT) of two Seawolves conducted an air strike with rockets and machine guns at the area indicated by the SEALs. Agent reports the next day counted twenty-seven VC KIA.

Of course not all of the SEALs' missions ran into as much trouble or ran up as great a body count. On April 3, four SEALs went out on a prisoner snatch raid. The prisoner snatches were turning out to be one of the best ways of gaining intelligence. Three SEALs from Mike platoon and a single SEAL from Delta platoon worked with six PRU (provincial reconnaissance unit) members on the snatch. Inserting and extracting by Whaler kept the noise level of the SEALs' operation very low.

Moving through an open area of rice paddies during the early evening after last light, the SEALs completed the entire operation in an hour. From a house in Phuo Khanh village, the SEALs abducted a suspected VC squad leader and liaison man. Exfiltrating quietly, the SEALs left no mark of their passage or what happened to the villager who had suddenly "disappeared."

Though some of the local VC thought that the SEALs had supernatural abilities, the Viet Cong in command were still trying to counteract the effectiveness of the SEALs' operating methods. The VC observed the SEALs' actions and kept trying new tactics against them. This fact became very clear to Squad Bravo 1 during one of its operations in April. On the night of April 25, a combined force of SEAL Squad Bravo 1 along with a Vietnamese LDNN went out on a twelve-hour ambush mission. Arriving at their target area at 2030 hours, the ambush team inserted from an armed LCM that stayed within range to give the team fire support.

The SEALs moved through an area of nipa palm and established their ambush site after patrolling through the area. As the night progressed, the SEALs noticed a small fire burning about seventy-five meters south of their ambush position. While listening to the radio traffic in their area, the SEALs learned that the VC had a new technique available.

While maintaining radio silence, the SEALs heard the LCM receive what sounded like an emergency extraction call from the SEAL squad! The VC must have either seen the SEALs' LCM or overheard radio traffic in the area that tipped them off. The Viet Cong were imitating the SEALs' radio procedures to try to deceive the LCM.

After contacting the LCM themselves, the SEALs were able to convince the crew of who they were and arrange an extraction. Though the results were not serious this time, the SEALs learned their lesson. All SEAL call signs and frequencies would be changed much more often than they had been in the past and authentication procedures would be followed closely.

Bravo, Delta, and Mike platoons continued their operations through the month of April. On April 20, Delta platoon returned to Nha Be and operations in the RSSZ. Mike platoon reported to CTF 117, the Mobile Riverine Force, on board the barracks ship APL 55.

From the end of April through the middle of May, SEAL Team 1 suffered a high number of casualties. BM1 Pope and BM3 Toms were mortally wounded while on classified operations, and a squad from Mike platoon was inserting on a patrol/ambush mission on May 5 when one of its members was killed in a freak accident.

SFP2 David Devine was acting as the Stoner machine gun operator for his squad during the patrol. While making an underway insertion from a PBR on the Ham Luong River, Devine drowned after entering the water. It was decided later that the heavy weight of his weapon and ammunition, combined with the darkness of the insertion area at 0300 hours, dragged Devine down under the surface before anyone could reach him. After the accident, Stonermen were recommended to wear two inflatable life jackets when making water insertions.

On May 12, SK2 Donald Zillgitt was killed in action while leading his PRU against a large VC force in the Tra Vinh province. The Viet Cong had overrun and occupied the hamlet of Giong Lon. Zillgitt was killed while successfully leading his PRU against the VC positions, forcing the VC to withdraw from the hamlet.

Mike platoon was aboard an LCPL on May 15 to patrol a suspected VC cadre meeting near Cho Lach. Besides ambushing the meeting, the SEALs were hoping to capture some high-level VC prisoners. When the LCPL began the insertion there was a sudden explosion from near the bow of the boat.

Later investigation indicated that a hand or rifle grenade had detonated just inside the bow of the LCPL. CSI Patrick was killed outright by the explosion. Lieutenant (j.g.) Beall and Lieutenant (j.g.) Brierton were both seriously wounded and five other SEALs were wounded to a lesser degree in the blast. The operation was immediately abandoned and the LCPL moved out.

Petty Officer Gordon Brown was killed on May 19 while he was leading his PRU on a patrol in the Kien Giang province. The PRUs had discovered a large box and Brown was moving forward to examine it when the box exploded. Brown was mortally wounded in the blast and six of his PRUs were injured. The box was suspected to have held a booby-trapped land mine.

Four SEALs arrived in Vietnam from CONUS to replace the losses Mike platoon had suffered. Two officers and several enlisted men from Bravo platoon had been temporarily supporting Mike platoon until the replacements arrived.

Juliet platoon arrived at Nha Be on June 6 and relieved Bravo platoon. Juliet continued on to Vinh Long in the Mekong Delta to conduct operations there. Detachment Golf moved its headquarters to the Naval Support Detachment at Binh Thuy. Two of Detachment Golf's platoons were now assigned to the Commander of the River Patrol Force (CTF 116) to support Operation Game Warden. The remaining platoon of Detachment Golf was assigned to the Commander of the Coastal Surveillance Force (CTF 115) for duties with Operation Market Time.

During the latter half of 1968, the SEALs of Detachment Golf continued operations in the RSSZ and expanded into the Mekong Delta. Stronger emphasis had been placed on the PRU and Phoenix programs since the Tet offensive earlier that year, and the SEALs were receiving greater quantities of higher-quality intelligence in a timely fashion.

Though the ambush continued to be a SEAL operation, the number of special operations, such as prisoner abductions and supply cache captures, increased in number. The special operations continued to show spectacular results. This success was directly attributed by the SEALs to the increase in available intelligence.

Besides numerous caches of supplies captured and prisoners taken, the increase in intelligence information itself resulted in more intelligence being gathered. Documents were captured from couriers, VC prisoners, and caches. In one operation, five kilograms of documents were taken, including such top secret data as battle plans and a complete VC battalion roster of personnel and operations.

The operation that resulted in the documents' capture was conducted by Hotel platoon after it had relieved Delta platoon on July 20. On September 14, Lieutenant (j.g.) Parrot took his squad out on an ambush mission. The squad, along with an LDNN interpreter, departed the Naval Support Facility at Qui Nhon in the II Corps area, in a PCF (Patrol Craft, Fast).

When the PCF arrived near the target area, the SEALs and the LDNN transferred to Boston Whalers for the insertion. After an uneventful patrol, the SEALs established their ambush site on the bank of a stream and awaited their target. Throughout the night the SEALs heard voices coming from the jungle fairly close by. The LDNN translated what he could hear and said the voices were VC, from what he could make out from the conversations.

Later, the SEALs ambushed a sampan coming from the area where the voices had been heard. Three Vietnamese males were aboard the sampan with at least one of the men having a weapon. The SEALs opened fire with everything they had available.

The ambush was a short but fierce one. In the after-action report, the SEALs listed 150 rounds of 5.56-mm ball (M16 rifle ammo), 145 rounds of 5.56-mm linked (Stoner light machine gun), six high explosive and two canister 40-mm grenades, 24 rounds of 9-mm, three concussion grenades (MkIII A2), and four white parachute flares as having been used in the operation.

After the ambush, the SEALs quickly searched the sampan and the bodies of the three Viet Cong. The SEALs left the area on foot and returned to their Whalers for extraction. During their outward patrol and extraction the SEALs were covered from the air by two Cobra gunships and an armed Huey helicopter. After the extraction was complete, the SEALs directed the helicopters to strike the area where the voices were thought to be located.

As it turned out later, the SEALs had ambushed a Viet Cong district chief, the company commander of the E2B

Battalion, and a district-level courier. In the five kilos of documents captured were the battle plans for a large-scale attack on Qui Nhon, the complete personnel roster and structure of the E2B battalion, a complete munitions inventory of the battalion, and the operational reports on the E2B from mid-August to September.

Using supplied intelligence, the SEALs would often move into hamlets undetected during the dead of night. Bursting into a house they had identified earlier, the SEALs would shake their man awake and then spirit him away. Using this technique, the SEALs had a tremendous psychological impact throughout their areas of operation (AOs). As the SEALs' AOs were expanding, the VC never knew where the SEALs would hit next.

The effect of such actions on a Viet Cong who was trying to spend time at home are obvious. Americans with black-and-green faces would come out of the water to seize the Viet Cong. Anyone could be taken, anywhere, anytime. These actions and their resulting rumors gave the SEALs an effect far out of proportion to their numbers. There were over five million Vietnamese in the delta and less than two hundred SEALs in all of Vietnam. Even though the odds were in their favor, a number of VC joined the Hoi Chanh program to avoid meeting the men with green faces.

SEAL Team 2 entered 1968 conducting operations in the Mekong Delta under the operational control of CTF 116. Detachment Alfa was the primary unit of SEAL Team 2 in Vietnam and was made up of three operational platoons and a headquarters group consisting of a single officer (OIC) and two enlisted men. Seven enlisted men from SEAL Team 2 were assigned to duties with Detachment Bravo of SEAL Team 1. These seven men conducted operations with the PRUs as part of the Phoenix program.

In January, Detachment Alfa's three operating platoons were spread out through the Mekong Delta. The Sixth platoon operated out of Vinh Long, the Seventh from My Tho, and the Eighth from Binh Thuy. The Headquarters Group of Detachment Alfa was also located at Binh Thuy, where it was assigned to the staff of CTF 116.

January was a very hard month for the SEALs of Team 2.

Three of the six SEALs killed in action during 1968 were killed during that month. On January 18, while conducting an emergency extraction under fire, GNGI Arthur G. Williams of the Sixth platoon was killed. A round entered under Williams's arm and lodged in his spine, killing him almost instantly.

On January 21, ADR Eugene T. Fraley was fatally wounded when the booby-trapped demolition charge he was preparing for use on a SEAL combat mission exploded prematurely. The device accidentally detonated as Fraley removed it from the sandbag enclosure in which it was assembled.

The third SEAL loss in January took place on the thirty-first. AMG3 Clarence T. Risher was fatally wounded in combat during the Tet Offensive. Risher was taking part in the fierce fighting during the liberation of Chau Doc when he was killed.

Tet, the lunar new year, is a widely celebrated holiday throughout Vietnam. The SEALs, as well as other U.S. services, had been developing intelligence for some time that the Communists were building up strength for a major push. How major was brought to light on January 30 with the start of the Tet Offensive.

Over 84,000 VC and NVA troops took part in the largest Communist operation of the war to date. The scale of the offensive was staggering to the U.S. military planners. By February 1, along with Saigon, 36 of 44 provincial capitals, 5 of 6 large cities, and 64 of 242 district capitals were attacked. In the Mekong Delta, Quan Long, Khanh Hung, Rach Gia, My Tho, Vinh Long, and Can Tho were among the major towns attacked. In all of the towns, the U.S. and ARVN forces fought back, and so did the SEALs.

During the entire Tet Offensive, the three SEAL platoons handled themselves capably and professionally. Much of the fighting consisted of heavy street fighting. The SEAL platoons in Vinh Long and My Tho, which were almost completely destroyed, were instrumental in thwarting the Viet Cong attempts to overtake the cities.

The Eighth platoon, in Chau Doc at the time together

with a small PRU force, succeeded in liberating the capital of that province. A commendation to the Eighth said in part, "The SEALs in vicious house-to-house fighting succeeded in breaking the hold that the Viet Cong had established on the city. The members of the CORDS (Civil Operations and Revolutionary Development Support) staff in Chau Doc have the deepest admiration for and extend profound gratitude to each member of this platoon of Navy SEALs." Toward the end of the Tet Offensive, the Ninth platoon departed Little Creek for Vinh Long to relieve the Sixth on February 17.

After Tet, the SEALs continued to conduct operations in the Mekong Delta. Things were different with the number of VC operating and the tactics they used. On February 11, Eighth platoon, along with an LDNN, a PRU advisor, and a scout dog, went out to establish ambushes on two suspected VC commo/liaison routes. Inserting by STAB at 2045 hours, the SEALs expected little difficulty in movement. The weather was clear, with the moon in its second quarter. The terrain consisted of treelines surrounding rice paddies and scattered hamlets.

The SEALs encountered an estimated two VC squads at both of the squads' insert points. The SEAL squads were able to fight free of the VC ambushes with the help of their PBRs' fire support. The SEALs aborted their mission due to an apparent compromise. Later, in their after-action reports, the SEALs stated, "[the] VC have not followed normal routes or procedures since the Tet Offensive." What the SEALs did not know was the extent of the VC losses. The Viet Cong had been almost wiped out as a functioning military unit from their losses during Tet. Not one Communist objective was captured and held permanently. It was from this point on that the NVA was running the war in South Vietnam.

With need for proper intelligence being so great, the SEALs of the Eighth platoon pulled off one of the more audacious patrols of the Vietnam War. On February 14, two SEALs inserted by Slick (Huey helicopter) into the Seven Mountains region, a VC stronghold in the Chau Doc province 110 miles west of Saigon. The mountainous area that was the SEAL objective was a few miles southwest of Chau Phu, the provincial capital, and was just across the border from Takeo province in Cambodia.

With the clear weather, the two SEALs were able to verify with American eyes the VC strength in the area. The SEALs noted the number of VC troops, their movement, strongholds, and tactics. The SEALs observed over four hundred VC and NVA troops in the area.

The SEALs did not engage any of the enemy units and, after a four-day patrol, extracted by helicopter. Wearing black pajamas, the field uniform of the Viet Cong, the SEALs had been carrying sterilized equipment, nothing of U.S. manufacture. Most of the equipment the SEALs had used had been of Soviet or Chinese manufacture. Later the SEALs learned from intelligence reports that their ruse had worked. The disguised SEALs had been seen and reported—as Russian advisors!

It was from operations such as these that the SEALs developed a reputation for the unorthodox. The UDTs of the 1950s, with their trash cans of demolition charges, would have felt right at home.

Bravo squad of the Seventh platoon was on an intelligence-gathering mission deep into enemy territory on March 13. The SEALs penetrated five thousand meters through VC-controlled countryside undetected to reach their objective, a VC base camp. The squad located a large barracks area that appeared to hold about thirty well-armed enemy troops.

Three SEALs entered the barracks hut to try to gather more information. An enemy sentry noticed the three SEALs and opened fire. During the violent firefight that followed the SEALs' discovery, at least sixteen of the enemy were killed. Five of the seven SEALs in the squad were wounded in the exchange, one of them so badly he couldn't walk.

While the SEALs were regrouping, a large force of enemy troops could be heard approaching. Withdrawing and eluding the enemy force, the SEALs moved out through more than one thousand meters of enemy territory without being discovered by the alerted VC. The SEALs found an open area where a helicopter would be able to land. Taking cover, they called in a "dust-off" medical evacuation.

All but two members of the squad were hit. During the withdrawal, less seriously wounded SEALs carried their more stricken comrades. The injured SEALs being carried were still prepared to use their weapons in defense of the squad in spite of their pain. The SEALs never left anyone behind, period.

The searching Viet Cong could be heard moving within thirty meters of where the squad was hidden. The enemy could be heard shouting to one another as they aggressively searched the area. But the SEALs still held their fire.

Helicopter gunships and dust-offs arrived but could not find the hidden SEALs. Normally a colored smoke grenade would be fired to indicate the squad's position. But if normal procedures were followed, the SEALs would be discovered by the enemy before the squad could escape.

Contacting the helicopters by radio, the SEALs fired tracers near the aircraft to indicate their position. The red tracers of the SEALs were noticed by the helicopters, who could distinguish them clearly from the Communists' green tracers. The move both signaled the helicopters and served to confuse the searching Viet Cong. The ruse worked, as the VC knew that an American unit would not shoot at its own rescuers.

As the helicopters landed, the SEALs held off the attacking enemy while the wounded got aboard. Under heavy enemy fire, the SEALs extracted successfully. Once safely in the air, the SEALs directed immediate air and artillery strikes against the Viet Cong positions. The base camp was destroyed.

The Eighth platoon inserted by helicopter near an ARVN Regional Force outpost on March 14 to gather intelligence for an upcoming operation. Personnel at the outpost had the location of a suspected supply route that led to a VC battalion staging area. The SEALs planned to ambush that route. The patrol left the outpost to move forward to a smaller listening post nearer to their objective. When night was approaching, the SEALs left the LP and moved out to their ambush site.

After moving three thousand yards through open rice fields, the SEALs reached their planned position next to a small canal. After only an hour in their ambush position, the SEALs noticed a lone Vietnamese landing his sampan near to where the SEALs were hiding.

The suspected Viet Cong was captured by two SEALs and taken to the ambush site. Immediate questioning confirmed that the man was a VC and was also a member of the battalion that the SEALs were investigating. The VC was bound and gagged and his sampan hidden.

In spite of the considerable enemy activity taking place around them, the SEALs remained at their ambush site. About a half hour after the first Viet Cong had been captured, six armed VC moved their sampans into the killing zone.

Initiating the ambush, the SEALs killed six VC and captured their sampans. Collecting the enemy equipment and their prisoner, the SEALs patrolled back to the LP and waited for daylight. After dawn had broken, the SEALs moved back to the ARVN outpost and extracted.

The operation resulted in six VC KIA, one VC prisoner, and a large amount of equipment captured. Among the gear taken were eight boxes of battalion communications equipment and battalion documents. The dead and captured VC were identified as the battalion deputy commander, a company commander, three battalion cadre, and a news reporter from Hanoi.

Later reports from IV Corps headquarters informed the SEALs of their operation's long-term results. The loss of the cadre and communications equipment forced the VC battalion to disrupt their scheduled operations against the Binh Thuy airfield. In one ambush, the SEALs had temporarily rendered an entire VC battalion inoperable.

The Seventh platoon returned to Little Creek in CONUS on April 27 after having been relieved by the Tenth platoon in My Tho.

On May 12, the Tenth platoon went on a prisoner-abduction operation guided by a VC prisoner. The prisoner had been made available by the Vietnamese National Police and was offering to lead the SEALs to a VC meeting. The SEALs arrived at the meeting place and detained all of the civilians in the area. While the SEALs held the civilians, the VC guide pointed out six Viet Cong. The Viet Cong were taken prisoner and turned over to the National Police for questioning.

The intelligence gathered from the six VC prisoners resulted in the SEALs' being able to capture thirteen more confirmed VC espionage/intelligence agents. Further interrogation of the new prisoners enabled the National Police and other allied agencies to arrest over one hundred VC agents. The VC agents were operating in and around the provincial capital of My Tho.

The Viet Cong agents had penetrated every U.S. and allied agency and military unit in the city. The removal of the agents completely blocked the VC from knowledge of U.S. and allied intentions in the Binh Thoung province.

The prisoner/guide originally used by the SEALs had a wealth of information on local infrastructure individuals and numerous Viet Cong contacts. The willingness to cooperate on the part of the prisoner was the beginning of a SEAL-run intelligence net. The net was expanded until the Tenth platoon was generating its own operational intelligence. The SEALs were even able to route pertinent intelligence to other U.S. and allied units.

On June 15, Third platoon opened a new field of operations for SEAL Team 2. Relieving the Eighth platoon at Binh Thuy, the Third platoon continued on to Nha Be. From Nha Be, the Third platoon extended their operations into the Rung Sat. This was the first time that SEAL Team 2 had been operating on a large scale in the Rung Sat since starting their operations in Vietnam in January of 1967. The other SEAL platoons of Detachment Alfa continued their operations in the Mekong Delta provinces.

The Ninth platoon made a night insertion on the evening of June 26 to conduct a search-and-abduction patrol. Entering a small hamlet, the SEALs searched for suspected VC who were known to be in the area. In one of the huts, the SEALs found four Viet Cong who were sleeping on their weapons. During the struggle to disarm the VC and take them alive, all of them managed to escape the hut.

Though the Viet Cong had left their weapons behind, one of their number still had two hand grenades. All of the escaping VC were killed by the SEAL security element after one VC threw a grenade that wounded one of the SEALs. Reorganizing quickly, the platoon continued its search of the hamlet, taking into custody five more suspects.

While patrolling to the extraction point, the SEALs took three more suspected VC into custody. None of the suspects taken had the proper ID for being in the area.

Spot interrogation of the local populace revealed that the four Viet Cong who had been killed were a propaganda team. The VC team had toured the area, downgrading the Republic of Vietnam and its allies. The four VC also tried to encourage the locals into giving greater support to the VC effort.

The three suspects captured during the extraction patrol turned out to be Cambodians. The three Cambodians had been brought into the area to attend a VC political indoctrination course.

The five hamlet suspects captured were confirmed as VC by interrogation. Also taken in the operation were two weapons, five grenades, ammunition, and documents.

The summer did not end well, as Seal Team 2 lost two more of their number. MM1 Joseph Albrecht was mortally wounded on August 2 by a grenade booby trap while on a combat patrol in the Seven Mountains area of the Chau Doc province. Another SEAL lost his life to a VC booby trap in September. Lieutenant Frederick Trani was fatally wounded by a booby trap while he was leading a group of South Vietnamese LDNN on a combat patrol.

In September, the Third platoon received information that a PRU intelligence agent had been captured by the Viet Cong. The agent had escaped his captors and was posing as a Viet Cong in an enemy-contested hamlet while awaiting rescue.

The SEALs went out on the rescue operation on September 15. Despite the heavy concentrations of VC and NVA troops in the area, the SEALs reached the hamlet and rescued the agent. In the fighting to reach the agent, the SEALs killed three of the enemy and captured an AK-47 along with an 81-mm mortar and ammunition.

Also captured in the rescue were three local Viet Cong who had been acting as guards. The three VC agreed to lead the SEALs to several arms caches they knew of in the area.

Over the next three days, the SEAL platoon conducted patrols while accompanied by a PRU unit. The prisoners guided the SEALs to five enemy weapons caches. Captured were a 60-mm mortar, two rocket launchers, three machine guns, two assault rifles, two semiautomatic rifles, fifty anti-armor grenades, and more than eight hundred pounds of assorted munitions.

The Fifth platoon arrived in My Tho on October 22 to relieve the Tenth platoon. The Tenth had been successful in convincing higher command to change the emphasis of operations from a body-count orientation to one of gathering intelligence and identifying VC infrastructure members.

October also held the last SEAL Team 2 fatality for 1968. ABH2 Roberto Ramos was mortally wounded during a combat operation on October 29. Ramos had been participating in a joint SEAL/PRU operation when he was hit.

Alfa squad of the Fourth platoon made a night insertion near the Cambodian border on November 26. The squad's mission was to obtain intelligence on a known enemy base camp area. After first light, the squad moved out to their planned observation point. While the squad was patrolling, a lone armed Viet Cong was seen standing in an open field.

Two SEALs, EN1 Toothman and QM3 Simmons, (later Commander Simmons, XO of BUD/S), from the squad formed a capture team and moved out to take the VC prisoner and pump him for information about the area. The VC noticed the SEALs approaching and opened fire. During the short firefight, the lone VC was killed and no SEALs were hit, but the enemy base camp was alerted by all the noise.

The base camp opened fire on the two SEALs that they could see in the field. An estimated two companies of VC opened up on the SEALs with mortars, .50-caliber machine guns, 40-mm grenades, and both automatic and semiautomatic rifle fire. The main body of the squad immediately lay down covering fire to allow the two SEALs in the open to reach cover.

As the SEAL patrol was forced back, a Viet Cong platoon was seen to leave the base camp in hot pursuit of the SEALs. Calling in a helicopter gunship, the SEALs managed to establish a secure perimeter with the gunship's help.

The squad's leader, along with one other SEAL, moved out to try to locate the missing capture team. The two separated SEALs were located and the entire squad was airlifted out of the area.

Later, on December 7, the entire Fourth platoon returned to the same area and established an observation point. Noting heavy enemy activity in the area, the SEALs called in and directed a helicopter air strike on the base camp.

An hour after the strike lifted, the SEALs saw more enemy movement in the area. A second strike was called in. During the second air strike, the SEAL platoon lay down a base of automatic weapons and mortar fire on the enemy positions.

As the enemy tried to encircle the SEAL platoon, the VC started putting down their own mortar fire on the SEALs' position. While under attack, the SEALs held off the VC and were able to successfully extract by helicopter. Both operations resulted in a total of fifteen VC killed, twenty-nine wounded, a base camp destroyed, and one weapon captured.

The year ended with the Sixth platoon arriving in Nha Be to relieve the Third platoon. The SEALs had a very successful year while conducting operations in South Vietnam. New tactics and techniques had been developed to combat the VC in the delta environment. New equipment was used, some of which held up better than others.

The SEAL Team Assault Boats (STABs) that Team 2 had brought to Vietnam the year before proved out the utility of having a light, heavily armed boat available for the exclusive use of the SEALs. But the hard usage the STABs received over an extended length of time wore them out and rendered the boats inoperable.

The outboard motors proved to be reliable, but the hulls tore apart due to their flat-bottomed construction. A new type of boat was developed that combined the capabilities of the larger support boats and the maneuverability of the old STABs. The new boats were called Light SEAL Support Craft (LSSC).

By the early part of 1969, SEAL Team 2 had twelve of the new LSSCs in-country. The boats had a greater range, more firepower, better communications, and sturdier weather protection than the earlier craft used by the SEALs. The new "V" hulls with inboard engines were proven to be more stable, quieter, and had a longer service life than the STABs or other SEAL boats.

During 1968 SEAL Team 2 experienced one of its biggest equipment allocations. Four hundred thousand dollars had finally been budgeted by the Navy to bring the team up to strength in terms of equipment on hand. Though this meant a great deal of additional material for SEAL Team 2, it was still not enough to bring the team up to its full allowance of equipment. The team was growing faster than it could obtain equipment.

Several of the new pieces of equipment that the SEALs did receive in 1968 were new weapons and munitions. A pistol and silencer was produced that, when used with special ammunition, had an undistinguishable noise level when fired. The weapon was later called the "Hush Puppy" and became something of a SEAL trademark. SEAL Team 2 now had silencers for both rifles and pistols. Special ammunition was also developed for the SEALs' shotguns in the form of twelve-gauge CS and flare rounds.

Vietnam: 1969

This was the year that marked the beginning of the end of SEAL activities in Vietnam. A new president was in the White House and new actions were taking place in Vietnam. The new Secretary of Defense, Melvin Laird, along with the new MAC-V Commander, General Creighton Abrams, were ordered to implement programs of troop withdrawals and a gradual turning over of the war effort to the South Vietnamese. "Vietnamization" had begun.

SEAL Team 1 still had three operational detachments in Vietnam. Detachment Golf was the primary detachment and it had moved its headquarters to the Naval Support Detachment at Binh Thuy. Two of Golf's three operational detachments were assigned to operations with the River Patrol Force (CTF 116) and were under the operational control of that group's commander.

Detachment Bravo had expanded in size. Authorized manning for Detachment Bravo had been expanded to thirteen officers and twenty-one enlisted men as of October 4, 1968. Bravo SEALs advised PRUs throughout the Mekong Delta. Of the twelve PRU advisory billets, SEAL Team 1 filled eight of them while SEAL Team 2 filled the remaining four.

Due to the severe shortage of SEAL qualified officers, Detachment Bravo never reached its assigned manning level of commissioned officers. Only four SEAL officers were in Bravo at any one time. The balance of Bravo's manpower was made up of enlisted men.

Detachment Echo was also part of SEAL Team 1's Vietnam commitment and was under the operational control of the Commander of MAC-V. Located at the Naval Advisory Detachment at Da Nang, Detachment Echo consisted of one officer and five enlisted men. The detachment advised Vietnamese military personnel how to conduct unconventional warfare against a guerrilla force.

On January 21, Delta platoon moved out to Cam Ranh Bay, where it was to take up operations with the Coastal Surveillance Group (CTF 115). CTF 115 ran Operation Market Time, the use of a variety of naval forces to block Viet Cong arms and equipment from being brought in to the south by sea.

Delta platoon SEALs were receiving accolades from the command staff by February as they conducted successful operations in areas that were untouched by earlier efforts. The SEALs assaulted the Than Phu Secret Zone, a VC-infested area on the east coast of Vietnam, for the first time during the war. Striking deep within the Viet Cong sanctuary, Delta platoon accounted for twenty-one VC KIA (body count), the capture of several weapons, and the destruction of two VC structures.

Part of the Delta platoon was called the Kerrey Raiders after its leader, Lieutenant (j.g.) Joseph Kerrey. Lieutenant Kerrey was very soon to become famous as a SEAL. In March, Lieutenant Kerrey was leading his squad in an operation against the VC on an island in the bay of Nha Trang. Wounded severely during the operation, Kerrey continued to lead his men. This action was later to make him the first SEAL to receive the Congressional Medal of Honor.

Missions for Detachment Golf remained much the same as the year before. The primary emphasis was on gathering intelligence, not just running up a VC body count. The SEALs preferred to operate this way; as one SEAL put it,

"Anyone can just go in there and kill someone." This statement agreed with the SEALs' confidence in their own abilities and also went along with another SEAL motto: "You can't get information from a corpse."

So the ambush and the prisoner snatch were still the primary SEAL operations. Detachment Golf, now operating in the Mekong Delta, was working primarily on intelligence it had gathered through its own network.

The new Light SEAL Support Craft (LSSC) had arrived in the country and was well received by the SEALs. The LSSC was twenty-six feet long with a beam of nine feet six inches and could fit in the cargo hold of a C-130 aircraft Armored against .30-caliber rounds, the LSSC had withstood .30- and .50-caliber armor-piercing rounds and even a hit with an RPG-2 (B-40) on its self-sealing gas tank during development tests. Powered by two 300-HP inboard engines running two water jets, the LSSC could turn within its own length and reach a speed of twenty-six knots.

With a normal crew of three, the LSSC could also carry an entire SEAL squad of seven along with equipment. Normally armed with two M60 machine guns and a 40-mm machine grenade launcher, the LSSC fit the SEALs' requirements well.

The LSSC ran very quietly. The radar dome the LSSC was equipped with actually made more operating noise than did the engines. Besides the radar, the LSSC had an integral communications setup and storage areas for supplies.

The first operations the SEALs had with the LSSC went well, with the SEALs developing new procedures to take advantage of the crafts' capabilities. Detachment Golf's Alfa platoon used the LSSC during several operations in January. On January 19, one squad from Alfa platoon used the LSSC to set up an ambush on a canal used by the VC as a commo/liaison route. The squad patrolled to the ambush up the targeted canal using the LSSC as their transport. After-action reports listed this method of patrolling as very quiet when using the new boats.

Intelligence reports had stated a VC battalion was using the canal as one of their routes down from the north. The SEALs reached their planned location and set up their ambush by 2145 hours, well after dark. The squad did not have to wait long for a target as several sampans moved down the canal and beached just one hundred meters from the ambush site. Sampans could be heard by the SEALs moving on the main river behind them. Troop movements were also heard coming from along the banks of the main river.

Just after 2300 hours, three sampans, two of them heavily laden, moved down the canal directly in front of the SEALs' ambush. The SEALs initiated the ambush and sank two of the sampans. The third sampan was seen drifting down the canal after the ambush. One of the SEALs fired a 40-mm HE round that scored a direct hit on the drifting sampan. A violent secondary explosion indicated that the sampan had been carrying some cargo a bit more energetic than just rice.

The SEALs counted five VC bodies and suspected that an additional two VCs had been in the sampan at the time of the explosion. The enemy activity in the area caused the SEALs to extract quickly. A later PBR and Seawolf strike was called in by the SEALs on the area while the Viet Cong were still there.

Further operations by Alfa demonstrated the flexibility and usefulness of the LSSC when used by the SEALs. At midnight on January 25, a fire team of four SEALs from Alfa platoon used their LSSC to stage another canal ambush on a suspected VC liaison route. The LSSC was guided to the proper location by a nearby PBR that used its radar to guide the smaller craft. The LSSC also had a small radar set to help it locate targets and its own position.

The SEALs established the ambush directly from the LSSC using the mounted weapons on the craft. Two medium-sized sampans were seen to approach the SEALs' position. While the SEALs kept watching the approaching sampans, the two craft turned and beached just seventy-five meters from where the SEALs were hidden. Later, noticing movement that indicated the sampans were preparing to get under way, the SEALs illuminated the area with flares and approached the two boats.

When they reached the sampans, the SEALs found only

fishermen with proper ID and no weapons. Letting the Vietnamese go, the SEALs returned to their base. Though the ambush had not turned up any VC, the SEALs were pleased with the way the new LSSC could be used as a small base of operations.

Other systems of insertion and extraction were still used by the SEALs, especially as so few, twelve in all of Vietnam in January, of the new LSSCs were available. Alfa platoon used a PBR for insertion on a prisoner snatch operation on February 3. Accompanied by two LDNNs, the SEALs were moving in to abduct three suspected VC from their hootch. A Vietnamese fisherman, acting as an intelligence agent, had identified the VC and pointed out their hootch to a PBR crew.

At 0430 hours the SEALs moved in for their prisoners. After patrolling the hootch and surrounding area and finding no VC home, the SEALs decided to set up an ambush nearby.

At 0730 hours, two VC were seen approaching the house along the path on which the SEALs had established their ambush. One VC was caught immediately but the other was killed as he attempted to flee. As the SEALs left the area with their POW, he admitted to being a VC and said he would cooperate with the SEALs. The prisoner said he could lead the SEALs to the VC village chief's house the next evening. The SEALs agreed to the idea and prepared for the next night's mission.

The next evening, the SEALs moved out to try to capture the VC chief. Accompanying the SEALs were two LDNN and a member of UDT-11, who had gone along to gather field experience.

The team patrolled back to the same area as the night before, again using a PBR for insertion. Guided by their prisoner, the SEALs inserted at 0430 hours and patrolled to the VC village chief's house. Again finding the house empty, the SEALs set up an ambush; the time was 0630 hours.

After an hour's wait, two VC were noticed approaching the house. The two men passed within five feet of where the SEALs were hiding. The SEALs tried to capture the men but both VC broke away and fled. Taking the fleeing VC under fire, the SEALs killed both men. The two dead VC turned out to be the village chief and his assistant.

The SEALs learned from their prisoner that the VC in the area slept in the boonies at night to try to escape the SEALs. To account for this, the SEALs started establishing their prisoner ambushes before dawn and waiting until 0800 or 0900 hours. The VC in the area the SEALs were presently in normally returned to their homes at daybreak, about 0715 hours.

SEAL Team 1 still had relatively few losses as compared to their effectiveness in the field. Six men from Team 1 were listed as KIA during 1969. These six deaths were a particularly gruesome loss for the SEALs. A group of SEALs from Charlie platoon out of My Tho were working at the MAC-V compound in Rach Gia City on May 18. The SEALs were working to remove the explosive charge in an 82-mm ChiCom mortar round that was in the compound when it suddenly detonated.

Killed outright in the blast were ATW1 Kenneth E. Von Hoy and MM2 Lowell W. Meyer. Severely wounded in the explosion were QM2 Ronald E. Pace and HM1 Lin A. Mahner. Heroic efforts were used to try to save Pace but he succumbed to his wounds that same day. Mahner died of renal failure in a military hospital seven days later.

On October 17, Lieutenant (j.g.) David L. Nicholas was killed while leading a combat patrol. A member of Kilo platoon stationed at Cam Ranh Bay, Lieutenant Nicholas was patrolling six and one half kilometers southeast of old Nam Can when the incident occurred.

The unit Lieutenant Nicholas was part of was conducting a sweep of a suspected VC area. The sweep was being directed toward another unit that was acting as a blocking force. As Lieutenant Nicholas and his unit approached the blocking unit, the blockers opened fire. Though the firing ended quickly, Lieutenant Nicholas was hit in the upper left chest and died within two minutes.

The last member of SEAL Team 1 to die in action during 1969 was HM1 Richard O. Wolf. On November 30, Wolf, a member of Mike platoon, was leaving with his unit on a standard patrol. The team was going in by a helicopter insertion. While approaching the LZ (landing zone), the helicopter developed difficulty and crashed. Wolf was killed instantly by the impact.

Vietnamization was well under way by later in 1969. But the SEALs' operations were continuing. In July, Detachment Echo was reduced from having one officer and five enlisted men to having just two enlisted men assigned to it. The men of Detachment Echo now worked with a cadre of Vietnamese to assist them.

Detachment Bravo was placed under the operational control of the South Vietnamese Ministry of the Interior. The SEALs of Detachment Bravo still operated in support of the PRU program. With the turnover of control from MAC-V, and the overall Vietnamization of the war effort, the manning levels of Detachment Bravo had been reduced. There were now three officers and ten enlisted men from SEAL Team 1 at Bravo, down from a high of four officers and twenty-four enlisted men.

The SEAL platoons were still subject to a six-month rotation. Delta platoon was relieved by Kilo platoon on July 20. Echo platoon was relieved by Mike platoon on August 20. And Charlie platoon was relieved by Golf platoon on May 20. Golf platoon in turn was relieved by Bravo platoon on November 28.

The SEAL commitment for Vietnam grew during the latter part of 1969. Alfa platoon, which had been relieved earlier in the year, returned to Vietnam on October 6 to act as an augmentation platoon for Detachment Golf.

Charlie platoon returned to Vietnam on December 27, also to act as an augmentation platoon. Detachment Golf ended 1969 with five operational platoons in-country with a total of eleven officers and sixty-three enlisted men aboard.

Seal Team 2 still supported two detachments in Vietnam during 1969, Detachments Alfa and Bravo. Detachment Alfa consisted of seven officers and thirty-four enlisted men divided into three operational platoons and a command element. The command element consisted of a single officer, the detachment commander, and two enlisted men.

The command element of Detachment Alfa, along with

one operational platoon, operated out of the Naval Support Facility in Binh Thuy. The other two operational platoons of Alfa were stationed, one each, at My Tho and Nha Bè. Operations were conducted throughout the Mekong Delta from the RSSZ to the east and west past the Plain of Reeds to the Cambodian border.

Detachment Bravo was continuing its work with the PRUs. Several SEALs from Team 2 were operating with Detachment Bravo through the year. The only two fatalities SEAL Team 2 suffered in 1969 were both from the Bravo detachment. GMG1 Harry A. Mattingly was killed in action on January 16 while conducting operations with his PRU.

The second SEAL loss was in December when AE1 Curtis M. Ashton was killed. Ashton had been leading his PRU on a combat patrol when he was fatally wounded on December 27. In spite of the spreading antiwar sentiment in the United States, Ashton was posthumously honored in his hometown of Sweetwater, Texas. In accord with the mayor's proclamation, there was a suspension of business activity in the town during the SEAL's funeral.

A new effort had been launched by the Navy in 1968 to try to take advantage of the capabilities of the Brown Water Navy, the Seawolves, and the SEALs. Called SEALORDS (for Southeast Asian Lake, Ocean, River, and Delta Strategy), the effort was intended to cut off the VC supply lines running from Cambodia and disrupt VC operations in the delta. Since the Game Warden and Market Time operations were appearing successful at cutting off the VC's sea supply routes, the higher command thought the same could be done for the land routes.

SEALORDS was formally designated Task Force 194 in December 1968. In that same month Operation Giant Slingshot was started. Giant Slingshot was intended to block supplies from coming through Cambodia at a point known as the "Parrot's Beak," west of Saigon. That portion of Cambodia extended into Vietnam and was the southern end of the Ho Chi Minh Trail.

The Tuan Co Dong and Vam Co Tay rivers ran to either side of the Parrot's Beak area and became the main channels of movement for the forces used in Operation Giant Slingshot. The operation got its name from the shape of the fork that the two rivers took when they channeled into the Vam Co River running south of Saigon. The SEALs were involved with the operation from its beginning and proved extremely useful in gathering intelligence to base larger operations on.

On January 10, a seven-man squad from the Sixth platoon was conducting a patrol in support of Giant Slingshot. The squad was performing their patrol in the early morning near the Vam Co Dong River. After moving inland about one kilometer, the SEALs located and uncovered a large VC munitions cache. Over the next three hours, the SEALs removed several thousand pounds of munitions from the cache. The squad took over 620 rounds of mortar, rocket, and recoilless rifle ammunition along with 27,000 rounds of small arms ammunition and more than sixty-five hand grenades.

The SEALs proved so useful to Giant Slingshot that, in April, a platoon was moved to Moc Hoa to continue operations in closer proximity to the area. Giant Slingshot ran for 515 days until it was turned over to the Vietnamese in May of 1970. The operation did prove successful and the flow of supplies to the VC in the delta slowed down to a bare trickle.

In February, Fifth platoon was informed by a local about a group of VC holding a village nearby. One squad from the platoon went out on a reconnaissance patrol on February 16 in response to the information. The patrol moved in the early-morning hours to within sight of the reportedly enemy-held village near the My Tho River.

As the squad approached a home on the outskirts of the village, they noticed two armed men working in the front yard. The squad approached closer to the building and saw several more armed men inside of the house.

As the SEALs were closing in to the house, one of the men inside of the house saw the squad's radioman and called out a warning. Rather than stay and fight the SEALs, the VC fled. The SEALs took the escaping VC under fire, killing all five of them.

As the SEALs searched the house, they found a quantity

of mail and other papers. The house turned out to be a VC/ NVA postal station. Two automatic rifles, several hundred rounds of ammunition, and fifteen pounds of mail and documents were captured in the operation.

The SEALs continued to operate on intelligence they were gathering through their own nets. It was becoming occasionally difficult to take prisoners as the VC were tending to run away rather than surrender or fight. The reputation of the SEALs was such that the average Viet Cong did not want to face them given any choice at all.

A squad from the Fifth platoon went out on patrol on February 22, reacting to information they had received from one of their agents. The squad went on patrol shortly after evening fell and moved up to within sight of a Viet Cong village near the My Tho River. Seeing the level of activity in the area, the SEALs quickly set up a hasty ambush.

As the squad was establishing their ambush, eight men walked through the ambush site. The men were not carrying any weapons that could be seen and so the SEALs let them pass unmolested.

Soon after the first group of men had passed the SEALs, another group of seven men came along the same trail. Seeing that the men were armed, the SEALs initiated the ambush.

The ambush resulted in the killing of five very high ranking Viet Cong officials and the wounding of two more VC. Two semiautomatic rifles, one pistol, and two pounds of documents were captured after the ambush.

On March 2, a Fifth platoon squad conducted an intelligence-gathering patrol near the My Tho River. After about one hour of patrol, the SEALs approached two houses. The squad's interpreter was sent into one of the houses to speak to the occupants, who were seen to be unarmed.

The interpreter returned with the information that there were armed VC in the neighboring house. Moving to the nearby building, the SEALs set up a hasty ambush around the house. As the SEALs were moving into their ambush positions, one of the enemy soldiers inside of the house spotted them and opened fire.

Warned by their comrade's fire, the other Viet Cong ran

from the house. As the VC were fleeing, they were taken under fire by the SEALs around the house.

The operation resulted in ten Viet Cong KIA and one VC wounded. The unit recovered three automatic rifles, one semiautomatic rifle, two pistols, five B-40 rockets with boosters, and several hundred rounds of ammunition.

Though the SEALs could, and often did, defeat enemy forces much longer in number than themselves, it was a situation they preferred to avoid. When the target was an enemy force of unknown size, prior preparation for the mission helped prevent the SEALs from getting into a situation from which they could not escape.

On March 25, a squad from the Fifth platoon was on an operation to locate an enemy force of unknown size. The force was reported to be on the Thoi Son Island in the My Tho River. The SEALs patrolled toward the island in a Vietnamese sampan to avoid easy detection.

Noticing a large force of armed men in an open field, the SEALs quickly landed on the bank of a nearby canal and established a hasty ambush. When the SEALs opened fire on the visible enemy troops, the squad suddenly began receiving heavy automatic weapons fire from many different locations.

Realizing that they were in a difficult position, the SEALs called in and directed an air strike on the surrounding enemy positions. As the helicopter gunships kept the VC occupied, the SEALs were able to extract without any casualties. The enemy force was later found to have been in excess of two hundred men.

The SEALs were able to take on and defeat such large forces only with proper preparation and a high level of training. Helicopter gunships, usually Seawolves, were almost always alerted to be on call before a patrol went out.

Through superior tactics, training, firepower, and the surprise inherent in the ambush, even a small group of SEALs could successfully defeat an enemy force two or three times their size.

On June 9, the Eighth platoon put out a platoon-sized patrol in reaction to prior intelligence. The SEALs patrolled 1,500 meters north into the Binh Thong province to ambush a much larger enemy force. The platoon broke down into three fire teams in order to encircle the area where the enemy was located. The enemy force was estimated at fifty men and the SEALs only numbered fourteen.

Just before dawn, activity was seen by the SEALs in the hootches at the center of their ambush site. The amount of movement indicated a large force was in the buildings. The SEALs initiated their ambush and took the hootches under fire.

The return fire from the hootches was very heavy and the SEALs called in helicopter gunships to strike at the enemy forces. The gunships also covered the SEAL's safe extraction. The operation resulted in twenty-eight Viet Cong killed and nine wounded. The SEALs suffered no casualties.

In November, SEAL Team 2 suffered its last casualty of 1969. Lieutenant (j.g.) John Cook Brewton was critically injured while on patrol on November 25. Brewton was a member of the Tenth platoon, Detachment Alfa, when he was hit. On January 11, 1970, Lieutenant Brewton died of his wounds while at a military hospital in Vietnam.

On July 23, 1971, eleven officers and seventeen enlisted men from SEAL Team 2 attended the launching of the U.S.S. *Brewton* DE-1084 in New Orleans. The destroyer escort had been named in honor of Lieutenant (j.g.) John C. Brewton.

SEAL Team 2's Third through Tenth platoons continued a six-month rotation schedule throughout the year for duty with Detachment Alfa. The augmentation that SEAL Team 1 and Detachment Golf had at the end of 1969 did not take place with Detachment Alfa. There were always three platoons from Team 2 in Vietnam at any one time during 1969. The schedule for rotation was as follows:

PLATOON	IN-COUNTRY DATES	RELIEVED BY
4th	12 Aug 1968 to 12 Feb 1969	7th Plt.
5th	12 Oct 1968 to 12 Apr 1969	8th Plt.
6th	12 Dec 1968 to 12 Jun 1969	9th Plt.
7th	12 Feb 1969 to 12 Aug 1969	10th Plt.
8th	12 Apr 1969 to 12 Oct 1969	3rd Plt.

Presidential Unit Citation—SEAL Team 2

By virtue of the authority vested in me as President of the United States and as Commander-in-Chief of the Armed Forces of the United States, I have today awarded
THE PRESIDENTIAL UNIT CITATION (NAVY)
FOR EXTRAORDINARY HEROISM TO
SEAL TEAM TWO

SEAL Team TWO distinguished itself by exceptionally meritorious and heroic service from 1 July 1967 through 30 June 1969 in the conduct of unconventional warfare against an armed enemy in the Republic of Vietnam, although often required to conduct their operations in almost impenetrable terrain and in a violently hostile environment, this small, elite fighting unit nonetheless accounted for numerous enemy casualties and the capture of large numbers of troops, weapons, ammunition, and documents of significant intelligence value. The outstanding valor, professionalism, and esprit de corps of SEAL Team TWO are illustrated by the following instances: On 13 March 1968, a seven-man SEAL squad engaged an enemy force numbering approximately thirty men. During the fierce firefight, although five SEALS were wounded, heavy casualties were inflicted upon the enemy. Exposed to a withering hail of fire by the pursuing enemy, the SEALs withdrew through 1,000 meters of enemy-occupied territory to an extraction point, with the less seriously wounded carrying their stricken comrades to safety. On another occasion, a six-man SEAL squad carried out an offensive patrol deep into the enemy-infested Rung Sat Special Zone and accounted for six enemy casualties. On still another occasion, a SEAL squad penetrated 4,000 meters into a Viet Cong base camp and overcame two of the enemy, one in hand-to-hand combat, before withdrawing to an extraction point 2,000 meters away, eluding a twenty-man element of the enemy which swept within fifteen meters of their position while attempting to locate them. Engaging this larger force, the SEALS accounted for ten enemy casualties before they were extracted. The distinguished and heroic combat record achieved by the officers and men of SEAL Team TWO reflects the highest credit upon themselves and the United States Naval Service.

Richard Nixon

The Ambush

The ambush was only one of several field operations on which the SEALs commonly went in Vietnam. Often several types of action would be prepared for use on a patrol such as a listening-post/ambush mission or an ambush/prisoner abduction. The experience the SEALs gathered while in Vietnam allowed them to refine the ambush to a near science. Using the proper techniques would allow a small team of SEALs to defeat a much larger enemy force.

The ambush, combined with the SEALs' penchant for night operations, made movement very difficult for the Viet Cong who used the many trails, canals, and rivers of the delta and Rung Sat. Used to being almost untouchable in parts of the Mekong Delta and RSSZ, the VC quickly learned that the SEALs were able to use their own tricks against them.

The following is an example of a typical ambush mission as it was performed in Vietnam. The team described would be a squad from any of several deployed platoons. The operation takes place in March during the last years of the 1960s. It is based upon several after-action reports, though contains no more than might happen in a single action.

At 1325 hours the last man of the squad was awakened

from a deep sleep. Told by the CPO of the squad that a warning order was on the way, the SEAL got up to a new "morning."

Gathering with the rest of the squad at the head, the men found out that they had a mission coming up and they began to prepare. Collecting their equipment, some of the squad quickly shaved or showered and grabbed a quick cup of coffee before packing their gear.

1525 Hours

The six enlisted members of the squad assembled in the "bull pen" (briefing room) to receive the briefing on the upcoming mission from their "wheel" (officer, either the platoon leader or his assistant). Four members of the PBR (Patrol Boat, River) crew who would provide transportation to the squad also attended the briefing. The PBR crew was part of the local Mobile Support Team and came from the Brown Water Navy.

With the room sealed off, the "boss" began the briefing.

The mission was to be the culmination of a six-week project from Army intelligence. Early the next day, a group of five sampans carrying ten to fifteen Viet Cong, including the local paymaster, was expected to use a section of a nearby river. Besides carrying the VC, the sampans would also be loaded with arms and ammunition for local operations. The job of the SEALs would be to destroy the shipment and capture any of the VC that they could. According to Standard Operating Procedure (SOP) the SEALs would try to capture and preserve any intelligence data that they could.

The squad poured over detailed air recon photographs and picto maps (maps made from aerial photographs) of the area of operations. Using charts and maps, the team decided to place the ambush site thirty meters north of a narrow point in the river.

The briefing continued with the weather report for the area. The wind would be coming from the south-southwest at five miles per hour. There would be a high overcast cloud cover with the possibility of rain. The air temperature would be eighty degrees and the water temperature seventy-one degrees. There would be no moonlight, a slack tide, and a river current of eight knots.

The terrain was heavy jungle, dense brush cover, and low hills. There were no special obstacles.

The enemy would be ten to fifteen men, all of them considered armed. The first and last boats in the convoy would be armed escorts. The nearest friendly troops would be twenty-three kilometers away. The SEALs would be operating deep in enemy-controlled territory.

After making note of the day's call signs and authentication codes, the squad sterilized the briefing room.

The blackboard was washed to remove all traces of chalk. All charts, photographs, and maps were removed. All scraps of paper and notes were taken or destroyed. Within a few minutes, the briefing room was secured and no trace of the upcoming operation was left where it might fall into unfriendly hands.

1602 Hours

The squad and its equipment inventory for the operation were assembled.

The "Boss": Platoon Leader Lieutenant Alex Brown

Brown was thirty-four years old and had been a SEAL for seven years. He would be carrying the following: an M16A1 with 200 rounds of ammunition, including a magazine of tracers, a S&W model 39 pistol with 40 rounds of ammunition, an AN/PVS-2 Starlight scope that could be mounted on an M16 (the scope will be in a special waterproof case), one red and one green parachute flare, two M26A1 fragmentation grenades and one MK 3-A2 offensive (concussion) grenade, and a small penlight with a red lens.

Chief Petty Officer Charlie Deckert

This was Deckert's second war. He was in the UDTs during Korea and was the oldest and toughest member of the squad. As one of the two automatic weapons men,

Deckert carried an M60 machine gun. The M60 had the barrel cut back to the gas piston to lighten it. Deckert also carried 400 rounds of 7.62-mm ammunition and two M26A1 fragmentation grenades.

1st Class Gunner's Mate Ed Fox

As the point man (scout) of the squad, Fox preferred a shotgun. Along with his Ithaca Model 37, Fox would carry 40 rounds of #4 buckshot and 10 rounds of slugs. Ed would also have two M26A1 fragmentation grenades, two AN-M8 HC white smoke grenades, one prisoner-handling kit, and a 100-foot coil of 5/16" nylon rope. Ed was occasionally razzed by the rest of the squad for his habit of wearing panty hose while on operations to keep the leeches off his legs.

1st Class Electronics Technician George Halls

Halls would act as the squad's RTO (Radio Telephone Operator) and would carry the AN/PRC 77 radio. For weapons, George had a S&W Model 76 submachine gun with 216 rounds, six magazines, of 9-mm ammunition; an S&W Model 39 pistol with 40 rounds, five magazines, of 9-mm ammunition; two M26A1 fragmentation grenades; and one red and one green parachute flares.

Hospital Corpsman 1st Class Indigo Jose

As the platoon's medic, Jose would carry a medical kit as well as a prisoner-handling kit. As a SEAL, Indigo would be carrying an M16A1 rifle with an M203 40-mm grenade launcher mounted under the barrel. SEAL medics took an active part in all SEAL combat operations. To support his part in the operation, Indigo would have with him three high-explosive 40-mm rounds and three white, one red, and one green 40-mm parachute flares.

Boatswain's Mate Kevin Lees

As the squad's other automatic weapons man, Kevin also carried a chopped-down M60 machine gun. To feed the gun Kevin carried 400 rounds of 7.62-mm ammunition as well as two M26A1 fragmentation grenades "just for fun."

1st Class Diver Mike Nelson

Mike carried a Stoner Mk23 with a short barrel and fitted with a 150-round belt box. Along with a spare 150-round belt, Mike had a prisoner-handling kit, two M26A1 fragmentation grenades, one AN-M8 HC smoke grenade, and an M18A1 Claymore mine fitted with a thirty-second fuse and an M60 pull igniter. In case the squad had to run from the ambush while being chased by the enemy. The Claymore could be placed near the squad's back trail with the fuse pulled. With the blast radius of a Claymore, the chances were that any pursuing Viet Cong would be caught by the trap.

Along with their specialized equipment, each member of the squad would carry two to four canteens, camo sticks, individual first aid kits, a wristwatch, a sheath knife, and a survival kit. The survival kit was usually carried in an M14 magazine pouch and included a folding knife, flint and matches, ten feet of copper or steel wire, fishhooks, and a small mirror. Additional items were added to the kit according to the wants of the individual. Sheath knives carried were usually either an issue Ka-Bar or a Randall Model 1, 2, 14, or 16.

To carry all their equipment and ammunition, each man wore a special buoyant ammunition-carrying coat according to his assignment. Each coat had, along with numerous pockets, a built-in inflatable flotation vest. Each man also had several self-sealing waterproof plastic bags to hold any maps, documents, or other intelligence materials that they might capture.

1640 Hours

The squad's lieutenant had finished his inspection of the men and their equipment. Everything checked out okay.

1720 Hours

The squad test fired all of its weapons. As gunfire happened every day around the base camp, any nearby Viet Cong would not think anything particular about it. Each man removed all rate and rank insignias and any form of identification, including dog tags. A SEAL never left anyone behind, so ID was not considered necessary and this eliminated one possible source of information for the enemy.

1800 Hours

The squad was now dressed and ready for their mission. Though there was great leeway in what the men wore into combat, T-shirts and shorts were not unusual; most men wore long-sleeved shirts and field pants. The clothes protected the men from the abrasive plant life in the delta as well as preventing any white skin from shining accidentally. Many of the men did not wear boots or sneakers as they could get sucked off by the mud and leave a distinctive trail that the VC could follow.

1830 Hours

The men went to mess and fixed their own chow. Several of the squad members ate native food, fish and rice, every day because the VC claimed to be able to smell an American "beef eater" a distance away. Other members of the squad ate C rations or LRRPs (Long-Range Reconnaissance Patrol dehydrated rations) as their tastes dictated.

1900 Hours

Rehearsal: To minimize any verbal communication in the field, the squad carefully planned its deployment for the ambush and studied every move. Long hours spent working together, and even longer hours spent in training, allowed each of the men to know exactly what the others would do in a given situation. Teamwork was *the* method of operating

Early UDT training (1950s) with dry suits for protection from
the cold. DEPARTMENT OF THE NAVY

Navy helicopter performing a water pickup of a combat
swimmer. DEPARTMENT OF THE NAVY

With astronauts James A. Lovell and Edwin E. Aldrin in raft, swimmers secure flotation gear to GT-12 space capsule, 1966.
DEPARTMENT OF THE NAVY

A crewman aids a member of the underwater demolition team to return to an inflatable boat during cast and recovery operations. This is part of Operation Springboard, 1972.
DEPARTMENT OF THE NAVY

SEALs conducting a raid on a Viet Cong base. They destroyed an estimated 40 to 50 bunkers and numerous camp structures—including a Viet Cong propaganda center and two tax collection stations—and detained 51 Viet Cong suspects, 1968.

SEAL examining a Viet Cong mine. It was to prevent attacks with mines like this and others that the SEALs started operations in the Rung Sat.

A PBR Mark II conducting trials off the Vietnamese shore.

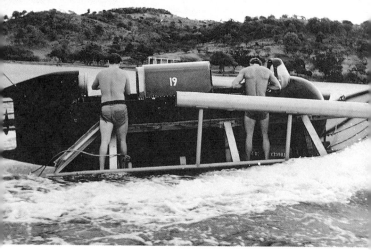

The "sea sled" method of inserting an SDV behind a normal boat. When the towing boat stopped, the sled would sink down to its floatation tanks, and the SDV could drive off or on.

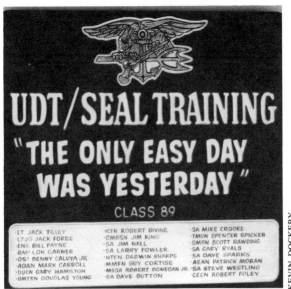

UDT/SEAL TRAINING
"THE ONLY EASY DAY WAS YESTERDAY"
CLASS 89

·LT JACK TILLEY·   ·ICEN ROBERT DIVINE   ·SA MIKE CROOKE
·LTJG JACK FORDE·   ·CMGSN JIM KING   ·TMSN SPENCER SPICKER
·ENS. BILL PAYNE·   ·SA JIM NALL   ·SASN SCOTT RAWDING
·BM¹ LON GARNER·   ·SA LARRY FOWLER   ·SA GARY RYALS
·OS³ BENNY CALUYA JR·   ·HTFN DARWIN SHARPE   ·SA DAVE SPARKS
·AOAN MARK CARROLL·   ·MMFN GUY CORTISE   ·AEAN PATRICK MORAN
·BUCN GARY HAMILTON·   ·MSSA ROBERT DONEGAN JR·SA STEVE WESTLING
·GMTSN DOUGLAS YOUNG·   ·SA DAVE SUTTON   ·CECN ROBERT FOLEY

KEVIN DOCKERY

Plaque given by Class of '89.

A pair of combat swimmers (swim buddies) outfitted with the new Draeger rebreather system.   KEVIN DOCKERY

A view looking forward
from the bridge of the
U.S.S. *Grayback*. These bow
hangars used to contain
the SDVs.

One of the "after actions"
reports on the first SEAL POW
rescue.

CONFIDENTIAL
(WHEN FILLED IN)

Coronado, California. Underwater demolition team recruits
eat their lunches as they sit in filthy water at the naval
amphibious base. The occasional explosion (outside the
picture) is set off to stimulate the students' appetites.

Combat swimmer, Nato breathing gear, and weight belt.

KEVIN DOCKERY

DEPARTMENT OF THE NAVY

A mud-coated underwater demolition team recruit enjoys a moment of humor during his rigorous training at the naval amphibious base.

Combat swimmers landing from CRRC.

Persian Gulf . . .
An Iranian command
and control platform is
set afire after a raid in
response to a missile
attack on a reflagged
Kuwaiti tanker.

for the SEALs, and many of their successes could be attributed directly to it.

1950 Hours

Rehearsal was complete and the men finished their final gear preparations. Those SEALs who could grabbed some rest while the time was available.

2115 Hours

Those members of the squad who slept were awakened and the team moved out to the docks. Gathering on board the PBR that would transport them, the SEALs took up positions in the bow on either side of the .50-caliber gun tub. The loose uniforms and many weapons of both the SEALs and the PBR made the group appear to be a bunch of Southeast Asian pirates rather than a military unit.

2200 Hours

The PBR was well on its way to the ambush site. Traveling first along a river, then a tributary, and finally canals and streams, was a difficult feat of navigation. The Mekong Delta had five different branches of two major rivers and hundreds of smaller branches and streams as well as thousands of canals. It took skill and experience on the part of the PBR crew to locate the exact stretch of water that would lead to the target area. To qualify as a captain of a PBR could take two years of training and even then field experience was necessary. The captain of this PBR was very experienced and his crew was more than competent. The SEALs realized this and spent their time watching the banks for an ambush.

Often the Viet Cong would prepare booby traps designed especially to nail PBRs and boats like them. The VC would place two B-40 rockets (RPG-2s), one on either side of a stream. The rockets would face toward each other and be connected by a trip wire across the water. The loose wire

would be pulled taut by a passing boat and fire both of the
rockets. The rockets would strike amidships, where most
of the crew was, and blow the boat in half. When the SEALs
chose to sit in the bow they were hoping that if the PBR
tripped a rocket trap they would be blown forward and off
the boat rather than be caught in the main part of the blast.

The PBR was crewed by four men. One man was forward
in the gun tub and controlled a pair of twin .50s. One man
was at the rear of the craft manning the single mounted
.50-caliber machine gun, and another was amidships at the
mounted M60 machine gun. The coxswain was in the small
cabin directing his craft.

2355 Hours

The PBR had finally reached the planned insertion point
and edged up to the bank. The SEALs jumped off the boat
and immediately sank hip-deep into the mud. Carefully
holding their weapons out of the mud, the SEALs moved
up onto the bank. As the squad moved about ten meters
from the shore, the PBR moved into midstream, where it
could better cover the area with its weapons. The squad
waited quietly for at least ten minutes, listening for any sign
of an enemy ambush.

Seeing and hearing nobody, the squad moved out to its
ambush site and the PBR moved upriver, away from the
insertion point. The SEALs went several kilometers in a
semicircle toward the ambush point. As they traveled
through the jungle, the SEALs were making sure that there
were no Viet Cong behind the ambush site as well as no
civilians near the combat zone.

0104 Hours

After having traveled three kilometers in a circle, the
squad arrived at the ambush site one kilometer upstream
from the insertion point. As they reached the position, a
small narrow point in the stream, the squad deployed automatically without any orders. The two automatic weapons

men with the M60s moved one to each flank. Ed Fox tied one end of his nylon rope to the bank and entered the waist-deep mud and water of the stream. The lieutenant stood in the center of the line formation spread out along Fox's rope. The RTO stood behind the lieutenant to cover their rear. The entire squad had spread out on either side of the lieutenant for a distance of about thirty meters.

0325 Hours

The natural sounds of the jungle had returned by that time, disguising the fact that the SEALs were in the area. In spite of the swarming mosquitoes and other insects, the squad remained still, standing in the warm waters. Some of the men chewed tobacco to help stay awake while others chewed gum or beef jerky to accomplish the same thing. None of the SEALs would smoke while in the field. Tobacco smoke carries for a long distance, especially at night.

0404 Hours

The moonless sky combined with the cloud cover had made the night extremely dark. The men could not see more than a few feet in front of them, except for the lieutenant. He had attached the Starlight scope to his M16A1 and was using the night vision device to scan the waters upstream. Watching through the Starlight scope made the entire area seem illuminated by dim, greenish daylight. Watching upstream, Lieutenant Brown would see the VC before the rest of the squad could. He would be the one to trigger the ambush. Though the expected rain did not show up, the SEALs could not be much wetter. They had been standing in the mud and water, without moving, for over three hours.

0404.15 Hours

The slight put-put sound of an approaching motor alerted the SEALs. Even though all the men were combat veterans, many of them had their mouths go dry, and their heartbeat

sounded loudly in their ears. Scarcely daring to breathe lest
they be heard, the SEALs waited silently for the signal to
open fire.

Suddenly the night was torn by the rapid fire of the lieu-

tenant's M16A1 on full auto. The tracer fire, aimed with
the help of the Starlight scope, indicated clearly the lead
sampan. There was a thump as Jose fired his M203. A burst
of stark white light from Jose's parachute flare illuminated
the VC from the far side, silhouetting them perfectly for
the rest of the squad.

Controlled pandemonium erupted as the rest of the squad
opened fire. The thunder of the two M60s was partially
drowned out by the deep booming of the twelve-gauge shotgun. Several VC were knocked out of one sampan as the
loads of #4 buckshot slammed into them. A blast roared
out as the middle sampan was nailed with an MK 3A2
grenade. A second illuminating flare popped into life above
the chaotic scene. Splashes and noise were everywhere as
tracers streaked toward the confused enemy. A sampan was
suddenly blasted into two pieces as it was struck squarely
by a 40-mm high-explosive grenade.

0405 Hours

As suddenly as it began, the firing stopped, as if on
command. The air was full of smoke as the SEALs quickly
moved out to their target. With their ears ringing from the
noise and their hands tingling from the bucking of their
weapons, the SEALs moved to gather materials and prisoners. One VC was spotted as he moved in the water and
a SEAL secured him. Other wounded VC were seen and
dragged in to shore by means of the rope that the SEALs
were holding their position with. Even with the corpsman
there to help, one of the wounded VC succumbed to his
injuries. The SEALs did not want to simply kill all of the
VC (you cannot get information from a corpse), and Jose
moved to help the other wounded VC. Several of the squad
moved to the wreckage of the sampans, quickly picking up

anything of interest that might sink. Anything that might have been missed would be watched for by the PBR waiting downstream. The wounded VC was only stunned from the MK 3A2 grenade and had nothing worse than a bloody nose and a monumental headache.

After quickly questioning the unhurt VC (two of the SEALs spoke Vietnamese), the prisoner was secured with a handling kit. The entire event only took six minutes from start to end with forty-five seconds of firing.

0411 Hours

The PBR was radioed to move to the extraction point two hundred meters downstream from the ambush site. Equipment and materials were gathered up and the squad moved out with their prisoners.

0420 Hours

Aboard the PBR, the squad felt good about their success; the large sack of currency they'd captured told them that they got the paymaster. The boat was still deep inside of "Indian country" so the men did not relax their vigilance. Worn out and covered with mud, the SEALs felt satisfied with their evening's work.

0740 Hours

The PBR had arrived back at base and the prisoners were turned over to Intelligence for detailed interrogation. The squad reported for debriefing and each man stated what he saw and thought. This time debriefing was over quickly and the SEALs had a chance to grab some chow and rest. They all knew it would only be a short time before they were again told that they had a mission.

Vietnam: The Last Years

The 1970s saw the end of the Vietnam War and the last of the SEALs left Vietnam. During 1970, the SEAL detachments in Vietnam saw major cutbacks in personnel and operations as Vietnamization resulted in more SEAL programs' being turned over to the South Vietnamese. The SEALs increasingly took on the role of advisors as the native Vietnamese performed the combat actions.

The first SEAL detachment to be dissolved during Vietnamization was Detachment Bravo. Since June of 1969, SEAL and other U.S. advisors were ordered not to accompany their PRUs into the field. Knowing that the only proper way to lead men is to be with them, some SEALs had themselves put on other units' duty rosters for administrative purposes. Higher headquarters either did not know of or chose to ignore this practice. The SEALs would continue to lead their PRUs in the field for as long as possible.

During the remainder of the year, the SEALs continued their operations with a constantly increasing emphasis on turning over operations to the Vietnamese. Emphasis was also placed on two new SEAL operations, Bright Light and downed pilot recoveries.

The Bright Light operations were the attempted rescues

of American POWs held in Viet Cong prison camps. Though no American POWs were ever recovered by the SEALs, they successfully attacked several camps and liberated a large number of South Vietnamese servicemen. The recovery of downed airmen was also becoming an important SEAL mission.

The continuing SEAL raids and missions against the Viet Cong were netting good results with few losses. SEAL Team 2 suffered no KIAs during 1970 but did have eighteen SEALs wounded during that year. Records for SEAL Team 1's operations in Vietnam are unavailable for the first years of the seventies, but it is known that they too had few losses.

The SEALs were still augmenting their combat capabilities during 1971. SEAL Team 2 alone received a number of new weapons, including M203s to replace their XM148 grenade launchers. Team 2 also received forty-five Hush Puppy silenced pistols and twelve Stoners. The number of Stoners available to Detachment Alfa then gave each deployed platoon two weapons per squad.

SEAL Team 2 ended 1970 with a complement of twenty-three officers and one hundred and fifteen enlisted men. Detachment Alfa had a headquarters group of one officer and one enlisted man, as well as three full platoons. This was to prove the last year of full SEAL operations in Vietnam. The rules of engagement had been changed and no longer would SEAL platoons operate in combat. Standing orders now stated that SEALs "were not permitted to actively participate in combat missions."

1971 saw the last three operational platoons of Detachment Alfa complete their Vietnam commitment. The year began with the Eighth platoon at the Navy base in Dong Tan, conducting its operations primarily in the Dinh Tuong province. Alfa squad of the Ninth platoon operated entirely out of the MAC-V district compound in Ca Mau and ran its operations in the An Xuyen province. Bravo squad of the Ninth platoon also operated in the An Xuyen province but was located at the MAC-V district compound in Hai Yen. After the creation of two Navy huts in the MAC-V compound at Vi Thanh, the Tenth platoon moved in during mid-January. The Tenth operated in the Chuong Thien province.

In February, the Eighth platoon was the first SEAL Team 2 platoon to leave Vietnam without being relieved. The Dinh Tuong area of operations was turned over to Victor platoon of SEAL Detachment Golf. Victor platoon conducted its operations based out of the Navy facility in Dong Tan.

The U.S. Navy senior advisor to the Operation Breezy Cove area of operations served as the commander of the Ninth platoon until it was relieved by Detachment Golf in April. The detachment commander's position for Detachment Alfa was finally dissolved on April 8 as all the detachment's platoons had either turned their operations over to Detachment Golf or had left Vietnam for CONUS.

By early spring, the only SEAL Team 2 detachment left in Vietnam was a four-man LDNN advisory group. This group was later to become Detachment Sierra. The LDNN advisory group was under the command of NAVSPECWARGRU-V and led by Lieutenant (j.g.) Frederick.

From August 14, 1971, to February 5, 1972, SEAL Team 2 had a single four-man unit in Vietnam. Detachment Sierra conducted operations with the South Vietnamese LDNN to prepare them for when the United States was gone completely. Although they were not to conduct combat operations, the four men of Sierra returned to CONUS with three of them having been recommended for the Bronze Star. As of February 1972, SEAL Team 2 had no men in Vietnam.

SEAL Team 1 was also cutting back on its Vietnam commitment. Though available records are sketchy, by 1973 there were no SEAL detachments in Vietnam. Operations were still conducted in 1972, as two SEALs performed acts that later won them the Medal of Honor.

In 1975, Saigon fell to the North Vietnamese. SEAL-trained LDNNs, former PRUs, and other South Vietnamese units moved into the Mekong Delta area and continued their fight against the Communists. The Communist government of Vietnam is still trying to eliminate them all, a final tribute to the SEALs and the men they trained and worked with.

The SEAL Bull Newsletter

The *SEAL Bull* newsletter was a monthly sheet put out in Vietnam by members of SEAL Team 2: The newsletter was started by HMCE Riojas, who was considered the unofficial team cartoonist in Vietnam. The monthly newsletter was not an official publication but was looked forward to by many of the SEALs as a source of news and gossip. *SEAL Bull* did pass on a considerable amount of information to the men, both official and unofficial. Each issue's cover depicted a team joke that was making the rounds that month. The following is from the first issue of *SEAL Bull*.

Short-Time News
SEAL Team Newsletter

Greetings to the officers and men of the Can Tho staff! This little composition is our first effort to put out a little local news for all you boys out in the boondocks, and we hope to publish on a continuing basis if everything works out all right. We cannot guarantee regularity but with any luck at all, we should be able to send the hot skinny out at least once a month.

The skipper has been in Ft. Bragg for about a month now and it appears that he will be extended there for a few more weeks. He's involved in some type of staff job with the Army making some sort of plans. During his absence we have worked the soccer team into No. 1 shape; any smiles?

LT Bailey has extended for three months and is seriously considering a UDT/SEAL billet in Panama. Mr. Boyce is now LTJG Boyce and married, as is the old perennial bachelor, Bill Garnett. Garnett just slipped

"FRIDAY MORNING SOCCER WAS NEVER LIKE THIS!"

THIS NEWSLETTER EDITED:
THE HEAD QUARTERS
GUERILLA STAFF

Cover art from the Seal Bull Newsletter published in Vietnam

around and got hitched without anybody knowing about it, but he will be back one of these days and when he gets back, stand by— At any rate, it looks like several kegs of beer are in order for the near future, but there just ain't enough guys around here at any one time to drink them all! Wish you were here—Lt. Rhinebolt returns from leave in a few days to take over the XO billet and Lt. Kochey will move over (or down) to take over Ops. LTJG Marcinko now has the 8th Platoon and will relieve LT Trani. Ens. Yeaw from UDT-21 is scheduled to come over any time now, as are Albrecht, Johnson, Neault, Keith, and Cyrus, all from UDT-22. We will pick up the additional men later in the quarter. As of now, we have no names.

The following men will go to Ranger School on 13 SEP.: Rangers Fox, Atkinson, Rabbit, and Detmer. On 2 SEP., Kennedy and A. J Ashton will depart for Judo School. Eighth Platoon just returned from Jungle Warfare School last weekend, where, after attending a few classes, they acted as aggressors against the rest of the class. Needless to say, Frank Scollise really raised hell down there, treating officers above the rank Ensign with the respect usually accorded Seamen.

The training group has just completed a week at Camp Pickett where much good training was undergone. On one of the live ambushes, Newell caught a piece of shrapnel from an M-79 round in the belly, but he will be all right; he thought he was a goner for the first few seconds, from all reports. We're trying to figure out a way to give him the Purple Heart, but so far nobody's come up with any suggestions!

The Seventh Platoon is on the way to "Moccasin Manor" (Union Camp) for some real good swampland training. Should be there about ten days or so. How are your own swampland maneuvers coming along? Any trouble getting in your practical factors? As soon as 7th gets back they will undergo Rapelling training and will shortly deploy to relieve 4th Platoon (LTJG Boitnott). Au revoir!

Everything else around here is in good shape except

for Cozart's front lawn; with Garnett in the Bahamas on his honeymoon there ain't nobody around to mow it for him—sorry about that, Diz.

In the near future we're sending a minimum of three men per platoon to a 120-hour Vietnamese Language School at Ft. Bragg, with the intention of upgrading it to at least 4 men per platoon. As you're sure to have found out already, this should really increase our operational capabilities over there. Chief Blais just returned from a special interrogator's school at Ft. Holabird, Maryland and is scheduled to go to the Language School as soon as we can send him.

The most recent UDT Training Class just graduated— 70 men. We hope that the standard of training was of a high level, but we'll just have to wait and see. At least the numbers game was won with that many graduates coming out; maybe we'll be able to get the men we need with such an increased input to the UDT's.

O'Brien, HM2, has just reported on board for duty and will be assigned to the 9th Platoon upon completion of Jump School. Supply has a shore duty type seaman assigned to them, which just tickles R. A. and Saunders to death; fellow by the name of Broadway. He'll be followed by a Storekeeper second at a later date. R. A. Tolison thinks that these boys will be his way out, but the Skipper has just ordered a set of Mk1 Mod O leg-irons for him with just enough chain to let him walk to the file and to the telephone. The allowance List has just been updated for the umpteenth time and more and more gear is coming in, especially in the Electronics and Ordnance fields. Also the Gatling Gun (5.56 model) will be brought down by the GE tech reps on the 8th of SEP and, barring problems, the weapon will be deployed with Mr. Peterson's platoon in October. Watch out, Charlie! Things look real good toward obtaining a high-velocity automatic 40mm. grenade launcher around the first of next calendar year (January, for those of you who don't understand that).

Chief Watson is going to the West Coast in conjunction

with the development of a combat-type life jacket. This piece of gear is covered with camouflage material and has pockets and attaching devices for just about all our combat gear; takes the place of web gear. When the bugs are ironed out of it, we plan to send a few prototypes out to you for your own evaluation and comments. We're also working on a small pair of fins which will fit over a pair of combat boots—no doubt about it, we're getting on with the "lessons learned."

We're experiencing quite a bit of difficulty in jumping due to the shortage of aircraft and bad weather. Maybe we'll be able to get a jump in one of these days, but at the moment, Helicopters are just about impossible to come by.

J. P. Tolison left this week for Knife-and-fork School at Newport, Rhode Island, and upon completion will be sent to SEAL one—another West Coast Puke! Before long an East Coast Warrant Officers' Association will be formed with headquarters in Coronado, California.

KESTNER, CS2, from the base galley is still supplying us with gedunks from the galley—what a good man to have on the inside. The pastry-makers are getting better and better, too; their doughnuts are better than Krispy Kremes at this stage.

The Dog Training Program is coming along real well; one of them bit the Phiblant Chief of Staff when he stopped by one day to show the dogs to his wife. We are training them to hate officers in general, by the way. Boesch and Blais passed the tests for E-9 as did Gallagher Dearmon and Riojas for E-8. All are due to have their records appear before the selection board in the near future.

Porter, RM1, found out a few weeks ago that after his 37-month tour in VN he was suffering from malaria, so keep taking the pills; they're a small price to pay to keep from getting in Porter's condition.

In closing, we'd like to admonish you not to forget the "lessons learned" aspect of the war; jot them down and send them to the Team so that either Ops or the

Training Group can act on them for insertion into the Training curriculum. Until next time, keep your heads and asses down, and keep up the good work. Let us know about any personal problems you'd like taken care of at this end (like wives that need helping out, etc.), and we'll try our best to take care of them.

POW Rescue

The POW question was strong in the minds of the American public during 1970. Letters, petitions, and ranking dignitaries were sent to the North Vietnamese government to try to get some news of the POWs, some of whom had been prisoners for over six years. Since Vietnam was not a signatory of the Geneva Convention, the North Vietnamese government felt no obligation to follow conventional guidelines. In point of fact, they felt the public outcry meant that the POWs could be used as a bargaining chip with Washington. The Army Special Forces started planning a raid into North Vietnam early in 1970, with the raid to take place in the fall of the same year.

On November 22, 1970, a large force of Green Berets, backed by a squadron of helicopters, gunships, and jet fighters, attacked the Son Tay prison camp south of Hanoi. Though no prisoners were rescued, this was the first indication to the public that the military was putting forth a major effort to locate and rescue POWs.

There were earlier attempts made before the Son Tay raid by other forces who could not afford to publicize their activities. The operations conducted by the Navy SEALs under the code name Bright Light had been mentioned but, as much of their operations have remained classified, their rescue attempts have received little publicity.

The MAC-V had an advisory team, Team 80, on station in the Mekong Delta area of Vietnam for some years before 1970. SEAL Team 2, Detachment Alfa, had several platoons assigned to MAC-V and operating in the delta region. Sixth platoon was made up of two officers and thirteen enlisted men under the command of Lieutenant Louis Boink. During the summer of 1970, Sixth platoon was stationed at Ca Mau in the An Xuyen province of South Vietnam.

At approximately 1000 hours on August 21, Sixth platoon received information from a low-level source that indicated the size, location, and personnel strength of a Viet Cong prison camp. The camp was located in the Dam Doi district of the An Xuyen province. Included was information that there were several American POWs being held at the camp. It was known at the time that the VC held several American servicemen captive in the Mekong Delta area and that they tended to move them quickly from camp to camp.

Though not confirmed by this author, the information probably came from a prisoner captured by a provincial reconnaissance unit (PRU). The PRUs worked closely with advisors from the SEALs and other units as part of the Phoenix program and the intelligence they gathered was usually of good quality. But even with the "quality assurance" the SEALs had, they must have confirmed the information about the camp from at least one other reliable source before they acted.

Realizing the time-sensitive nature of the intelligence he had, Lieutenant Boink, rather than going through the time-consuming route of official channels, reacted according to his SEAL training. Quickly organizing the necessary forces, Boink prepared to stage a rescue operation for the POWs. Coordination was immediately organized with province forces and other local assets. Fire support would be supplied by a U.S. Navy destroyer, U.S. Army helicopter gunships, and a unit of Royal Australian Air Force B-57s.

The plan was to have the raiding force land on the beaches to the east of the camp while the Australian bombers struck to the south of the camp. At the same time, the Army gunships would saturate the areas to the west and north of the prison camp with rockets and minigun fire. The intention was to overwhelm the VC forces with approaching gunfire, forcing them to break and run from the camp.

Since the number of prisoners was reported to be substantially greater than the number of guards, it was hoped that the guards would abandon the prisoners rather than be slowed down by taking them along. The rapid approach by the raiders' ground forces would also help prevent the VC guards from simply killing the POWs. The rescued POWs and the ground forces would be extracted by helicopter after the camp had been secured.

In the morning hours of August 22, 1970, the fifteen SEALs of the Sixth platoon, supported by nineteen Vietnamese from the 974th Regional Force company, landed by helicopter on a beach on the South China Sea. As the raiding party was landing, the B-57 bombers were dropping their bombs to the south of the camp, cutting off any enemy movement in that direction.

As the helicopter gunships were making their runs, completing the supporting units' circle of blocking fire, the SEALs were coming under fire from a hidden VC bunker just off the beach. One SEAL, Petty Officer Slator Blackiston III, took the bunker under fire, while the other members of the team maneuvered to bypass the emplacement and move on to the camp.

The force continued to move westward and soon found themselves inside the heavily camouflaged prison camp. No guards or prisoners were to be seen, but a clear trail of footprints leading into the jungle was found. As the team followed the trail into the swampy jungle, naval gunfire was directed to the south of the camp to reinforce the blockage of any VC taking that route of escape. When the force had moved deeper into the jungle they started to find abandoned personal equipment and bundles of clothing dropped along the trail by the retreating guards. The condition of the materials indicated that the fleeing VC were only minutes ahead of the pursuing SEALs.

Heavy rocket fire was called for by the SEALs from the circling gunships to intensify the pressure on the escaping VC. After the fire was lifted, the patrol had moved forward only a short distance before finding twenty-eight Vietnamese POWs whose guards had just left the area. Fast interrogation of the POWs indicated that there were no other prisoners with the guards and no American POWs in the immediate area.

Petty Officer Blackiston, who was acting as the squad radio operator, secured a small pickup zone that had been quickly chopped out of the surrounding jungle. Calling in the recovery helicopters, Blackiston helped coordinate the quick extraction of all the liberated prisoners as well as the raiding force. Blackiston, who had defeated the enemy bunker on the beach, was later to be awarded his fourth Bronze Star medal in recognition of his actions during the raid.

The bodies of three VC were found and listed as KIA, with no casualties on the part of the raiding force. Twenty-eight Vietnamese prisoners were liberated, some of whom had been held captive for over four years. Though no American POWs were rescued, the operation was considered a success and a classic of its type. Subsequent operations in the delta area resulted in a total of forty-eight Vietnamese POWs being liberated during 1970, but no American POWs were reported found.

The raid by Sixth platoon is considered the first of the Bright Light operations conducted in Vietnam. The Bright Light program was intended as a series of raids by the SEAL forces to rescue any American POWs whose locations could be determined. The rescue program was considered one of the most compelling reasons for the continued SEAL presence in the Mekong Delta area long after other American combat forces had ceased operations. The SEALs were the last American combat unit to be operating in the Mekong when they finally officially ceased operations in 1972.

When the POW camp was taken, a small amount of weapons and equipment was also captured. Of primary interest to the American public back home were the first pictures of the now infamous bamboo "tiger cages" where the American POWs were reported to have been held. The Sixth platoon received a Navy Unit Commendation for their actions during the raid itself as well as for the professional manner in which they conducted all of their operations in the delta. SEAL Team 2 also received a Presidential Unit Citation for the second year in a row. There is specific mention of the rescue attempt and its results in the citation document.

It is a testament to the high level of professionalism and dedication of the SEALs that a single platoon, led by a lieutenant, was able to quickly gather the resources needed for a specialized operation. The training and skill of the men is shown by the platoon's being able to effectively take advantage of a sudden opportunity. Lieutenant Boink assembled a multinational, multiservice strike force on short notice and was able to take advantage of intelligence the SEALs had gathered from their own sources.

Presidential Unit Citation—SEAL Team 2

By virtue of the authority vested in me as President
of the United States and as Commander-in-Chief
of the Armed Forces of the United States, I
have today awarded
THE PRESIDENTIAL UNIT CITATION (NAVY)
FOR EXTRAORDINARY HEROISM TO
SEAL TEAM TWO

For extraordinary heroism and outstanding performance of duty in the conduct of unconventional warfare against enemy forces in the Republic of Vietnam from 1 July 1969 to 30 June 1971. While conducting swift and daring operations into enemy strongholds and sanctuaries located in and about the riverine environment of the Mekong Delta, SEAL Team TWO accounted for large numbers of enemy casualties, enemy troops captured, weapons, ammunition and documents of significant intelligence value. Characteristic of the courage, professionalism and dedication of SEAL Team TWO's personnel were their actions during the morning hours of 22 August 1970. While units of the U.S. Army and Australian Air Force provided blocking-force air strikes, a SEAL Team platoon successfully liberated twenty-eight South Vietnamese prisoners of war from a prisoner of war camp deep inside the violently hostile Dam Doi District of the Mekong Delta. On another occasion, a SEAL Team squad engaged a platoon of prisoner of war camp guards in a firefight during which the guards fled, leaving four casualties and six individual weapons behind. On a third occasion, U.S. Navy helicopter gunships and destroyer fire, reacting to intelligence received from a SEAL squad, resulted in eighty enemy casualties. The exceptionally distinguished combat record achieved by the officers and men of SEAL Team TWO reflected the highest credit upon themselves and the United States Naval Service.

Richard Nixon

The Medal of Honor

In today's armed forces there are a number of medals and decorations to signify an individual's bravery in combat. In general, the ratings start with the Bronze Star and move up through the Silver Star, Distinguished Service Cross, Navy Cross, and the Medal of Honor. Various other decorations exist for the different services to indicate deeds performed by the wearer. For all the services, it is the Medal of Honor that stands above all others as an indication of valor.

The Medal of Honor has been awarded to 3,394 men since its inception during the Civil War. Eighteen men have won it twice. During this century, the medal has been awarded to soldiers whose individual acts of heroism were at great risk to their own lives, above and beyond the call of duty.

During the years of American involvement in the Vietnam War, 238 men won the Medal of Honor; 150 of them died performing the acts that later earned them the medal. Medals of Honor went to 155 Army soldiers, 57 to Marines, 12 to airmen (some of them POWs), and 14 to sailors in the Navy.

During their years in Vietnam, the SEALs never went out actively seeking medals. The SEALs performed their duties to the best of their abilities. During their time in

Vietnam, the SEALs were awarded a quantity of decorations. Besides several hundred Purple Hearts for wounds received, SEALs earned 2 Navy Crosses, 42 Silver Stars, 402 Bronze Stars, 2 Legions of Merit, 352 Navy Commendation Medals, 51 Navy Achievement Medals, and 3 Presidential Unit Citations. Almost all of the medals were awarded for acts of valor. Three SEALs won the Medal of Honor, none of them posthumously.

Joseph R. "Bob" Kerrey was a new officer when he reported for BUD/S training on June 18, 1969. Six months later, Ensign Kerrey had graduated BUD/S and was assigned to SEAL Team 1. As one of Delta platoon's two officers, Lieutenant (j.g.) Kerrey proceeded to Vietnam and duties with Detachment Golf. He was well liked by the men under his command; "Kerrey's Raiders" considered their officer to be an "operator's operator."

In March 1969, Delta platoon was conducting operations based out of Cam Ranh Bay as part of the Coastal Surveillance Group (CTF 115) and Operation Market Time. While performing operations in the mountainous Khanh Hoa province, Lieutenant Kerrey learned of a local meeting of VC on an island in Nha Trang Bay. Intelligence indicated that this would be a high-level meeting of key VC figures from the local area. Such a target was not to be missed. The official citation for the subsequent operation reads as follows:

For conspicuous gallantry and intrepidity at the risk of his life above and beyond the call of duty on 14 March 1969 while serving as a SEAL Team Leader during action against enemy aggressor (Viet Cong) forces in the Republic of Vietnam. Acting in response to reliable intelligence, Lieutenant (j.g.) Kerrey led his SEAL Team on a mission to capture important members of the enemy's area political cadre known to be located on an island in the bay of Nha Trang. In order to surprise the enemy, he and his team scaled a 350-foot sheer cliff to place themselves above the ledge on which the enemy was located. Splitting his team in two elements and coordinating both, Lieutenant (j.g.) Kerrey led his men in the treacherous downward descent to the enemy's camp. Just as they neared the end of their descent, intense enemy fire was directed at them, and Lieutenant (j.g.) Kerrey received massive injuries from a grenade which exploded at his feet and threw him backward onto the jagged rocks. Although bleeding profusely and suffering great pain, he displayed outstanding courage and presence of mind in immediately directing his element's fire into the heart of the enemy camp. Utilizing his radioman, Lieutenant (j.g.) Kerrey called in the second element's fire support which caught the confused Viet Cong in a devastating crossfire. After successfully suppressing the enemy's fire, and although immobilized by his multiple wounds, he continued to maintain calm, superlative control as he ordered his team to secure and defend an extraction site. Lieutenant (j.g.) Kerrey resolutely directed his men, despite his near-unconscious state, until he was eventually evacuated by helicopter. The havoc brought to the enemy by this very successful mission cannot be overestimated. The enemy who were captured provided critical intelligence to the allied effort. Lieutenant (j.g.) Kerrey's courageous and inspiring leadership, valiant fighting spirit, and tenacious devotion to duty in the face of almost overwhelming opposition, sustain and enhance the finest traditions of the United States Naval Service.

Richard Nixon

After his hospitalization, Bob Kerrey left the service and returned home to his native Nebraska. Not being one to let physical handicaps hold him back, Kerrey worked and exercised with his artificial leg. As in BUD/S training, fortitude won out and Kerrey ran a marathon just to prove he could do it.

After establishing a successful chain of popular restaurants in the Omaha area, Kerrey looked to the field of politics. Throwing his hat into the political arena in November 1982, Democrat Bob Kerrey was elected Governor of Nebraska. Even this was not enough, and in 1988 Bob Kerrey became the Democratic Senator from Nebraska.

Thomas R. Norris wanted to fly. Joining the Naval Reserve in 1967, Norris volunteered for active duty in 1968. Reporting to Pensacola, Florida, for flight school, Norris washed out of the program due to faulty depth perception. While waiting for reassignment, Norris came across an article on the Navy SEALs. Deciding that this was a worthwhile alternative to flying, Norris volunteered for BUD/S.

After a tour in Vietnam, Norris returned to CONUS for language school. In March of 1971, Norris returned to Vietnam for another combat tour with SEAL Team 2's in-country detachment.

It was during the 1972 NVA Easter offensive that Lieutenant Norris moved north with his team to assist ARVN forces. It was in the northwest section of Quang Tri province, the most northern province in South Vietnam and the closest to the demilitarized zone, that Norris conducted the action that was later to win him the Medal of Honor. The award citation reads as follows:

For conspicuous gallantry and intrepidity in action at the risk of his life above and beyond the call of duty while serving as a SEAL Advisor with the Strategic Technical Directorate Assistance Team, headquarters, U.S. Military Assistance Command, Vietnam. During the period 10 to 13 April 1972, Lieutenant Norris completed an unprecedented ground rescue of two downed pilots deep within heavily controlled enemy territory in Quang Tri Province. Lieutenant Norris, on the night of 10 April, led a five-man patrol through 2,000 meters of heavily controlled enemy territory, located one of the downed pilots at daybreak, and returned to the Forward Operating Base (FOB). On 11 April, after a devastating mortar and rocket attack on the small FOB, Lieutenant Norris led a three-man team on two unsuccessful rescue attempts for the second pilot. On the afternoon of the 12th, a Forward Air Controller located the pilot and notified Lieutenant Norris. Dressed in fishermen disguises and using a sampan, Lieutenant Norris and one Vietnamese traveled throughout that night and found the injured pilot at dawn. Covering the pilot with bamboo and vegetation, they began the return journey, successfully evading a North Vietnamese patrol. Approaching the FOB, they came under heavy machine gun fire. Lieutenant Norris called in an air strike which provided suppression fire and a smoke screen, allowing the rescue party to reach the FOB. By his outstanding display of decisive leadership, undaunted courage, and selfless dedication in the face of extreme danger, Lieutenant Norris enhanced the finest traditions of the United States Naval Service.

Gerald R. Ford

After his rescue mission, Norris continued his tour in Vietnam. Six months later, Lieutenant Norris found himself again in a situation that resulted in a Medal of Honor award—although this time the medal went to someone else.

While acting as the senior advisor to a joint SEAL/LDNN mission, Norris was severely wounded. Another SEAL member of the team, Michael E. Thornton, maneuvered to where the stricken lieutenant lay and moved him to safety. Struck in the head by a bullet, Lieutenant Norris was in very bad shape. The actions of Thornton were later to win him the Medal of Honor.

This created the first time in the history of the medal that a man won the Medal of Honor by saving a Medal of Honor winner.

The very serious injuries Norris sustained kept him in hospitals for two years. Retiring from the Navy in 1975 on a medical disability, Norris continued to work to overcome his handicap. Today, Thomas Norris is a special agent of the FBI, which he joined in September 1979.

Michael E. Thornton enlisted in the Navy in the fall of 1967 after he graduated from high school. For almost two years, Thornton served as a gunner's mate apprentice aboard destroyers. In November 1968, Thornton reported to Coronado and BUD/S training.

After graduation from BUD/S, Thornton was assigned to SEAL Team 1, where he began a series of tours in Vietnam. From January 1, 1970 to December 1972, Thornton spent most of his time serving in Vietnam and Southeast Asia.

On October 31, 1972, Halloween night, Thornton; his senior advisor, Lieutenant Norris; and three LDNNs set out on a prisoner snatch and intelligence-gathering raid near the DMZ on the coast of Quang Tri province. It was during this mission that Norris was hit while calling in naval fire support for the team. Thornton went after Norris as reported in the following citation:

For conspicuous gallantry and intrepidity at the risk of his life above and beyond the call of duty while participating in a daring operation against enemy forces in the Republic of Vietnam on October 31, 1972. Petty Officer Thornton, as assistant U.S. Navy advisor, along with a U.S. Navy lieutenant serving as senior advisor, accompanied a three-man Vietnamese Navy SEAL patrol on an intelligence gathering and prisoner capture operation against an enemy-occupied naval river base. Launched from a Vietnamese Navy junk in a rubber boat, the patrol reached land and was continuing on foot toward its objective when it suddenly came under heavy fire from a numerically superior force. The patrol called in naval gunfire support and then engaged the enemy in a fierce firefight, accounting for many enemy casualties, before moving back to the waterline to prevent encirclement. Upon learning that the senior advisor had been hit by enemy fire and was believed to be dead, Petty Officer Thornton returned through a hail of fire to the lieutenant's last position, quickly disposed of two enemy soldiers about to overrun the position and succeeded in removing the seriously wounded and unconscious senior naval advisor to the water's edges. He then inflated the lieutenant's lifejacket and towed him seaward for approximately two hours until picked up by support craft. By his extraordinary courage and perseverance, Thornton was directly responsible for saving the life of his superior officer and enabling the safe extraction of all patrol members.

Richard M. Nixon

After his award, Thornton was the only SEAL Medal of Honor winner who remained on active duty. Later, Thornton was to volunteer for service with SEAL Team 6 when it was formed for counterterrorist duty. Lieutenant Thornton took his commission as a Navy officer in 1983 and is still with the SEALs at the time of this writing.

Phoenix

The Phoenix program was probably the most misunderstood and maligned SEAL operation in Vietnam. U.S. news correspondents and antiwar activists both labeled the Phoenix program as "organized assassination" that tortured and killed thousands of innocent civilians. The reality of the Phoenix program was considerably different than the media's story.

Since the Viet Cong were fighting a guerrilla war, they were very difficult to spot among the general population. Guerrilla-style warfare has a greater need than standard combat for an efficient command structure and leadership. Without their leaders, guerrilla groups cannot act as a cohesive unit and usually quickly fall apart into simple marauding bands, which can be quickly neutralized. The objective of the Phoenix program was to eliminate the command-and-supply infrastructure the Viet Cong had so carefully built up over the years. A second objective of the Phoenix program was the collection and confirmation of high-level intelligence.

The need for an organization of the intelligence efforts in attacking the Viet Cong infrastructure (VCI) was clearly stated as early as 1961. Sir Robert Thompson served with the British Embassy in Saigon during the early 1960s and was recognized as a leading counterguerrilla expert. The opinion of Sir Robert was that the VCI was the primary target of the counterinsurgency effort in Vietnam and could be successfully attacked by a concerted effort of all of the allied intelligence services in Vietnam. At the time of Sir Robert's statement there were seventeen intelligence services from several allied nations operating in Saigon alone.

It was in 1966 that a concerted effort by the United States began to attack the VC infrastructure. Protection of the general Vietnamese public from VC reprisals was considered mandatory for a successful campaign in Southeast Asia. U.S. Ambassador Henry Cabot Lodge knew in detail of the intelligence situation in Vietnam at the time and stated, ''Getting at the VCI is the heart of the matter.''

Reorganization of the intelligence community against their new target was begun with the establishment of the Intelligence Coordination and Exploitation program (ICEX). ICEX was a joint MAC-V/CIA operation that was the immediate forerunner of the Phoenix program.

The Vietnamese who worked in the field for the ICEX program were native to their assigned areas. These personnel received training from the U.S. Army Special Forces or the SEALs before being assigned to a unit. Gathered into armed reconnaissance teams, the men would be assigned to their home area as a provincial reconnaissance unit (PRU). Together with the Vietnamese National Police and police field units, the PRUs made up the action arm of the ICEX program.

SEAL Team 1 began sending entire platoons to Vietnam for duty in the field as combat units in 1966. Five platoons were initially sent and each was assigned to one of three operational detachments: Golf, Bravo, or Echo.

Detachment Golf was the first and largest operational SEAL detachment in Vietnam. Located at Nha Be, Detachment Golf ran reconnaissance and intelligence-gathering patrols against the Viet Cong operating in the Rung Sat Special Zone. Consisting of three operational platoons of two officers and twelve enlisted men each along with an

Officer in Charge (OIC), Detachment Golf was under the operational control of the commander, U.S. Military Assistance Command, Vietnam (COMUSMAC-V) and—or, depending on the mission—the Commander, Naval Forces, Vietnam (COMNAVFORV).

Detachment Echo was the smallest SEAL detachment in Vietnam during the early years of the war. Consisting of one officer and five enlisted men, the detachment was under the control of the COMUSMAC-V. Operating out of the Naval Advisory Detachment at Da Nang, Detachment Echo would advise indigenous personnel in the art of conducting special warfare in a riverine counterinsurgency environment.

Detachment Bravo consisted of a platoon of one officer and twelve enlisted men during its early operations. Under the operational control of the COMUSMAC-V, all the personnel assigned to Bravo acted in direct support of the PRUs. The SEALs of Detachment Bravo would be assigned to PRUs throughout the Mekong Delta, the IV Corps Tactical Zone (IV CTZ). Each individual SEAL operated with a PRU in the field, acting as an advisor and instructor. With this system, the SEALs of Detachment Bravo were able to conduct ICEX operations in twelve of the sixteen delta provinces.

Since part of their mission centered on the gathering of intelligence, the SEALs of Detachment Bravo preferred capturing members of the VCI as opposed to simply killing them. Once the SEALs had convinced their PRUs that information couldn't be obtained from a corpse, their operations became very successful. Utilizing native and local sources of information, the SEAL/PRU teams started conducting regular operations against the VCI. Viet Cong tax collectors and local leaders were favorite targets of SEAL snatch raids where prisoners were ambushed or kidnapped while seemingly secure in their village huts.

With prisoner snatches, ambushes, and increasing VC defections, the ICEX program and SEAL Detachment Bravo were proving a successful combination. By 1968, Detachment Bravo and its PRUs were neutralizing eight hundred members of the VCI every month. Unfortunately, intelligence gathered in these operations was not being properly processed and evaluated by the higher commands of the various intelligence agencies. This situation came to a head on January 31, 1968—the unleashing of the furious attacks known as the Tet Offensive.

Though the Tet Offensive was stopped by the U.S. and South Vietnamese forces and proved to be a military disaster for the Viet Cong, the fact that it had surprised the intelligence services was ominous. The situation could not be allowed to be repeated.

South Vietnam's President, Nguyen Van Thieu, used the Tet Offensive as part of his rationale for pushing ahead the Phoenix program. Thieu wanted a more coordinated intelligence network with the South Vietnamese in overall control. The U.S. would provide advisors and support for Phoenix but command would be in South Vietnamese hands. Phoenix would be set up with a high proportion of Vietnamese to American advisors. Intended ratios would be as high as five hundred Vietnamese for every one U.S. advisor.

The U.S. did have a strong role in the planning and organization of the Phoenix program. U.S. officials involved with the planning included the U.S. Ambassador to Vietnam, Robert W. Komer; William E. Colby, who later became the Director of the CIA; and John Paul Vann, the senior civilian advisor. Earlier, Ambassador Komer had worked with President Thieu and the two men had actually launched the Phoenix program before the Tet Offensive began. Little had been accomplished to advance the program before the sudden Communist onslaught.

Named "Phuang Hoang" by the Vietnamese after a mythical bird, the Phoenix program was restarted on July 1, 1968. Most media reports list that date as the beginning of the program, because the earlier ICEX and other operations were highly classified.

Even though it created a new bureaucracy, the Phoenix program was considered a major step forward in the efficient processing of field-gathered intelligence. All the intelligence gathered by the action arm would be collated and analyzed by a joint Vietnamese/U.S. team at each province head-quarters before being sent up to higher commands. Each province had a Province Intelligence Operations Coordination Center (PIOCC) that reported its findings to the district centers. Each district had a District Intelligence Operations Coordination Center (DIOCC) that reported to headquarters in Saigon.

The neutralization of the VCI throughout South Vietnam was the stated goal of the Phoenix program and the number of possible targets was dangerously high. It was estimated that there were between 65 and 80,000 members or sympathizers of the VCI in South Vietnam during 1968.

Combating the VCI in the urban areas was the task of the National Police Force, backed up by the Police Field Force. The field force was a paramilitary arm of the National Police that was able to both operate in the cities and function efficiently in the countryside surrounding the urban areas. The PRUs operated throughout the country in the rural areas and were the primary action force of the Phoenix program as they had been for its predecessor, the ICEX program.

Under the tutelage of their SEAL advisors, the PRUs in the Mekong Delta region continued increasing their combat effectiveness. While the majority of the PRU forces were made up of Vietnamese, there were also a large number of humong (montagnards) from the mountains, Cambodians from across the border, some Chinese, and even deserters from the Army of the Republic of Vietnam (ARVN). The deserters were often drawn by the higher pay offered by the PRUs as well as the chance to defend their home areas. North Vietnamese and Viet Cong deserters also entered service with the PRUs through the Chieu Hoi (Open Arms) program, which was another part of the overall Phoenix strategy. The Chieu Hoi program was started in 1963. Offering amnesty to all VC defectors, it resulted in some excellent intelligence for the U.S. forces as well as trained, experienced men for the PRUs.

The PRUs quickly became some of the most effective native troops of the Vietnam War. Generally organized into teams of ten to twenty men, the PRUs would be able to quickly act on "hard" or confirmed intelligence on a specific VCI target. With their small size and close organization, the PRUs could act decisively where larger units would be bogged down by their own size. Moving deep through enemy territory, the PRUs would take prisoners, set ambushes, kidnap prominent VCI members, gather intelligence, and set up and maintain networks of native agents.

The effectiveness of the ICEX program might have contributed greatly to the Viet Cong defeats during the Tet Offensive. There is no question of the effect that the PRUs and the Phoenix program had against the VCI. By 1969, the Communists launched a concerted effort against the Phoenix program, which they believed was devastating their leadership. It is interesting to note that this was also the time that the stories about the "assassination squads" began appearing in the U.S. media.

The success of the SEALs of Detachment Bravo and their PRUs is demonstrated by the almost complete elimination of the Viet Cong as a functional force in several parts of the Mekong Delta. With military units, including other SEAL detachments, attacking the enemy forces throughout the delta region and the Bravo SEALs and Phoenix PRUs removing the VCI, areas of the Mekong Delta that had been under Communist domination for ten years found themselves free of the Viet Cong.

The phrase "Charlie doesn't live here anymore" came out of the delta and is a testament to the effect that the SEALs, Phoenix, and the PRUs had on the Viet Cong.

Detachment Bravo proved to be such an important operation that their personnel levels were increased in 1968. Bravo went from being authorized a single officer and twelve enlisted men to having four officers and twenty-four enlisted men on October 4, 1968. Of the twelve PRU advisory positions, eight were manned by SEALs from Team 1 and four were manned by SEALs from Team 2. The result of this situation was that SEAL Teams 1 and 2 reported a Detachment Bravo in Vietnam at the same time.

By the end of 1968, the IV CTZ PRUs were almost entirely advised by SEAL personnel. The SEAL advisors were accompanying their PRUs on an average of fifteen operations each month. During most of these operations, the SEALs would often be the only Americans operating in their area.

Almost no information is officially available regarding specific operations that the SEALs conducted as part of the Phoenix program. All records from the field operations of individual PRUs are still listed as classified and are still unavailable for publication in this book. Several SEALs were awarded decorations for their part in the PRU operations, and it is only through the award statements that we are able to gather some insight into the interaction between the SEAL advisors and their PRUs.

SEAL Petty Officer John S. Fallon was serving with Detachment Bravo as a PRU advisor during the spring of 1969. Working with locally produced intelligence, Fallon took his PRU on a mission deep into enemy-held territory on March 20. Inserted by helicopter into their target area, Fallon and his PRU dismounted from their choppers and moved out to their objective.

While crossing a rice paddy, the PRU came across a well-entrenched unit of VC who immediately opened fire on the PRU and their SEAL advisor. Caught in a withering hail of automatic weapons fire, the PRU quickly dove for cover, but not before two of the PRU men were hit and went down.

In complete disregard for his own safety, Fallon left his position behind cover and ran across the open paddy to the stricken men. Fallon administered first aid to the wounded PRUs and then used his radio to call for a "dust-off" (medical air evacuation). When the MEDEVAC chopper arrived, Fallon, while still under heavy fire from the Viet Cong, carried the most severely wounded man to the helicopter and put him aboard.

Returning to his PRU, Fallon rallied his men and led an assault on the VC positions. The VC broke and ran, leaving four dead. Fallon's PRU also captured a VC prisoner as well as two rocket launchers. Fallon's performance earned him the unswerving devotion of his PRU followers and is representative of the SEALs' general level of professionalism and loyalty to their PRUs. Though he received the Silver Star for his actions in the field that March 20, Fallon's greatest reward was the value the PRU placed on him and his leadership.

Occasionally, individual PRUs would be gathered together into company-size units to accomplish a particular objective or conduct a more standard military task. They proved to be the most effective of all the South Vietnamese military and paramilitary organizations. Not only did the PRUs have the lowest desertion rate in the South Vietnamese military, they also had the lowest casualty rate. The losses the PRUs inflicted on the enemy, especially those PRUs operating in the Mekong Delta, were far out of proportion to those losses they received.

The ambush was probably the most common and primary PRU tactic used when attacking the enemy. Though it could be very difficult to positively identify individuals as Viet Cong when they were in their normal village surroundings, the PRUs found other means for confirming their targets. For example, when a suspect was found moving through the jungle at night, armed with an AK-47 and accompanying other Viet Cong, it was a relatively simple task to identify him as a member of the VCI.

One ambush that resulted in elimination of unknown VCI members took place in the Vinh Loi district of the Bac Lieu province during the summer of 1969. The SEAL Phoenix advisor later stated that the PRU was acting on intelligence received that a VC propaganda team would be in a certain village on a particular night. Plans were made to intercept the unit outside of the village.

The ambush team, consisting of ten PRU members and two American advisors, took up positions overlooking a trail the VC unit was expected to use. The ambushers had been in position for about two hours when they heard the VC unit approaching the ambush zone. The SEALs were shocked to see that leading the VC unit was the chief of the local village, who had convinced the local authorities that he was not a Viet Cong sympathizer.

As soon as the fifteen-man VC unit had entered the ambush killing zone the PRU opened fire. The village chief, along with several Viet Cong, went down in the initial fire of the ambush. The remaining Viet Cong who had not been wounded or killed in the opening shots of the ambush broke ranks and fled into the jungle. Several of the Viet Cong who had been wounded were captured by the PRU as they tried to take cover in the surrounding brush. While later being interrogated by the local intelligence team, the VC prisoners admitted that the village chief had been an active member of the Viet Cong for over ten years.

The numerous losses that the Viet Cong were sustaining among their clandestine field agents due to the Phoenix program were proving severe by 1969. Combined with the losses sustained by the VC during the Tet Offensive, the Phoenix program was causing some VC field units and areas to go without effective leadership. Documents (#6-029-0451 71) captured from the Viet Cong in the Long Khanh province in 1971 showed that the Phoenix program's success had weakened the Communists' position, even though the Americans were largely no longer involved. Besides outlining countermeasures to be used against the Phoenix program, the documents also listed compromised Phoenix agents and informers; local VC were also "sent special underground security agents to check on [Phoenix] activities," indicating that the VC hierarchy was willing to expend valuable assets in opposing the Phoenix program.

It was due in no small part to its success that Phoenix became such a point of controversy in the United States. With the operations and methods of the Phoenix program being, of necessity, highly classified, no reports about them could be officially confirmed, or even effectively denied. Eighty-five to ninety percent of the VCI neutralized by Phoenix operations had been either killed or captured during field military operations by the PRUs. Regardless of this, the public image of the Phoenix program portrayed a CIA "spook" leading a team of criminal Asian mercenaries into helpless villages at night. The silenced pistol shot to the head of an innocent sleeping villager was the picture told to the American public, not the story of American SEALs

Results of SEAL Combat Actions in Vietnam, 1966–1971

	1966	1967	1968	1969	1970	1971	(72)*	Totals
SEAL TEAM 1								
Enemy KIA (body count)	86	60	187	235	N/A	N/A		568
Enemy KIA (probable)	15	30	52	122	N/A	N/A		219
Enemy WIA	—	—	—	—	—	—		—
Captured personnel	N/A	24	96	114	N/A	N/A		234
Captured weapons	N/A	40	24+	N/A	N/A	N/A		64+
Captured documents	some	some	20 kg	20 kg	N/A	N/A		40 kg +
SEAL TEAM 1 LOSSES								
KIA	1	5	6	6	N/A	4(1)		23
WIA	16	26	15	19	N/A	0(1)		7
SEAL TEAM 2								
Enemy KIA (body count)	N/A	163	477	285	52	49		1,026
Enemy KIA (probable)	N/A	49	161	164	25	20		419
Enemy WIA	N/A	56	119	91	10	23		299
Captured personnel	N/A	98	382	270	29	67		846
Captured weapons	N/A	40	200	131	12	38		421
Captured documents	N/A	some	some	52.5 kg	149 kg	37 kg		237.5 kg +

SEAL TEAM 2 LOSSES

KIA	N/A	0	6	2	1	9
WIA	N/A	19	40	28	18	105

SEAL TEAM TOTALS FOR OPERATIONS IN VIETNAM, 1966–1972

Enemy killed in action (confirmed by body count)	1,594
Enemy killed in action (probable, body not found)	638
Captured enemy personnel	1,080
Captured enemy weapons	over 485
Captured documents (intelligence)	over 277.5 kilograms

SEAL LOSSES

Killed in action	32
Wounded in action	182

RATIO OF SEAL LOSSES (KIA) TO ENEMY LOSSES (KIA, BODY COUNT)

1 SEAL per 50 Enemy

*SEAL Team 1 records are still classified for these years. The one SEAL KIA in 1972 was Lt. Melvin S. Dry. Killed in action in the Gulf of Tonkin on June 6, 1972, Lt. Dry's loss was originally listed as due to an operational accident. Lt. Dry was the last SEAL listed as a KIA in the Vietnam War.

standing for hours in chest-deep water alongside their PRU companions, waiting for an armed, but unsuspecting, VC unit. Those opposed to U.S. involvement in Southeast Asia refused to believe that a classified operation could be successful due to professionalism and a high level of training. It was far more sensational to accuse Phoenix of committing atrocities even if there was no hard proof.

Public outcry and negative press reporting was such that the American involvement in the Phoenix program was ordered ended in the early 1970s. SEAL Detachment Bravo was dissolved in March of that year and its Phoenix operations were turned completely over to South Vietnamese control.

In spite of several congressional inquiries into reported excess of the Phoenix program, no evidence of American involvement in assassinations has ever been brought to public view or proven. Most of the Phoenix deriders could only state hearsay evidence from individual "agents" with no government records to back up their atrocity horror stories.

The SEALs still state unequivocally that their mission was to gather intelligence and conduct combat operations, not commit assassinations. The SEALs were the only U.S. unit in Vietnam with the ability to gather their own intelligence, conduct a combat operation based on that intelligence, and then analyze the results, all with the blessing of those in command.

Critters

In the swamps, mud flats, and waterways of Vietnam there was far more to threaten the SEALs' successful operations than the Viet Cong. Sudden death moved silently through the waters, slithered through the grass, or just lay in wait.

Saltwater crocodiles, recognized man-eaters, could grow to a length of twenty-five feet and infested many areas along the coast of Southeast Asia. Snakes ranged from the massive Burmese python to the small, but highly venomous, krait. Insects were plentiful in the humid environment of Southeast Asia. The threat from insects could be anything from disease-carrying swarms of mosquitoes and flies to spiders the size of dinner plates, and scorpions over six inches long.

All the living dangers aside, the areas in which the SEALs operated were almost impassible. In the mangrove swamps, such as those found in the Rung Sat Special Zone (RSSZ), plants grew thick and heavy. The plants combined with the watery terrain to create a barrier to movement anywhere but on the open waterways. Even a well-conditioned squad of SEALs, working very hard, would only be able to cover a few hundred yards in a single day in some parts of the RSSZ.

It was the inhospitable terrain that first attracted the Viet

Cong to the RSSZ. The VC's simple forces were able to move and hide in an area where normal military units would quickly bog down. It was in these areas that the SEALs had to operate. The SEALs faced tropical animals, insects, and diseases as well as booby traps, punji stakes, and direct contact with the enemy during their missions.

During one operation in the RSSZ, a platoon of twelve SEALs, led by Lieutenant David Janke and a chief petty officer moved deep into the four-hundred-square-mile swamp. The platoon was investigating information that a Viet Cong arms cache was located near an old pagoda.

Approaching the site of the arms cache, the SEALs ran across a small unit of six Viet Cong. The VC took cover in a nearby hut and opened fire on the SEALs, who were still in their transport boat. Seaman Gary Gleason, who was armed with a 57-mm recoilless rifle, placed several accurate high-explosive shells into the hut, which quickly ended the fight.

Unknown to the SEALs, however, the six Viet Cong were the rear guard to a nearby VC battalion that was using the arms cache. As the SEALs moved ashore, a large number of the enemy appeared farther along the riverbank. When the VC saw the SEALs and their boat they immediately opened fire. Faced by a superior enemy force, the SEALs went on the attack. The actions of the SEAL platoon worked and drove the enemy force away.

The SEALs pursued the fleeing VC for some distance into the jungle before stopping their chase. Concerned that the platoon could be caught in an ambush while short of ammunition, Lieutenant Janke ordered his unit back to the river. When the platoon arrived back at their transport boat the men immediately restocked on ammunition from the supplies on board. Informing higher command of the situation, Lieutenant Janke decided to continue the mission.

Ordering the boat back to the base, the SEALs set out to reach the pagoda and the enemy supply cache. After several hours of quiet movement through the jungle, the platoon suddenly stopped when their scout approached. Ahead of the platoon, the scout noticed a group of enemy soldiers approaching the SEALs' location. Using hand signals for silent communications, the scout informed the SEAL platoon that about twenty of the enemy were approaching from the direction of the pagoda. The VC were heavily laden with arms and ammunition from the pagoda cache and offered a tempting target for the forewarned SEALs.

The Viet Cong were only about fifteen minutes away when the SEALs quickly established an ambush site and settled down to wait. As the Viet Cong entered the killing zone, Gleason initiated the ambush with a high-explosive round fired from his 57-mm recoilless rifle. The first VC were instantly killed from the blast of the 57-mm shell. Four more of the enemy were quickly cut down by the withering hail of bullets coming from the SEALs' positions. The surviving Viet Cong dropped their bundles and fled from the scene.

Lieutenant Janke figured the platoon had pushed their luck about as far as it would go that day and ordered the platoon to withdraw. Quickly stripping the enemy dead of any items of intelligence value, the SEALs destroyed the abandoned supplies before pulling out.

Moving south, the SEAL platoon penetrated deeper into one of the densest areas of mangrove swamp in the RSSZ. The lieutenant thought that if the remainder of the VC battalion took up after the SEALs, the platoon would have its best chance in the deep swamp. The SEALs were using the Viet Cong's own method of operation against them. Since the SEAL platoon was a relatively small number of men, they would be able to move in the areas where the larger battalion of VC could not easily go.

While moving along the swamp, just before dark, one of the SEALs became stuck in the mud on the bottom of a canal. While trying to work his legs free, the SEAL noticed what was apparently a log moving upstream toward him. The stuck SEAL silently signaled another member of his platoon over to where he was standing in the water. The trapped SEAL quickly removed the magazine from his M16 and ejected the round in the weapons chamber. He realized that if an accidental shot was fired, the searching enemy forces would immediately know that the SEAL platoon was still in the area. With his weapon empty, the trapped SEAL could safely use the weapon as a club, a desperate measure at best. Seeing the situation, the approaching SEAL also unloaded and cleared his weapon.

As the approaching log moved closer, it became obvious why it could move upstream. The "log" was a hungry crocodile! When the crocodile was within a few feet of his position, the trapped SEAL struck the reptile between the eyes with his rifle butt. The large reptile twisted away from the sudden blow, directly into the path of another descending rifle butt, this one swung by the other SEAL on the scene. Confused by the rain of blows, the crocodile thrashed around until it was finally able to swim away. After all this commotion, the SEAL who had been stuck in the mud found his legs had been freed during the struggle. Turning to cross the canal, the two SEALs saw the rest of their platoon on the opposite shore. The platoon was convulsed with silent laughter at the show the two "Tarzans" had put on against what turned out to be a rather timid crocodile.

Finding a mangrove clump that was a little higher than the rest of the swamp, the SEAL platoon moved in for the night. After putting out sentries, the platoon settled down onto the relatively dry ground to try to get some rest before continuing their mission the next day.

Before dawn, the platoon was on the move again. The SEALs once more worked their way north to their original objective, the pagoda.

Arriving in the vicinity of the pagoda by 1000 hours, the SEALs took up positions around the building and prepared to wait. Three hours later, the SEALs were still waiting patiently and had not moved from their positions. With all of the activity in the area the day before, there was a very real possibility that the Viet Cong were waiting in ambush for the SEALs to return. The SEALs intended to observe the area until they were satisfied no one was waiting for them. During this long wait, there was another encounter with the local wildlife.

The chief petty officer of the platoon lay crouched next

to a large tree where he had an excellent view of the pagoda. Next to the chief, about fifteen feet to his left, Lieutenant Janke lay hidden. Fifteen feet behind both the chief and the lieutenant were a gunner's mate and a boatswain's mate, both men in a location to be able to watch the rear and flanks of the SEALs' position.

After having been in position about twenty minutes, the men heard a strange sound. The chief heard it first and turned toward the boatswain's mate behind him to see if he had also heard the noise. The chief saw that the boatswain's mate was watching something in the tree above the chief's head. Before he could move to look above himself, a large python slipped down from the tree a few feet away from the chief.

All of the men who saw the snake swore that it was at least thirty feet long. The chief agreed that the snake was big, but all he saw was the reptile's head staring at him from two feet away. The SEAL and the snake stared at each other for over two and a half hours. Finally, bored with the situation, the massive snake slowly slithered away. The chief had not been bored!

With the python gone, the SEALs moved out to examine the pagoda. Finding several enemy booby traps but no cache, the SEALs made up and left some traps of their own before leaving the area.

While moving back to the river, the scout reported to the lieutenant that there was a large number of Viet Cong up ahead, apparently waiting in ambush for the SEALs' return. Carefully maneuvering for more than an hour put the SEALs in a position to outflank the ambush.

Throwing a grenade toward the other flank of the ambush site was the signal for the SEAL platoon to open fire on the surprised Viet Cong. During the fierce firefight, eleven of the enemy were killed before the rest of the VC broke ranks and fled into the jungle. One of the VC was not fast enough and was captured by one of the SEALs, the same SEAL who had fought the crocodile the day before.

Calling in an airlift back to base, the SEALs left the area by helicopter, accompanied by their prisoner. Though the platoon had not received any casualties during the operation, one SEAL was permanently marked by the mission. From that day on, the chief was known as The Python.

Not all of the SEALs' encounters with the natural dangers of Vietnam turned out so well, with nothing more than a nickname and a good story afterward. During one operation, listed as report #275, the results were quite different.

During the morning of August 11, 1967, a squad of Team 1 SEALs from Detachment Echo were setting up an ambush along a trail in the jungle. An enemy patrol was expected to use the trail and the SEALs were digging in to establish their ambush site and kill zone.

While clearing his position in the muddy terrain, a SEAL named Hertenstein was bitten by a spider that was hidden in the brush he had been pushing away. Within minutes Hertenstein was having difficulty breathing, blurred vision, and had swollen up over most of his body. Rapid evacuation by LCM and then MEDEVAC by helicopter to a hospital site managed to save the SEALs' life. With the position blown, the remainder of the SEAL squad moved to a secondary position to again attempt the ambush. After having received no enemy contact by the next day, the SEALs returned to their detachment's headquarters in Da Nang.

Besides combating the local fauna in Vietnam, the SEALs also put animals to work for them. In late December 1967, Silver, a two-and-a-half-year-old German shepherd attached to SEAL Team 2, became the first Navy dog to earn his parachute wings. The award was given after Silver had completed a sixteen-week course of instruction at the Army Canine School in Fort Benning, Georgia.

Silver's SEAL handler, Quartermaster Third Dewayne G. Schwalenberg, was already parachute-qualified when he reported to the Canine School. Schwalenberg had to learn a whole new method of jumping and landing to successfully operate with the sixty-two-pound dog.

To make a parachute jump, Silver was fitted with a special harness from which he could hang without any danger of slipping out and falling. After securing Silver's harness, Schwalenberg would attach the dog's harness to his own with a twenty-foot length of line. On board the jump aircraft,

Schwalenberg would again attach Silver's harness to his own by means of a quick-release buckle.

Schwalenberg would exit the craft with Silver in his arms and then the dog would hang at his side during the descent. When the pair was two hundred feet from the ground, Schwalenberg would lower Silver to the end of his tether line. At the last moment before impact, Schwalenberg would pull up on Silver's line, cushioning the dog's landing.

Silver had already proved himself an intelligent and capable animal even before he completed training. During a practice jump, Schwalenberg had a bad landing and was lying on the ground stunned. When his parachute canopy filled from the wind and started dragging the helpless SEAL across the ground, Silver jumped on the dragging chute and collapsed it, saving Schwalenberg from possible injury. Even though it had not been part of his training, Silver was able to size up the situation and "think" quickly.

The training Silver did receive at the Army school included basic obedience, patrolling, attack, booby trap detection, scouting, and helicopter rappelling. All the time and training spent on the dogs was considered worthwhile, especially taking into account a German shepherd's several natural fighting advantages over a normal man, even a SEAL. Silver's hearing was 20 percent greater than a man's, his sense of smell 40 percent greater, and his eyesight 10 percent greater. Silver's natural armament also was nothing to be scoffed at. The jaws of a healthy German shepherd can exert pressure of up to five hundred pounds per square inch, enough to hold even a strong man firmly.

Silver was one of a number of dogs fielded in Vietnam by SEAL Team 2. The first of these dogs, Prince, stands out even above the rest. It was Prince who proved the effectiveness of SEAL/dog teams in combat and set the standards that Silver and the other dogs had to live up to.

Starting out in life as a family pet, Prince soon grew too large and was considered too aggressive for the family's children. A Virginia Beach police officer, Gene R. Griffith, obtained Prince from his original owners in 1965, intending to train him as a police dog.

Griffith considered Prince "one of the smartest dogs I've

ever seen, with unusual smelling and tracking ability." According to Officer Griffith, Prince "could smell a man upwind, fifty to sixty yards away."

Prince entered into the Norfolk K9 program with Officer Griffith as his handler, and that is where the SEALs found him. Chief Boatswain's Mate William Bruhmuller had been sent by SEAL Team 2 to train with another dog at the Norfolk K9 facility. The first SEAL dog, a shepherd named Duke, did not work out during training and was dropped from the program. Bruhmuller was impressed with Prince and took over his training. The animal quickly proved himself up to the task.

With police K9 school behind him, Prince was shipped out in 1966 for his first six-month tour in Vietnam with Bruhmuller as his handler. This was the first time any Navy unit had used scout dogs in combat in Vietnam. While on his first tour, Prince caught a Viet Cong agent outside of a Mekong Delta river patrol base at Binh Thuy. The man was dressed as a South Vietnamese soldier and had been riding away from the base on a bicycle when detected by Prince. Responding to the dog's actions, the SEALs detained and questioned the man, who turned out to be an agent in disguise. The agent was taken to military headquarters and turned over to Intelligence.

While successful in the field, Prince was considered promising but not as useful as he could be. Arrangements were made with the Army Canine School, and Prince reported for training along with his new handler, Seaman Mike Bailey.

Prince and his handler went through the sixteen-week course at Fort Benning, where the dog learned to detect booby traps, among other military skills. After completing training, Prince and Bailey returned to Vietnam for a six-month tour in the latter half of 1967.

During one patrol, Bailey allowed Prince to run loose while the squad stopped to eat. While the patrol was eating, Prince came back into the area carrying a hand grenade in his mouth! Following the dog, the patrol was led to large enemy cache of automatic weapons, ammunition for small arms and mortars, rockets, medical supplies, and a quantity of enemy documents.

It was also during his second tour in Vietnam that Prince was wounded in his chest and legs by an exploding booby trap during a patrol and, as a result, was awarded his first Purple Heart. The SEAL moving in front of the dog set off the booby trap that injured Prince before he had a chance to detect it. Prince recovered from his wounds and returned to combat duty.

In 1968 Prince returned to Vietnam for his third tour of duty. Prince is credited with twice warning his patrol about an enemy ambush ahead of them. The dog would warn his handler by "alerting." When a trained dog alerts he becomes nervous and agitated, holds his head high with his ears standing up. It is the handler's job to determine what it is that the animal is bothered by.

During this third tour of duty, Prince won his second Purple Heart. When the SEALs were taking on an enemy force near a tunnel complex, Prince was struck by hand grenade fragments. Newspaper articles back in the States enjoyed showing photos of the black-and-tan SEAL dog wearing his two Purple Hearts hanging from ribbons around his neck.

In August 1970 Prince was seven years old. He had survived three tours in Vietnam, had received two awards for wounds received in combat, and had proved the feasibility of the SEALs' scout dog program. Not bad for a dog who had started life as a family pet.

The SEALs used more dogs in combat than just Prince and Silver. Primary training was given to the dogs at the Army Canine School, but the animals received some special training from their handlers, some of the instruction being very original. One shepherd assisted its SEAL handler during prisoner interrogations.

The Vietnamese people, though tough and hardy, are physically small in stature. When a Viet Cong became a prisoner of "the men with green faces," the VC's nickname for the SEALs, he would already be in a very tense frame of mind. When a large, berserk dog suddenly appeared and began ripping the prisoner's clothing with its jaws, most prisoners told their interrogators anything just to keep that dog away from themselves. The prisoners normally didn't notice that the dog had never touched the flesh under the clothes but had only ripped the cloth, exactly what his SEAL handler had taught him to do.

The SEALs successfully used the man/animal combination during several operations. One of these operations was Stable Door, and it resulted in the most unusual military use of trained animals in U.S. history. Operation Stable Door was the protection and patrolling of key South Vietnamese harbors and the shipping they held. Both the SEALs and the UDTs operated with other Navy forces during this operation, described in the following 1968 Department of the Navy press release:

> STABLE DOOR units maintain a 24-hour visual and radar surveillance of harbor approaches and anchorage areas. STABLE DOOR harbor patrol boats intercept and search local indigenous craft, maintain a vigilant watch for enemy swimmers or floating objects which could be mines, and carry Explosive Ordnance Disposal (EOD) diver personnel for inspection of ships' hulls and anchor chains.

Many of the patrols conducted for Stable Door were routine and boring, the stopping and searching of sometimes hundreds of sampans in a single day. During random sweeps of some harbors, the Navy men would toss grenades into the water and watch for the bubbles that indicated an enemy swimmer was in the area. The body of an enemy swimmer would occasionally wash up on shore as a bloody indication of the effectiveness of these operations.

By far the most unusual patrolling took place at Cam Ranh Bay under the direction of the SEALs and the UDTs.

Cam Ranh Bay, in II Corps area, was a billion-dollar U.S. naval base on the South China Sea. It was the largest Navy base west of Subic Bay in the Philippines and could accept major-size Navy ships. As such the base was a prime target for Viet Cong combat swimmers. The Navy used a unique experimental system as part of their protection forces for the base: teams of specially trained, armed, killer dolphins.

Former Chief of the CIA's Office of Dolphin Research James Fitzgerald released some information about the guard-dolphins in an interview after the war. "With their built-in sonar," Fitzgerald stated, "the dolphins detected enemy demolition divers on sabotage missions. They impaled them [the divers] with long hypodermic needles connected to carbon dioxide cartridges. The frogmen just blew up."

Exact details of when and how many of the dolphins were used at Cam Ranh Bay are not available and the Navy considers the project still classified. The dolphins have been unofficially credited with killing up to sixty enemy swimmers, according to some unofficial estimates.

It is easy to see how the dolphins would be able to run up such a body count. The average adult bottlenosed dolphin, the type used at Cam Ranh Bay, weighs in the neighborhood of four hundred pounds and can move through the water at speeds of twenty-four knots (twenty-eight miles per hour). To help guide and direct this much muscle, the dolphin has a brain slightly larger than man's and has highly developed senses for use in his water environment.

The eyesight of a dolphin is so sharp that they can be trained to jump twenty feet up from a tank of water and take a small cigarette from a trainer's mouth. Their most successful weapon is an extremely acute hearing coupled with their natural sonar.

A dolphin can detect sounds ranging from 20 cycles per second to as high as 150,000. A human, on the average, can only hear sounds up to about 16,000 cycles per second. It is this range of hearing ability that the dolphin uses for his sonar sense.

Since water is so much denser than air, sound moves more efficiently through it. Dolphins unconsciously use this aspect of their environment in their highly precise echo-location system, far superior to our most advanced sonar systems.

When a dolphin uses its sonar on an object it can immediately tell the object's size, shape, texture, density, direction, and distance. Testing shows that a dolphin can even tell the difference between some metals, such as copper and aluminum, underwater. The difference in size between a ball two and a half inches in diameter and one two and a quarter inches in diameter is almost impossible for a person to judge when standing only ten feet away. A dolphin can tell the difference between the two balls from over twenty feet away.

It was the dolphin's natural abilities that first brought them to the attention of the Navy and the CIA. For the Navy's requirement for an offensive capability, the trainers studied the dolphin's natural instincts and methods of attack. One of the few natural enemies of the dolphin is the shark, and the dolphin has developed an efficient method for dealing with its enemy.

The only weak points in a shark's exterior are the gill openings just behind the head. A group of dolphins will attack a marauding shark by ramming their snouts into the shark's gills until they have either killed the marauder or driven it away. Working together, dolphins can even kill the huge Great White shark with their ramming method.

The Navy trainers decided to work with the dolphins' ramming attack but had to increase the attack's lethality. Unless an enemy swimmer could be killed quickly, the diver could detonate any charges he would have with him, either causing damage or killing the attacking dolphin. Using an explosive device, such as a commercial Bang-stick that fires a shotgun shell on impact, would probably injure the dolphin as well as the enemy. Any spear or knifelike object would have to be far too accurately placed to have an instant effect and the blood released would attract sharks to the area.

The problem was solved with a simple harness affair that a dolphin could easily carry on its head and snout. A short, thick, hollow needle would be attached to the end of the harness and connected to a standard cartridge of carbon dioxide. When the dolphin rammed the enemy diver, the needle only had to hit the main part of the body, the same target the dolphin would naturally go for. When the needle struck the target, it would puncture the gas cartridge, releasing the gas into the target's body. The sudden massive gas injection would kill an enemy diver almost instantly, before the individual knew he was under attack.

The system was effective—there was never a successful attack on any shipping in Cam Ranh Bay by enemy swimmers. The Navy still trains dolphins at its research facility near San Diego, but for other applications—including the rescue of lost divers. No official information is being released on the Navy's use of trained dolphins in combat. It is thought that the use of combat-trained dolphins is still part of possible future SEAL operations.

The Seawolves

During the earliest discussions about CTF 116 and its applications it became obvious to the Navy planners that the Fast Patrol Craft would need a partner for operations. The vast network of waterways in the Mekong Delta and Rung Sat were too complex for the patrol craft to be able to quickly move from one trouble spot to another. If a PBR came under fire in an ambush, other patrol craft might not be able to reach the stricken boat fast enough to save it. The fast partner to the patrol boat was planned to be the armed helicopter—the gunship.

The plan was for proper helicopters to be obtained by the Navy and for Navy pilots to be trained as part of a PBR-helo team. The helicopter would use its high visibility, speed, and maneuverability to gather intelligence on VC sampan and troop movements and to spot clandestine sampan infiltration. As the PBRs and ground forces would move to contact the VC the helicopter gunships would be nearby, ready to apply their firepower where it was most needed.

The Navy had no suitable helicopters available for gunship duty in the mid-1960s. Navy helicopters tended to be large and stable for use in antisubmarine warfare or search and rescue. The U.S. Army came to the Navy's aid and agreed to supply the Navy with twenty-two Utility Helicopter 1Bs (UH-1Bs) for the Game Warden operation. The 197th Army Aviation Company supplied the aircraft and the 120th Aviation Company the trainers.

Originally eight UH-1Bs were supplied by the Army and sent on to their Navy assignments. Four detachments of eight pilots and eight crew members each left Imperial Beach, California, in mid-1966 and reported to Tan Son Nhut Airfield near Saigon for training. The first detachment, Detachment 29, arrived for training in July 1966. The Navy pilots were taught how to fly and their crews how to maintain the UH-1B aircraft. The pilots also received advice from the Army as to what were then the best tactics to use against the Viet Cong.

The four detachments, each with two aircraft, were assigned to waterborne bases in the delta. The bases were specially built barges with facilities for both PBRs and helicopters, and had barracks and personnel-support capabilities as well. Operations began in September 1966 with the Navy pilots working as part of the HC-1 Detachment at Vung Tau. It was while working in these first operations that the Navy units came to be called the Seawolves by their Army trainers.

The UH-1B, "Huey," was a common sight in Vietnam. The single-turbine-engined aircraft had a length of fifty-three feet with a main rotor span of forty-four feet. The cargo capacity of the UH-1B was four thousand pounds with a maximum laden speed of ninety knots. The troop carrier, or "Slick," was the most common version of the UH-1B. The crew of a Slick was a pilot, co-pilot, and two doorgunners, one of whom was the crew chief. The two doorgunners each had an M60 machine gun. The Slick could easily transport eight combat-equipped soldiers. The UH-1B version used by the Seawolves was the armed gunship.

The gunship was the standard UH-1B fitted with the M16 armament system. The armament system consisted of two gun mounts, one attached to each side of the aircraft. Each mount held two M60C machine guns and one M158 rocket pod. The rocket pods each held seven 2.75″ FFAR rockets that could be fired in pairs, one from each side, or multiple rocket "ripples." Each M60C had three thousand rounds of ammunition available to it and fired at a cyclic rate of six hundred rounds per minute. The machine guns could track inboard eleven degrees and outboard seventy degrees; elevation was either plus-eleven or minus-sixty-three degrees. If the machine guns were pointed at any portion of the aircraft, limit switches automatically stopped their firing. Rocket pods were fixed to fire dead ahead and were aimed by the pilot through a manual reflex sight and by pointing the aircraft. Weapons were controlled from the control stick with the machine guns automatically cutting out when the rockets were fired.

The gunship's crew was a pilot, co-pilot, crew chief, and door-gunner. The pilot fired the rockets, the co-pilot the mounted machine guns, and the crew chief and door-gunner each had an M60 machine gun. The door guns were originally hung from slings in the open side doors, one on each side of the helicopter. Later gunships had the door guns on a pintle mount. The crew chief made sure the aircraft was working properly and the door-gunner made sure all of the weapons systems were working. Along with the mounted weapons, the aircraft had two M79 grenade launchers, one for each door-gunner, a spare M60, and an M16 and pistol as personal weapons for each crew member.

In June 1967, the HC-1 detachments were gathered into a new squadron commissioned at Vung Tau. The new unit was named the Helicopter Attack Squadron, Light Three (HAL-3). The air crews assigned to HAL-3 served twelve-month tours of duty in Vietnam in harsh conditions. In spite of this, many of the Navy personnel assigned to HAL-3 volunteered for several tours with the unit. Crews served in rotation, twenty-four hours on duty, twenty-four hours off duty. While a crew was "on call" the men often slept in their flight suits because an emergency "scramble" call could come in at any time. In the Seawolves, crews flew an average of six hundred missions, 3,500 hours of flight time, per year-long tour.

Seawolves flew in two normal patrol formations. A Light

Helo Fire Team (LHFT) was the most common formation and consisted of two aircraft. The Heavy Helo Fire Team (HHFT) was less commonly seen and consisted of three aircraft. By early 1968, HAL-3 had twenty-two UH-1Bs stationed in detachments of two aircraft each. Detachments were at Nha Be, Binh Thuy, Dong Tam, Rach Gia, and Vinh Long. Three detachments were stationed on mobile floating bases in the delta. The remaining helicopters were retained at Vung Tau for use at all of the detachments on a rotating maintenance schedule.

In 1969 HAL-3 headquarters moved from Vung Tau to Binh Thuy in the central delta. The squadron also received nine UH-1Cs for duty as Slicks, freeing up the gunships for other duties. Until then, the gunships of the Seawolves would spend part of their time infiltrating and exfiltrating SEAL teams on missions. The gunships of the Seawolves were never more than a few minutes away from any point in the delta. More than one SEAL team or PBR crew owe their lives to the quick reactions and abilities of the Seawolves.

By the time the Seawolves were disbanded in 1972, they had nine operational detachments in Vietnam. The Seawolves had been considered a vital part of the triad that was known as the SEAL package: the SEALs, the PBRs, and the Seawolves.

In July 1976, HAL-4, the Redwolves, were commissioned in Norfolk, Virginia, as part of NAVSPECWARGRU-TWO. HAL-4 started out equipped with seven HH-1K gunships armed with the M21 weapons system. In the M21 system, two 7.62-mm miniguns, each capable of firing three thousand rounds per minute, replaced the mounted M60Cs of the M16 system. On the West Coast, HAL-5, the Blue Hawks, were assigned to NAVSPECWARGRU-ONE and maintained the reputation founded by the Seawolves in the swamps and marshes of Vietnam.

The Brown Water Navy

The Brown Water Navy was another Navy special warfare unit developed as part of the American effort in Vietnam. The term "Brown Water" refers to the riverine environment that the special unit was expected to operate in. Riverine encompasses all the inland waterways, rivers, streams, lakes, canals, and wetlands that were found in abundance in the southern portion of Vietnam. To operate in this environment, the Navy developed new small gunboats that would allow the battle to be taken to the Viet Cong in their sanctuaries deep in the watery jungle maze. The most common of these small boats was the PBR.

The first PBRs—for Patrol Boat, River—were the Mark 1 versions that arrived in Vietnam in March 1965. The PBR design was based on a commercial thirty-one-foot fiberglass hull with modifications to allow it to operate and fight in the harsh Vietnamese terrain. Primary modifications to the hull were the fitting of a water-jet propulsion system and gun mounts for weapons placements.

The water-jets were originally Jacuzzi tub pumps fitted to a tunnel system for directing the water jet and driven by two 440-HP GM diesel engines. The "hydrojet" propulsion system could drive the PBR to speeds of twenty-five knots plus.

The boat was not shorted in the weapons department either. In the bow of the craft was a sunken gun tub that could rotate to cover either side of the boat. The tub held twin .50-caliber machine guns and a large supply of ammunition. On the PBR's rear deck was mounted another .50-caliber machine gun, this one on a pedestal mount, giving the weapon a 360-degree field of fire. Amidships, just behind the small cabin, was another pedestal mount, this one intended to hold a 40-mm machine grenade launcher or an M60 machine gun.

One hundred and sixty of the Mark I PBRs were built in 1966 and the boats were well received by their users in Vietnam. Fast and maneuverable, the PBRs could rapidly approach an area and saturate enemy positions with the firepower they had on board. The water jet propulsion system left the bottom of the PBR smooth, allowing it to be used in waterways too shallow and choked with debris for conventional propellers to operate in. Though the Mark I performed well and proved out the design of the PBRs, it had some major flaws as well. The water jets and pump became too easily clogged for constant use in a combat environment and the fiberglass hulls were easily damaged. To address these problems, the Mark II PBR was soon developed.

Making their appearance in Vietnam in December 1966, the PBR Mark IIs were first deployed in the Mekong Delta with the CTF 116 forces and Operation Game Warden. The improved water jet system in the Mark II gave the craft a top speed of twenty-nine knots. The aluminum hull of the Mark II also proved to be more durable than the earlier fiberglass hull.

The PBRs quickly became the workhorses of the Brown Water Navy. Operating as part of the Game Warden forces, the PBRs could move in and strike anywhere in the delta that their four-man crews wanted to take them. The Raytheon 1900/W radar units and two radio communications systems on board the PBRs gave them an effective, all-weather, twenty-four-hour operations capability. The mounted weapons on board the PBRs were augmented by the M79s, M60s, M16s, and other weapons brought aboard by the boats' crews.

Further out to sea, the Market Time forces needed a larger, more seaworthy craft to support their operations as part of the Brown Water Navy. To reinforce the inshore units, the Navy developed the PCF—Patrol Craft, Fast—or "Swift" boats. The Swift boats were all-metal hulls fitted with weapons stations and cabin spaces for interdiction patrols. The twin .50s in the gun tub on top of the main cabin were backed up by an unusual weapon on the Swift's rear deck. Set on a pedestal mount in the center of the Swift's rear deck was a modified 81-mm mortar with a .50-caliber machine gun mounted on top. Though muzzle loaded like a conventional Army mortar, the Navy Mark 2 Mod 0 mortar had a pistol grip and trigger to fire it and could be fired in a horizontal position like a cannon. The .50-caliber machine gun backed up the potent power of the mortar, giving the Swift boats a powerful one-two punch.

Driven by twin 960-HP GM diesels, the SWIFT PCFs could move out at a top speed of twenty-eight knots. The six-man crews of the PCFs could take their craft out into the open ocean or deep into the delta's rivers and canals. So close did the PCFs work to shore that a special fléchette round, the Mark 120 Mod 0, was made for the boat's mortar. When caught in a sudden ambush, the mortar, which was carried loaded with the Mk 120 round, would be pointed at the ambushing forces and fired as a giant shotgun. The 1,300 finned steel needles of the fléchette round would open into a wide pattern, cutting a path through anything in their way.

Both the PCFs and PBRs were often used by the SEALs for insertions and extractions as well as for fire support during the mission. The operations of the Brown Water Navy took place throughout South Vietnam but were concentrated in several operations in the Mekong Delta and Rung Sat Special Zone.

The first operation of the Brown Water Navy, and the operation that gave it its start, was with Operation Market Time. Task Force 71, later redesignated CTF 117, was also known as the Coastal Surveillance Force and was tasked with the conduction of Operation Market Time. Begun on March 24, 1965, and running until 1973, Market Time was the United States's effort to stop the infiltration and supplying of the Viet Cong from the north by sea. Run as a naval blockade, Market Time was intended to break the waterborne supply routes from North Vietnam into South Vietnam.

Market Time, for coastal waters, was organized around eight, later nine, patrol sectors that divided the 120 miles of South Vietnamese shoreline that ran from the 17th parallel to the Cambodian border. Operating up to 40 miles out to sea, Market Time forces patrolled a vast expanse of ocean for all types of clandestine traffic.

Though the size of the operation was immense, the Market Time forces did prove successful at stopping the VC supply flow fairly early in their existence. By 1968, the seaborne supply routes were all but closed to the VC. This resulted in the Ho Chi Minh Trail's becoming even more important to the Viet Cong war effort.

Game Warden was the name of the operation to eliminate the Viet Cong's ability to operate in the Mekong Delta and the Rung Sat. The Operation Game Warden forces, CTF 116, operated deep inside of the delta and Rung Sat regions, reaching the Viet Cong in areas that they thought unapproachable. The specific mission of Operation Game Warden was to enforce curfews for shipping on the water, interdict VC infiltration, prevent taxation (extortion) of the civilian water traffic by the Viet Cong, and to counter enemy movements and supply efforts on inland waters.

Officially begun on December 16, 1965, Game Warden was the first naval operation in Vietnam to be assigned SEALs as part of its operational forces. Divided into two groups, Game Warden had Task Force 116.1 assigned to duties in the Mekong Delta. The other major Game Warden force was Task Force 116.2, assigned to operate in the RSSZ. It was with Task Force 116.2 that SEAL Detachment Golf began operations in Vietnam in February 1966.

When the first PBRs arrived in Vietnam in March 1965, they were immediately assigned to CTF 116 and Operation

Game Warden. Eighty of the PBRs were assigned to TF 116.1 with TF 116.2 receiving the remaining 40 boats. The PBRs proved so successful in their operations that the original allotment of 120 boats was raised to 250 boats by the CNO in February 1967.

The original plan of operation for Game Warden was for groups of ten boats, river sections, to work out of forward operating bases throughout the Mekong Delta and the Rung Sat. For operations in the Rung Sat, the river sections were based at Nha Be and Cat Lo. For the Mekong Delta, the original river section bases were at My Tho, Vinh Long, Can Tho, Sa Dec, and Long Xuyen. In addition to the bases in towns, there were four floating PBR bases, one at the mouth of each of the delta's four major rivers.

Activities by the Viet Cong in the Rung Sat took a sharp drop as the SEALs and the Brown Water Navy conducted operations. Originally, the ratio of Game Warden forces and PBRs divided between the Mekong Delta and the Rung Sat was two to one. By later in the war, successes in the Rung Sat allowed the ratio to be changed even more, with six units in the delta for each one in the Rung Sat.

Game Warden also fielded some of the most spectacular forces in the Vietnam War. For a short time, November through December 1966, Game Warden ran a division of air-cushion vehicles in the Plain of Reeds, a swampy portion of the Mekong Delta to the west of Saigon. PACV (Patrol Air Cushion Vehicle) Division 107 ran three SK-5 vehicles in Vietnam. The PACVs were fan driven and rode on a cushion of air contained by their billowing rubber skirt.

The cushion effect allowed the boats to travel over almost any surface that could be found in the delta. Besides having a high speed capability the PACV could cross a wide variety of obstacles. A twelve-foot ditch, a four-foot wall, five-foot waves, and six-feet-deep vegetation could all be passed by the PACV. Their main driving propellers gave the PACVs a top speed of sixty knots along with a high degree of maneuverability. Armed with machine guns and grenade launchers, the PACVs terrified the Viet Cong, who could hear them coming from a good distance away.

Called dragon-boats and monsters by the Viet Cong, the PACVs were stationed at Moc Hoa. The PACV crews were so taken with the effect they had on the Cong that they picked up the VC words for "monsters" as their radio call sign and named their major operation "Operation Quai Vat."

During the sixteen days of Operation Quai Vat the PACVs accounted for twenty-three confirmed VC kills, eleven VC captured, seventy enemy structures destroyed, and seventy enemy sampans sunk. The high noise level of the operating PACVs eliminated some of their advantages of speed as the Viet Cong would learn to quickly hide when they heard the Monsters coming. The operating noise level, combined with the million-dollar cost of each PACV, kept them from being used as much as they could have been in Vietnam.

The last major group of the Brown Water Navy was the Mobile Riverine Force. Established in September 1966, the Mobile Riverine Force, Task Force 117, was a combined Navy/Army unit. TF 117 conducted operations in the delta with units of the Army's 9th Infantry Division along with South Vietnamese forces. The task force was intended to transport the U.S. Army and ARVN ground forces to enemy-held areas in the Rung Sat and Mekong Delta using the Navy's small boat forces. After delivering the ground forces to the target area, the Navy units of TF 117 would remain on station to give close-in fire support during the operation.

All of the major Brown Water Navy task forces were ended in the early 1970s. TF 117 was the first to go, with its assets being turned over to the South Vietnamese in August of 1969. During their operations, the forces that made up the Brown Water Navy proved their value with their wide range of successes against the Viet Cong. Because of the actions of the SEALs, the Seawolves, and the Brown Water Navy, the VC and the NVA were almost completely driven out of the Mekong Delta and the Rung Sat Special Zone.

The Mekong Delta was one of the last areas to fall to the North Vietnamese forces in 1975. This was a far cry from the early days of the war when the VC had been able to operate with complete freedom almost anywhere in the delta region.

The capabilities of the Brown Water Navy were not ignored by the Naval High Command after the Vietnam War. Today, the Special Boat Squadrons (SBRs) continue the proud traditions begun over twenty years ago in the swamps and channels of Vietnam.

Special Boat Squadron 1 is assigned to NAVSPECWAR-GRU-ONE at Coronado and is made up of Special Boat Units (SBUs) 11, 12, and 13. Special Boat Squadron 2 is part of the forces of NAVSPECWARGRU-TWO at Little Creek. SBR-2 is made up of SBUs 20, 22, and 24. The squadrons work closely with all of the U.S. military's special warfare forces but most especially with the Navy SEALs.

SEAL Equipment

To assist in their assignment to "develop capabilities," the SEALs needed a great deal of specialized equipment, much of which did not exist. SEAL Team 1 listed over two hundred different pieces of equipment either under development or being field tested in a report issued in 1967. This material was for use by the SEALs in addition to those items they were able to get from normal supply channels.

The SEALs, like the UDTs during World War II, held a high priority when it came to requesting new equipment. The new material being developed specifically for the SEALs covered a wide range of applications to account for many possible mission assignments. Equipment ran from the prosaic, such as a waterproof individual first aid kit, to the exotic, such as the WOX-5 underwater gun that fired rocket-powered projectiles. Also listed for development were such items as specialized explosives, diving equipment, miniature submarines (SDVs), and small boats.

It was the small arms and individual weapons used by the SEALs that made them the envy of many of the troops in Vietnam. Given the limited number of SEALs available in Vietnam, and the small size of their operational units, maximum firepower was the SEALs' major requirement.

To achieve this firepower goal, the SEALs used many weapons not readily available to any other service unit.

The simplest weapon that can greatly increase an individual's firepower is the repeating shotgun. Every round fired from a shotgun releases a swarm of nine or more projectiles, each capable of downing an enemy. At longer ranges, the swarm of shot from the shotgun's blast expands in a ever widening pattern that greatly increases the chances of hitting a target. At close range, the shot strikes almost as a single projectile, tearing massive holes in a target.

The SEALs were familiar with these characteristics of shotguns and used the weapons to great effect during their combat operations. A variety of shotguns were initially used in Vietnam, whatever could be obtained from supply channels. As the war progressed, the SEALs settled on using the Ithaca Model 37 as their primary fighting shotgun. Initially, the five-round magazine of the Model 37 was considered a bit small by SEAL standards. After 1968, the SEALs began receiving new Model 37s with eight-shot extended magazines.

Today, the SEALs use the Remington Model 870 in either five- or eight-shot versions as their primary fighting shotgun. Most of the 870s have fixed wooden stocks, but the SEALs do have some available that have folding metal stocks for use in situations where size is an important consideration. The Remingtons have what is called a disconnector as part of their mechanism. The function requires the trigger to be fully released before the weapon can be fired again. The Ithaca 37 had no disconnector and the SEALs quickly found that a magazine could be fired as fast as a man could operate the pump action simply by holding the trigger back. This method of firing makes the shotgun appear an almost fully automatic weapon and is devastating when used where a maximum amount of firepower is needed in the shortest time.

In 1967, the Remington Arms Company put into the SEALs hands what is probably the most powerful and awe-inspiring close-in weapon ever devised, the machine-shotgun.

The Remington 7188 was developed with firepower in mind, and the weapon certainly delivered. The 7188, and 7188 Mark I, were both modifications of the sporting-use Remington Model 1100. Modifications to the 1100 to create the 7188 included an extended eight-shot magazine, a redesigned trigger assembly giving the weapon a select-fire capability, and, in the Mark I, a ventilated barrel shield and bayonet mount.

Fired on semiautomatic, the 7188 acted as a standard autoloading shotgun, one shot for each pull of the trigger. Firing on full automatic, the 7188 could spew out its ammunition at a cyclic rate of 420 rounds per minute. Using OO buckshot rounds loaded with nine pellets each, the 7188 could empty its magazine in just over a second. This rate of fire would put seventy-two .33-caliber "bullets" out of the weapon in under a second and a half. That's greater firepower than two men firing submachine guns on full automatic.

Though well liked by the SEALs who used them, and coveted by other military personnel who saw them, the 7188s did not prove a successful design. Difficulties in control when firing on full automatic caused the 7188 to be withdrawn from service after the Vietnam War. However, the concept of a full automatic shotgun was proved viable by the 7188, and the SEALs are presently studying several possible modern designs.

Shotguns are only as effective as their ammunition, and the SEALs had a variety of types to choose from. The most common combat load used was a twelve-gauge shell loaded with nine OO buckshot, .33-caliber lead balls. When available, the favorite shotgun ammunition used by the SEALs in Vietnam was the M19 OO buckshot shell with an all-brass casing. Developed during World War I, the M19's all-brass shell was almost completely waterproof, a characteristic highly prized by the often waterlogged SEALs.

Later in the Vietnam War, the XM162 and XM257 plastic-cased shotshell rounds were available and were used in place of the M19 round by the SEALs. The XM162 round carries twenty-seven #4 buckshot. The denser shot patterns of the #4 buckshot are considered superior to the OO buck. But penetration of the. 25-caliber #4 pellets is much less than the larger OO buckshot pellets, making OO buckshot more lethal to the target. Today, the SEALs' primary combat shotgun load is OO buckshot.

Other specialized shotgun loads were available to the SEALs for their weapons. Fléchette loads launching dozens of finned steel "needles" for combat and light birdshot rounds for training were all part of the SEALs' inventory. What was probably the most exotic round of ammunition ever made for the shotgun was developed to fulfill a specific SEAL request. The SEAL specification was for a low-signature round that could be fired from an unmodified, pump-action shotgun. In 1968, *Aircraft Armaments Inc*. (AAI) developed what they called the Silent Shotgun Shell to satisfy the SEAL requirements. The Silent Shotgun Shell used an expanding metal capsule to drive a plastic pusher piston. The piston drove the round's twelve #4 buckshot to a muzzle velocity of 450 feet per second. The expanding metal capsule prevented any gases from escaping the fired round and consequently the only sound heard when firing the Silent Shotgun Shell was the click of the shotgun's firing pin.

Next to shotguns, the SEALs liked using light machine guns to raise their combat firepower. The standard U.S. machine guns, the Browning M1919A4 and M60, were extensively used by the SEALs in Vietnam. Though preferred for their power and reliability, the Browning and M60 were both considered heavy for the hit-and-run tactics the SEALs used. To lighten the M60 machine gun, the SEALs often modified the weapons in the field by cutting off the portion of the barrel just in front of the gas system. This change removed several pounds of weight, including the M60's folding bipod, and made the weapon shorter and handier for close combat. On photographs of SEALs armed with the M60, an empty C ration can can often be seen attached to the left side of the weapon's feed tray. The can would help straighten out and feed the long belts of ammunition used on board the SEALs' combat boats. Today the SEALs have the M60E3 machine gun, which uses the same ammunition as the original M60 but weighs only 18.5 pounds as compared to the M60's 23.2 pounds.

To eliminate the weight problem of the M60 and still give their squads the sustained fire of a belt-fed machine gun, the SEALs turned to a whole new weapons system, the Stoner 63. Developed by Eugene Stoner, the original designer of the M16, the Stoner 63, and later 63A, was a unique system in the field of small arms. With one basic receiver and a kit of barrels and parts, any one of a series of weapons, from a short carbine to a light machine gun, could easily be assembled by the operator without tools.

It was the light machine gun version of the Stoner system that most appealed to the SEALs. The machine gun version of the Stoner uses the same caliber of ammunition as the M16 rifle, 5.56x45-mm. The rounds are held in a flexible metal link belt much like a miniaturized M60 belt. The ammunition belt was held in a number of containers of different capacities, all of which could be attached to the underside of the weapon. The SEALs' favorite container was a metal drum that held a 150-round belt securely to the weapon.

The Stoner 63 light machine gun held particular appeal for the SEALs because of its relatively light weight and firepower. Loaded with a 150-round drum, the Stoner 63 LMG only weighed about eighteen pounds. After field experience with the weapon, the SEALs made some suggestions for changes in the design to the manufacturer. The manufacturer, Cadillac Gage of Warren, Michigan, used some of the SEALs' suggestions in its new model, the Stoner 63A.

Included in the new 63A system was a special short-barreled version known as the Commando. The Commando Stoner was developed especially for the SEALs, who adopted it as the Mark 23 Mod 0. The Mark 23 had a much shorter barrel than the standard Stoner machine gun and was very quick to handle. Weighing 14.2 pounds loaded with 150 rounds, the Mark 23 was enthusiastically welcomed by the SEALs in Vietnam.

One of the major drawbacks of the Stoner system was that the weapons needed to be kept extremely clean, a requirement that was complicated by the fact that the Stoner had many small parts that could easily be lost when the weapon was stripped for maintenance under field conditions during jungle warfare. These disadvantages helped keep the Stoner from being generally issued by the U.S. military.

Because of their training, the SEALs religiously see to the routine maintenance of all their equipment. When using rebreathing equipment during the diving phase of BUD/S, all SEALs learn that the slightest slackening in proper maintenance of their equipment can be fatal to the operator. The lessons learned at BUD/S are extended to all of the SEALs' materials, especially their weapons. This philosophy of maintenance helped prevent the SEALs from having a great deal of trouble with their Stoners in Vietnam.

On board their insertion boats and riverine craft, the SEALs used a number of heavy machine guns. The .50-caliber Browning M2HB was popular but restricted by its need for a large enough firing platform to absorb the powerful weapon's recoil. The 7.62-mm minigun was well received by the SEALs and was used in situations where the minigun's high volume of fire was an advantage. The minigun, a modern version of the gatling gun, could fire its ammunition at the amazing rate of six thousand rounds per minute. That's one hundred rounds on target in one second! This high rate of fire consumed large quantities of ammunition and the minigun was, and still is, used in situations where the SEALs need an overwhelming coverfire.

The last piece of "firepower augmentation" used by the SEAL squads is the 40-mm grenade launcher. Developed as a possible replacement for the 60-mm mortar, the 40-mm grenade launcher fires a quarter-pound, high-explosive shell to a distance of four hundred meters with good accuracy. The first 40-mm grenade launcher to see service was the M79. This was the weapon the SEALs took with them to Vietnam.

The M79 is a single-shot weapon that resembles an oversized shotgun. Though highly respected by the SEALs, the

M79 had several drawbacks. The major problem was that the M79 was a single-shot and slow to reload. When the grenade had been fired, the operator had nothing, other than a pistol, he could use to defend himself. If the target was not worth a grenade—they were heavy and bulky—the M79 operator would not engage the target, cutting down on the squad's volume of fire. These problems were addressed by the weapon designers in the States and the SEALs began receiving new grenade launchers by 1967.

The first new launcher was a lightweight 40-mm system that could be mounted underneath the barrel of the standard M16 rifle. Enthusiastically received by the SEALs, the new weapon, the XM148, was quickly put to use by the men in the field.

The XM148 was easily attached to any M16 rifle and allowed the operator to fire either weapon by using one of two separate triggers. This gave the operator twenty or more rounds of 5.56 rifle ammunition to back up the 40-mm grenade in the launcher. Though popular, the XM148 suffered from several drawbacks and was replaced by the M203 in the spring of 1969.

The M203 is also a single-shot 40-mm launcher that mounts underneath the barrel of the M16. Simple to operate and reliable, the M203 has remained in the U.S. military inventory, and with the SEALs, to this day.

The SEALs still wanted a repeat-fire 40-mm launcher that could be used by one man to lay down a heavy pattern of fire. The weapon would have to be portable and as easy to handle as the average rifle. Several experimental repeaters and multibarrel models were made but only one had much success. The experimental 40-mm weapon most liked by the SEALs was a four-round, pump-action repeater that resembled a cartoonist's drawing of a shotgun. The weapon acted like anything but a cartoon since it could put out four rounds of high-explosive grenades as fast as a man could operate the action. Received by the SEALs in 1968, the pump-action launcher saw immediate field use. Reportedly, only about thirty of the special launchers were ever made and details on the weapon are still classified.

By the late 1960s the SEALs had their primary weapons selected and squad firepower somewhat standardized. The common weapons load for a three-man SEAL ambush team would be as follows: one eight-shot Ithaca 37 pump shotgun, one M16 with either an XM148 or M203 grenade launcher attached, a Stoner Mark 23 with either a long or short barrel and a 150-round belt. An assortment of hand grenades, ammunition, knives, a radio, and other survival/combat items would round out the squad's equipment.

The SEALs had special vests designed to carry all their materials. Built around an inflatable life preserver, the SEAL vests came in three models. One model had pockets to carry rifle magazines, the rifleman's model; another had multiple small pockets to carry 40-mm grenades, the grenadier's model; and the last had rifle magazine pockets on the front and a large waterproof pocket on the rear intended to carry the squad's radio, the radioman's model.

The SEALs had a great deal of leeway when it came to field uniforms. The most commonly worn combat uniforms were either locally produced "tiger-stripe" fatigues or Marine Corps-issue camouflage fatigues. Almost never wearing steel helmets, the SEALs favored wearing instead floppy-style "jungle" caps. A camouflage pattern beret was also occasionally worn by SEALs in the field and became something of an unofficial symbol of theirs. It was not uncommon for SEALs who were leaving for a mission to be wearing shorts, swim trunks, T-shirts, tennis shoes, or even to go barefoot!

Many other weapons and equipment were used by the SEALs in Vietnam besides those described above. G-3 rifles, M14s, AK-47s, M3A1 submachine guns, M1911A1 .45 pistols, and Mark 20 and Mark 19 full automatic grenade launchers were all part of the SEALs' combat arsenal. Two weapons in particular stand out because they were only seen in the hands of the SEALs. These weapons are the Mark 24 Mod 0 submachine gun and the Mark 22 Mod O pistol.

The SEALs were the only units in Vietnam to readily admit to using silenced weapons in combat. Records indicating earlier weapons used are sketchy but the weapons

were probably of World War II vintage. The first specially
designed silenced weapon made for the SEALs was the Mark
22 Mod O pistol. The Mark 22 is a modified Smith &
Wesson Model 39 9-mm semiautomatic pistol. The Model
39 was fitted with an extended, five-inch barrel, a slide lock
that could keep the weapon's slide closed when it was fired,
and raised sights. A Navy-designed Mark 3 Mod O silencer
was threaded onto the extended barrel. A special, subsonic,
heavy-bulleted 9-mm cartridge was developed for the Mark
22. The ammunition was adopted as the Mark 144 cartridge.

The Mark 3 silencer is a hollow can that holds a disposable
insert that does the actual sound suppression. The insert is
a cylinder containing four quarter-inch-thick, soft plastic
disks with a hole in the center of each. The disks act as
baffles and slow down the escape of the firing gases. Since
the escaping gases make most of the noise of firing, slowing
down their escape will suppress some of the sound. The
slide lock prevents the action from opening when the weapon
is fired, eliminating much of the mechanical noise of firing.
Since the Mark 144 ammunition has a bullet slower than
the speed of sound when fired, there is no sonic "crack"
from the bullet passing downrange. The insert will last for
about twenty-four rounds of Mark 144 ammunition before
it needs replacement. If standard ammunition is used, the
insert will last for only about six rounds.

The Mark 22, which became available in 1968, was nick-
named the "Hush Puppy" after its intended application, the
silent elimination of enemy guard dogs. Only about two
hundred Hush Puppies were made. Well received by the
SEALs who used them, the Hush Puppy is still found in
limited use by SEALs today.

The silencer insert, twenty-four Mark 144 cartridges, six
muzzle plugs, four chamber plugs, and several other items
were packed for use in the Mark 26 Mod O Pistol Accessory
Kit. The muzzle and chamber plugs would prevent water
from entering the barrel of a Mark 22 down to a depth of
two hundred feet. When surfaced, a SEAL would just have
to draw the Hush Puppy from its waterproof holster, draw
back and release the slide, which would eject the chamber

plug, and load a live round, and he would be able to safely fire the weapon through the muzzle plug.

By late 1969, Smith & Wesson had produced a stainless steel version of the Hush Puppy. The new weapon held fourteen rounds of ammunition compared to the Model 39's eight-round capacity. By 1971, Smith & Wesson had released this new design, minus the silencer and its attachments, to the public as their popular Model 59 pistol.

Along with their taste for 9-mm handguns, the SEALs also prefer 9-mm submachine guns. Though they had the Swedish-made Carl Gustav weapon available, the SEALs found the design heavy for its type, difficult to obtain in the quantities desired, and thus wanted a replacement. In June 1968, Smith & Wesson began producing the Model 76 submachine gun and made it available to the SEALs. Finding the Model 76 to their liking, the SEALs adopted the weapon as the Mark 24 Mod O submachine gun.

The Mark 24 was a lightweight, simple weapon that could be made compact by folding its metal stock. With the stock extended, the Mark 24 was capable of good accuracy when fired in the semi or full automatic mode. The distinctive perforated barrel jacket was removable, and many weapons had theirs taken off by the operator.

Several of the thirty-six-round magazines of the Mark 24 could be taped together for rapid reloading but this was not often done since it exposed the ammunition to dirt and made the weapons unwieldy. The simple action of the Mark 24 allowed the weapon to be easily carried underwater and quickly put into action on the surface.

The SEALs liked the light and handy Mark 24, presently replaced by more modern designs. The weapon became something of a recognition point for the SEALs since they were the only military unit to adopt the weapon.

Today the SEALs use many types of small arms, and most of the Vietnam era weapons are no longer used. The Heckler & Koch MP5A5, MP5SD5, and MP5KA4 have replaced the Mark 24 and most of the Ingram M10s the SEALs had available. The Stoner system no longer has parts available for its maintenance and only a few of the weapons are used for training.

The M16 and its variations are still widely used by the SEALs as their basic weapon, as is the M203 grenade launcher. The SEALs still use the M14 rifle for some applications and have had some of their weapons fitted with new stainless steel barrels.

Though there are still Hush Puppies available, new pistols are being used by the SEALs, some with silencers. The Heckler & Koch P9S and Beretta M92-F (M9) have both been used by the SEALs with the weapons fitted with slide locks and Qualatech silencers. New exotic sniper rifles in powerful calibers are also being used by SEAL snipers for precise firing at very long ranges.

The SEALs are constantly developing and evaluating new weapons and equipment. When the SEALs find something that works well for them, they stick with it until something else can prove itself superior. This could result in the SEALs' being the last users of certain items of equipment.

The SEALs are still issuing the old U.S. Mark II "pineapple" hand grenade developed prior to World War II. The Hagensen Pack, designed originally for use during the Normandy invasion, has had its explosive contents updated but is still basically the same item of ordnance issued in 1944.

Though some of the most modern equipment in the U.S. military is available to them, the SEALs still find themselves issued older materials still found in the Navy's log (inventory). This was especially true during the SEALs' early years in Vietnam. Captain Michael Jukowski, Director of the Naval Special Warfare Division at the Pentagon, stated in an interview with the author that sometimes the SEALs were issued strange items during his tours in Vietnam. Captain Jukowski said that sometimes you would just say, "How long has that been here? You figure it must have gotten here in the last shipment from World War II!"

The UDTs' Final Mission

The UDTs also served in Vietnam with some distinction. Sometimes facing combat situations and other times performing salvage and demolition work as well as beach surveys, men, and especially officers, would transfer from the UDTs to the SEALs and back again as the need arose. With the SEALs operating after the Vietnam War, the need for separate UDTs gradually became less and less

On May 1, 1983, the long history of the UDTs came to an end as the last teams were decommissioned. UDTs 11 and 20 became, respectively, SEAL Teams 5 and 4. UDTs 12 and 22 became SDV Teams 1 and 2, respectively.

The UDTs did more than just straight military duties in the 1960s and early 1970s. All of America's returning spacecraft were first met by UDT swimmers after splashdown. After spending weeks of training on new procedures, men from UDTs 11 and 12 were the recovery team for LCDR Schirra's Mercury flight on October 4, 1962.

All of the returning space capsules were met by men from either UDT 11 or 12 or combined teams from both. When the Apollo series began, UDT swimmers returned to the Manned Spacecraft Center in Houston for more specialized training. After weeks of studying decontamination and emergency procedures, the UDT group was ready.

When an Apollo capsule splashed down, UDT swimmers would jump from helicopters hovering nearby. Swimming to the floating capsule, the UDT men would be the first to greet the astronauts on their return to Earth. The swimmers would then quickly attach flotation collars to the space capsule, insuring it could not accidentally sink.

After putting out a sea anchor and inflating two rafts, the UDT men would help the astronauts out of their capsule. The UDTs would then remain with the capsule until it was recovered.

The first moon returns were handled differently. The UDT swimmers would wear decontamination suits when they approached the capsule. The threat of possible biological contamination forced the astronauts to remain inside the capsule until it could be opened on board the support ship. The UDT swimmers would attach to the capsule a cable from a waiting helicopter, which allowed the capsule to be hoisted from the sea.

From testing for the effects of weightlessness during the 1950s to recovering the first lunar explorers, the UDTs had a special role to play in America's space effort.

SEAL Team 6

The least-known SEAL unit is SEAL Team 6, organized as
a counterterrorism and rescue force for the Navy. Very little
specific information is available on Team 6, with the Navy
refusing to confirm or deny its existence officially. Established in November 1980, SEAL Team 6 drew its original
complement of men and officers primarily from SEAL Team
2. Assigned to Naval Special Warfare Group Two for administrative purposes, Team 6 receives its directives from
another source and is stationed at a different location than
at Group Two's headquarters at Little Creek.

Under the direct supervision of the headquarters of the
Unified Atlantic Command in Norfolk, Team 6 is tasked by
the Secretary of Defense and the White House. Physically
located at the Fleet Combat Training Center, Atlantic
(FCTCLANT), in Dam Neck, Virginia, Team 6 is gradually
developing its own training facilities separate from those of
the regular SEAL teams. It is construction projects for these
training facilities that first gave an "official" confirmation
that Team 6 existed.

The first project was the building of a swimming pool at
the FCTCLANT location, which had no swimming facilities
except for the nearby ocean. The request was for an indoor

pool where the team could test new equipment and techniques, ostensibly in an environment controlled from the weather but also to keep the equipment and techniques as closely guarded a secret as possible. The project, number P-327, was in the 1982 fiscal year's requests and was completed at a cost of $4 million.

The next official mention of Seal Team 6 was in an unclassified copy of the Naval Special Warfare Master Plan (NSWMP-U) for 1986. In this highly edited version of the NSWMP-U there is a listing for Project P-329, an indoor rifle/pistol range with an attached helicopter landing pad to be built at the FCTCLANT location. The construction was to be completed by September 1987 at a projected cost of $3.15 million. The type of defensive shooting and Close Quarters Battle (CQB) practiced by Team 6 is unique to counterterrorist rescue work and requires some sophisticated installations for proper development. The buildup of facilities dedicated to Team 6's operations indicates that they are expected to be at the FCTCLANT location for some time to come.

Though SEALs in general, and Team 6 in particular, do not come under the direct command of the Joint Special Operations Command (JSOC), they do work closely with the command and perform joint exercises with its units on a fairly regular basis. A Naval Special Warfare Command (NSWC) was set up on July 11, 1987, as the naval command link between the SEALs and the USCINCSOC (U.S. Commander in Chief, Special Operations, Command), Macdill AFB, Florida. The NSWC "oversees" SEAL training and readiness and incorporates the Navy's special warfare assets into the Joint structure.

Team 6 conducts a great deal of specialized training specific to the assignment and unlike much of the regular training received by the other SEAL units. Team 6 members have been to many of the country's finest civilian and police advanced marksmanship and combat craft schools. Individuals from Team 6 have also been notable competitors at many shooting events such as the annual Second Chance Shoot in Michigan, among others. It is at these courses and events that some speculative information has developed about Team 6. The team is broken down into the normal platoon/squad configuration of the rest of the SEAL teams with probably two to four squads per platoon. The squads are identified by a color, such as Red Squad, Green Squad, and so forth, and are approximately 8 men each further broken down into two 4-man teams. The actual manning level of Team 6 is highly classified, but there are probably at least 100 men in the unit with some estimates going as high as 175 to 200 men.

Mutual training is often conducted with the Army's Special Forces Operational Detachment Delta, commonly called Delta Force. The SEALs of Team 6 have worked with Delta Force on at least two known occasions: the invasion of Grenada and the *Achille Lauro* hijacking incident. Details on the actions of Team 6 are given elsewhere in this book in the sections about these two operations. Other field operations by Team 6 have not been divulged by the Department of the Navy and may never be known to the public.

It is known that the men of Team 6, called The Mob by insiders, are very competent at their assignment and are themselves a strong deterrent to marine-oriented terrorist actions directed against the United States and its allies.

Grenada

Grenada is a small island nation of only 133 square miles and a population of about 110,000 people. With the country's major industries being tourism and spice exports, most Americans had never known of the island's existence until the events of late October 1983 put the small nation in the news.

On October 25, 1983, President Ronald Reagan told the startled U.S. people that American troops, backed by a small contingent of forces from several Caribbean nations, had invaded the small island of Grenada in the southeastern Caribbean in an operation named Urgent Fury. The actions of the SEALs and other special units who played a role during Operation Urgent Fury are still, for the most part, classified—with little information being released to the public. The following is the most complete picture of SEAL operations on Grenada available from unclassified sources.

Grenada was under British rule until given her independence in 1974. Sir Eric Gairy, a former trade union organizer, was installed as the island's first prime minister. Gairy's regime was noted for corruption and the use of strong-arm tactics to suppress any political opposition. In March 1979, Maurice Bishop, a political rival of Gairy, overthrew the corrupt government in a bloodless coup. Taking his place as the head of the Provisional Revolutionary Government (PRG) of Grenada, Bishop soon turned to Cuba and the Communist sphere of influence to solve his country's financial problems. Bishop named his new political party the New Jewel movement, "Jewel" being an acronym standing for Joint Endeavor for Welfare, Education, and Liberation. Inviting further assistance from Cuba and the Soviet Union over the next four years brought Grenada into conflict with the United States' interests in the area. An ambitious airport construction project was begun by the PRG in 1979 for the stated purpose of increasing Grenada's tourist trade. Built by mostly Cuban workers, the airport would feature a nine thousand-foot-long runway, long enough for the largest jets. Later, captured documents indicated Cuba's intention to use the airport as a staging area for shipping troops to Africa as well as a refueling stop for Soviet aircraft going to Nicaragua.

The aid received from the Communists benefited Grenada's military the most, with the People's Revolutionary Armed Forces (PRAF) outnumbering the military forces of all the other eastern Caribbean nations combined by 1983. Disappointed with the economic assistance he was receiving, Bishop wanted to turn to the Western governments for greater assistance for his people. Deputy Prime Minister Bernard Coard led a faction of the New Jewel movement that demanded a faster conversion of Grenada into a true Marxist state. On October 13, Coard, having received the backing of the military, ordered Bishop out of office and had him placed under house arrest by the authority of Coard's People's Revolutionary Army (PRA).

The actions on Grenada seriously concerned the U.S. government, which held an interagency group meeting at the State Department on October 13, 1983, to discuss the situation. Of primary concern was the need for action to protect the lives of an estimated one thousand American citizens living and working on Grenada. About three hundred Americans lived on Grenada as full-time residents, with the rest being either students or faculty at the Saint George's University Medical School. On October 14, the

National Security Council ordered the Joint Chiefs of Staff (JCS) to plan a "nonpermissive evacuation," State Departmentese for a military rescue, of all U.S. citizens on Grenada. Since Grenada is an island, the JCS ordered Admiral Wesley McDonald, Commander in Chief Atlantic (CINCLANT) to draft the necessary proposal.

On October 18 two naval task forces left the United States for their assignments in the Mediterranean. The first was Task Force 124, assembled around the helicopter carrier *Guam*, and Amphibious Squadron 4 (PHIBRON FOUR), consisting of four landing ships. PHIBRON FOUR carried 1,700 combat-ready Marines of the 22nd Marine Amphibious Unit (MAU). Task Force 124 was going to Beirut, Lebanon, to relieve the 24th MAU. (The 24th MAU was the unit that would receive the terrorist truck bombing attack at the Beirut International Airport on October 23.) Also leaving for its assignment in the Mediterranean was the *Independence* Carrier Battle Group made up of the aircraft carrier *Independence* and her escort group of cruisers and destroyers.

The next day, October 19, proved to be the most eventful day leading up to the invasion. Grenadan Foreign Minister Unison Whiteman had just returned from New York, where he had cancelled an appointment to speak to the United Nations. Arriving in Grenada, Whiteman began gathering Bishop's supporters and speaking to people in the street, hoping to gain Bishop's release. As the crowd grew in size under Whiteman's oration, the listeners decided to go to where Bishop was being held and obtain his release themselves. Faced with a large angry crowd, Bishop's guards quickly gave way and Bishop was released to welcome his crowd of supporters, now numbering in the thousands. Returning to Saint George's, Bishop moved on toward Fort Rupert, where the few guards on hand were forced to permit the crowd to enter. As Bishop was greeting several of his ministers who had been held in the fort, three armored personnel carriers containing soldiers from the PRA arrived outside the fort. The officer leading the PRA troops ordered them to open fire into the crowd, hitting over one hundred Grenadians and killing more than fifty. As the survivors fled, Bishop, four of his ministers, and three of his most prominent supporters were taken into the interior court at Fort Rupert and shot.

Ambassador Bish, the American consul stationed at Bridgetown in Barbados, the nearest U.S. diplomatic post to Grenada, contacted the State Department immediately upon learning of the situation in Grenada. Bish stated that there "appeared to be imminent danger to U.S. citizens resident on Grenada." He went on further to describe the "deteriorating situation" in Grenada, which included rioting, armored personnel carriers patrolling the streets, and civilian casualties. Further recommendations from Bish were for an "emergency evacuation" of all U.S. citizens from Grenada.

On the evening of October 19, the JCS sent a warning order to CINCLANT to prepare for a "noncombatant" evacuation of Grenada. A request was also sent to the Joint Special Operations Command (JSOC) to prepare a contingency plan for the evacuation of Grenada by Special Forces. A meeting of the JCS was scheduled for the next morning with both groups to show their proposals. During the meeting on October 20, the assessment of the military strength of Grenada was sketchy, with little immediate hard intelligence. Grenada was thought to have about 250 Cubans and 300 Grenadians under arms. This was to prove to be the lightest assessment of the Grenadian military. The JSOC, seeing the small size of the opposing forces, had as their plan an operation completely performed by Special Forces. CINCLANT's plan, based on a larger assessment of the island's strength, would use only Marines in an amphibious landing. According to reports, the meeting became quite heated, with each side pushing hard for its plan. The final decision was for a compromise operation. In the initial assault the Rangers and Special Forces would take the southern half of the island and the Marines would take the northern half.

The JCS decided that the operation, for security as well as other reasons, would be commanded by the Navy. U.S. Atlantic Command in Norfolk, Virginia, was ordered to set up a command/planning group immediately with CIN-

CLANT having overall command of the operation. Once the decision to go ahead with the operation and produce detailed plans had been made, the JCS imposed complete operational security (OPSEC) on all aspects of the plan. The obsession with security, though justifiable, has been blamed for what was later described as inadequate planning. The only exceptions to the OPSEC directive were the *Independence* Carrier Battle Group and Task Force 124. Both units received orders at 0300 hours on October 21 to steam to map coordinates near the coast of Grenada and await further orders. If no further orders were received by October 24, the units were to continue on to their original assignments. No further clarification was given and the naval groups had no specific ideas of what awaited them.

On October 22, two State Department officials from the U.S. post at Bridgetown arrived in Grenada. The report they sent back listing a number of arrests as well as a twenty-four-hour shoot-on-sight curfew, reinforced the statements made earlier by Ambassador Bish. The next day the Organization of Eastern Caribbean States met and came to a joint resolution to ask the United States for aid in restoring order in Grenada. Finally, on October 24, Tom Adams, the Prime Minister of Barbados, reported receiving a letter from Governor General Sir Paul Scoon. Sir Paul had been appointed as the representative of Queen Elizabeth on Grenada by the queen herself in 1978. Queen Elizabeth is still considered as the official head of state by Grenadians. As the queen's representative on the island, Scoon had been mostly tolerated as a figurehead by Bishop's government. When Coard came to power Scoon was kept a virtual prisoner at Government House, the governor's mansion in Saint George's. The letter sent by Scoon was an official request for outside intervention to restore order and for personal protection for himself and his staff. The United States did not recognize the authority of Coard's Revolutionary Military Council as the government of Grenada and considered Scoon's letter as an official request for aid.

CINCLANT had by this time completed plans for the invasion of Grenada and had directed the JSOC to develop a special operation plan using both Delta Force and the

SEALs to complete specific assignments. The plan developed by CINCLANT specifically forbade any use of advance reconnaissance forces by the invading troops. This ban resulted in the 22nd MAUs not being able to utilize the SEAL detachment they had on board as part of their normal complement. Operations as planned would use elements from SEAL Teams 4 and 6, Delta Force, the 1st and 2nd Ranger Battalions, 82nd Airborne, the 1st Special Operations Wing of the Air Force, and the 22nd MAU. The operations in Grenada were considered especially significant because all four of the services would be operating together for the first time since the Vietnam War.

Vice Admiral Joseph Metcalf was put in charge of what was now called Operation Urgent Fury. Taking his place on the *Guam*, the flagship of what was now called Joint Task Force 120, Metcalf began operations on what was to prove a highly complex plan. There were five principal assignments of the Special Forces and SEAL elements.

1. A Delta detachment would parachute in before dawn and secure the airfield at Port Salines. Delta would secure the perimeter and clear the runway to allow the aircraft carrying the Rangers to land.
2. Another Delta detachment would attack the Richmond Hill prison and free the civil servants and other citizens being held there.
3. A detachment from SEAL Team 6 would attack the residence of Sir Paul Scoon, rescuing the Governor General and his staff and evacuating them from the island.
4. A platoon from SEAL Team 4 would capture the Radio Free Grenada station and keep it off the air until it could be used by the U.S. forces. RFG was the only major radio station on Grenada.
5. Another platoon from SEAL Team 4 would recon the beaches at Grenville and the area around Pearls Airport for the landings by the 22nd MAU.

At the last minute a change of plans was made and the SEALs assigned to the landing areas for the 22nd MAU would instead be used to insert an Air Force Combat Controller Team (CCT) at the Port Salines area before D day. The CCT would be used to help guide in the aircraft carrying the Ranger units.

Before dawn on Sunday, October 23, a team of twelve SEALs and four Air Force specialists parachuted into the Caribbean near Grenada to rendezvous with a Navy destroyer. Two USAF C-130s were used to fly the combined team to an area forty miles north-northwest of Port Salines, beyond the range of radar based on Grenada. At the rendezvous point the team would parachute into the water with their equipment as well as two inflated rubber boats. The team used the LAPES (Low Altitude Parachute Extraction System) method of exiting the aircraft into the drop zone, which had marginal weather conditions and a moderate sea. Exactly what happened next is unclear but four of the SEALs disappeared along with one of the rubber boats. Whether the SEALs had trouble with the jump or became entangled with the boat has not been released and indeed may not even be known to those in charge, but these four men became the first casualties of Operation Urgent Fury. The names of the men were released at a memorial ceremony at Coronado in 1984. They are: Machinist's Mate 1st Class Kenneth John Butcher, Quartermaster 1st Class Kevin Erin Lundberg, Hull Technician 1st Class Stephen Leroy Morris, and Senior Chief Engineman Robert Rudolph Schamberger.

The remainder of the team, along with the four-man Air Force CCT moved on toward Grenada and the beaches off Pearls Airport. The mission of the SEALs was to guide the CCT force to the shore, where they would scout the airfield and emplace radio beacons. The beacons would guide the first MC-130 Combat Talon special operations aircraft carrying the Ranger assault troops to the area where the CCT could direct the craft by radio to the airport. As the heavily laden boat moved to the island, the SEALs noticed a Grenadian patrol boat approaching that would pass close to the team. Quickly cutting power to the boat's outboard motor allowed the SEAL craft to slip past the nearby patrol boat without detection. The sudden drop in power caused the wake of the SEALs' craft, combined with the waves from the patrol boat, to swamp the small rubber raft, drowning the outboard motor. Strong offshore currents overcame the SEALs' efforts to reach the island and the rubber boat was carried out to sea. The team was later rescued by the U.S.S. *Caron* (DD 270) after they had been drifting out to sea for hours.

A second team of SEALs was quickly assembled from the platoon assigned to strike at the RFG station and was flown out to rendezvous with the U.S.S. *Caron*. After an uneventful parachute jump into the sea, the new team, along with another boat, combined with the remnants of the first team and attempted a new infiltration of the island. The new mixed team successfully navigated to the island during the darkness of Monday night, October 24.

Something happened during the final run to the beach that resulted in both boats' being swamped and the equipment of the CCT's being lost. The team was later recovered by friendly forces but had been unable to complete its mission. This left too few Team 4 SEALs to complete all of their special assignments and it was decided to allow the 22nd MAU to use its own SEAL detachment.

The commanders of the 22nd MAU were informed Monday night that they would not have advance intelligence on their target area supplied by other SEAL units and that they were allowed to send their own SEAL detachment ashore. The SEAL unit was from SPECWARGRU-TWO and had been assigned to the 22nd MAU as part of their standard deployment procedures. The CINCLANT plan for Urgent Fury specifically banned any use of advance reconnaissance forces who were organically part of the actual landing forces. This order was intended in part to fulfill OPSEC requirements as well as to keep command of all the Special Operations Forces under a single, centralized control. With the commitment of the second SEAL unit to the CCT infiltration at Port Salines, the Special Operations Forces were being spread too thinly and the Marines were allowed to use their own SEAL forces. The 22nd MAU SEAL detachment moved out to recon the landing sites at 2200 hours, Monday night, October 24.

The SEALs moved in toward the island from the fleet using their own Seafox raiding boats carried with the unit. After reaching a distance from the shore where the Seafoxes were still safe from detection, the team switched to inflatable rubber boats equipped with specially silenced outboard motors for the final approach to the island. The mission of the team was to first reconnoiter the landing beaches and conduct a hydrographic survey of the offshore waters. After the initial recon the SEALs would move inland and examine Pearls Airport, reporting its condition and defenses.

Landing on Grenada during a heavy rainstorm, the SEALs quickly found themselves within listening distance of a Grenadian work party. The Grenadians were digging beach emplacements as a defense against a possible American invasion. The workers were overheard by the SEALs complaining that the invasion would never happen and that their work was a waste of time. Within a few hours the Grenadian workers were POWs. By 0200 hours on Tuesday morning the SEALs had completed their mission and had sent back the code phrase "Walk Track Shoes" to their waiting commanders. The code words meant that there were reefs offshore of the intended landing sites, making the area unapproachable except by very-shallow-draft landing vessels. Vice Admiral Metcalf decided on a helicopter-borne landing by two companies of men, with Echo company of the MAU landing near Pearls Airport and Fox company landing at Grenville nearby. Originally planned landing zones were moved to avoid antiaircraft emplacements reported by the SEALs. Golf company, originally intended to land by boat, was held in reserve in a state of readiness. The landings by the Marines began at 0520 hours on Tuesday morning, October 25.

During the morning of the twenty-fifth, other SEAL units were performing their missions in support of Urgent Fury. The special operation that came off with the least number of problems was the raid by members of SEAL Team 4 on the Radio Free Grenada station. The SEAL team intended a night attack but delays, and the need to coordinate timing for all the attacks, forced the team to strike the station in daylight. According to some reports, the parachute drop by advance elements of Delta Force to take the Port Salines Airport took place as scheduled. Quick detection by ground forces and their heavier-than-expected resistance pinned down the Delta Force unit and alerted the Grenadian forces all over the island.

The delays in landing on the island, combined with the earlier Delta Force drop, caused the SEAL unit to arrive without the cover of darkness and into an area where the opposing forces were already alerted. The SEALs landed by rubber boat onto the shore of Grand Anse Bay, a short distance northeast of the Port Salines Airport, and proceeded inland to capture the RFG station. The team had moved toward the radio station when they suddenly came under heavy fire from Grenadian forces. In spite of receiving, according to some reports, as many as four men wounded out of an eight-man team, the SEALs continued their mission to capture the radio station.

The Radio Free Grenada facility was a 75,000-watt transmitter built from Soviet-supplied equipment and capable of blanketing a large area of the Caribbean. News reporters attempting to reach Grenada by chartered boat on the morning of the twenty-fifth heard RFG go on the air sometime before 0600 hours with a call to arms to the Grenadian people to repel the invasion. This same group of reporters heard the station suddenly go off the air about one hour after starting transmission. The SEAL team had reached the station, capturing it and closing it down, before the announcer had been able to send specific information about where the American forces were landing. Hearing the station go off the air caused a unit of Grenadian forces, including an armored personnel carrier, to investigate the situation. The lightly armed SEALs had been ordered to hold the station intact but were forced to withdraw, after destroying the transmitter, when faced by the much larger and more heavily armed Grenadian forces. The SEALs abandoned the area and moved out without receiving additional casualties. They were able to reunite with U.S. forces on the island some hours later. If the SEALs had been able to take the station earlier, before it had started transmitting, they would have most likely been able to hold it intact until relieved by arriving U.S. forces.

The primary special mission at Grenada for which the SEALs were especially qualified was the rescue of Governor General Sir Paul Scoon and his staff. The Governor General was being held under house arrest at the Government House on the outskirts of Saint George's. Scoon was considered the legitimate government authority on Grenada by the United States, and his rescue was given as high a priority as the rescue of the U.S. citizens also on Grenada. A group of men from SEAL Team 6 were chosen to go in and rescue Scoon on the morning of October 25. Originally planning to insert and exfiltrate by helicopter during the night, delays caused the SEALs to approach the chosen landing zone in near daylight.

The first Blackhawk helicopter carrying part of the SEAL rescue team arrived near the governor's mansion, where it immediately came under heavy fire from nearby PRA and Cuban troops. Badly shot up, the Blackhawk quickly dropped its team of SEALs by ''fast roping'' and pulled away. The initial fire received by the first Blackhawk did not cause any casualties but did damage the team's long-range radio, which was left aboard when the men left the aircraft. The second Blackhawk, carrying the balance of the team, was ordered away by the team commander on the ground. Just as the second helicopter was leaving, antiaircraft emplacements at nearby Forts Rupert and Frederick opened fire but did not strike the aircraft. The first team of approximately thirteen SEALs who were already on the ground fought their way across the lawn, which coincidentally had a Welcome U.S. Marines sign on it, and into the mansion, where they quickly barricaded themselves. The location of the mansion, on the top of a small hill surrounded by lawns, gave the SEALs a clear field of fire and a distinct tactical advantage over the surrounding PRA and Cuban troops.

Quickly bundling Governor General Scoon into a locked closet, ostensibly for his own security, the SEALs set up interlocking fields of fire surrounding the governor's mansion, effectively preventing any approach by PRA or Cuban ground forces. One SEAL, armed with a G3 SG/1 sniper rifle, moved to various positions at windows along the top floors of the mansion where he could hit any enemy troops that showed themselves. Using precision marksmanship, this individual SEAL is credited with between seventeen and twenty-one kills and was listed as instrumental in holding off the overwhelming ground forces. The PRA commander, realizing the difficulty in attempting to assault the mansion, settled for a temporary standoff while he called up reinforcements, including three BTR-60PB armored personnel carriers.

The original plan for exfiltrating Scoon and his aides by helicopter was abandoned after the Blackhawks were forced to leave the area. The loss of the long-range communications also limited the SEALs' communications with the rest of the U.S. forces on Grenada. The SEALs did manage to contact other U.S. units, according to some reports, by using the local telephone system, and they were able to inform Admiral Metcalf of their situation. The information received indicated that the position of the trapped SEALs was precarious, and Admiral Metcalf immediately sent two of his few available AH-1T SeaCobra helicopter gunships to give the SEALs some immediate air cover.

Arriving over Saint George's in the early afternoon, the first SeaCobra paused to engage the antiaircraft emplacements around Fort Frederick and the Cuban headquarters next door. Heavy fire from multiple 23-mm cannons as well as 14.5-mm rounds from a hidden BTR-60 ripped into the SeaCobra as it stopped to guide a fired TOW missile. The pilot, Marine Captain Tim Howard, was badly wounded when a 23-mm round exploded in the cockpit, severing his right forearm and seriously wounding his right leg. Howard managed to crash-land the SeaCobra in a soccer field in the middle of Saint George's.

The SeaCobra's weapons controller, Captain Jeb Seagle, was knocked unconscious when the helicopter took its disabling hits. Seagle came to after landing and managed to drag the wounded pilot from the burning helicopter. While

Seagle was going to signal the other helicopter he was cut down by small arms fire.

The second SeaCobra was shot down into the harbor when it tried to give covering fire for a MEDEVAC chopper attempting to reach Captain Howard. Howard was soon rescued by the MEDEVAC chopper and later recovered. Captain Seagle and the two-man crew of the SeaCobra that crashed into the harbor were the only Marine fatalities of Urgent Fury.

After the SeaCobras were shot down, the PRA commander of the troops surrounding the governor's mansion ordered an attack on the trapped SEALs. An AC-130 Spectre gunship arrived above the mansion as the attack began, and it immediately destroyed one of the BTR-60PBs and stopped the attack. The Spectre remained on station, circling above the mansion, for the rest of the day, staying just outside the range of ground-based antiaircraft. Metcalf ordered a full-scale air strike on the defenses surrounding Saint George's using A-7s launched from the carrier *Independence*. The air strikes demolished most of the antiaircraft emplacements that had been responsible for the downing of the two SeaCobras and also helped prevent the beginning of any organized attack on the governor's mansion. The PRA commander, unable to capture the governor's mansion, satisfied himself by surrounding the house and laying siege to the SEALs inside.

During the night of October 25, Admiral Metcalf ordered the LST *Manitowoc*, carrying Marine Company Golf, which had been held in reserve, to steam around the island and land its men at Saint George's to relieve the SEALs. A Navy commander who had spent some time sailing around the waters of Grenada some years earlier stated that there was a suitable amphibious landing site at Grand Mal Bay, just north of Saint George's, and this was decided upon as the site to land the amphibious troops. Fox Company, already on Grenada, crossed the island by helicopter and landed at LZ Fuel, next to Grand Mal Bay, at 0300 hours Wednesday morning.

Commander John Kolata pointed the stern of his LST at

the center of the unmarked beach in Grand Mal Bay and released his Marines for landing. The Marines' amtrac amphibious assault vehicles had only a short half mile of water to cross before they landed on the shores of Grenada at 0400 hours. Reinforced by five M60A1 tanks landed by the LSD *Fort Snelling*, the Golf Company Marines moved out to quickly group up with the Fox company teams landed earlier. The combined Marine team, reinforced with armored support, moved rapidly toward the governor's mansion and the trapped SEALs inside. While moving to the SEALs' location, the Marines ran into only light resistance. One Grenadian armored personnel carrier tried to hold up the Marines' advance but was quickly dispatched by one of the M60A1's 105-mm main guns.

An anxious night was passed by the SEALs in the governor's mansion. When dawn broke on Wednesday morning they were down to their last few rounds of ammunition. The long night had also proved a revelation to the commander of the PRA troops surrounding the mansion, who had learned the actual situation developing on the rest of the island. When the Marines' tank easily destroyed one of his APCs, the PRA commander decided on a better way of life—he and his force quietly slipped away. With close air support from Navy attack aircraft from the *Independence*, Golf company relieved the jubilant SEALs at 0712 hours. Governor General Scoon, his staff, and the SEALs were quickly evacuated by helicopter out to the *Guam*, waiting offshore.

With the relief of the SEALs and the rescue of Governor General Scoon, the special missions for the SEALs at Grenada were at an end and the units returned to their bases. The SEAL detachment assigned to the 22nd MAU remained with its ships at Grenada until November 2, when the squadron moved on to its original assignment, relieving the 24th MAU in Beirut, Lebanon.

One unit from SPECWARGRU-TWO did continue operations in Grenada after October 25 and these were the two Mark III fast patrol boats that had been carried as deck cargo aboard the LSD *Fort Snelling*. Assigned to the 22nd MAU in the same manner as the SEAL detachment, these two ships from SPECBOATRON-TWO were manned by a surface warfareman detachment who ran the boats in Grenadian waters.

The two Mark IIIs ran hard for several days, interdicting small boats carrying former revolutionary militiamen trying to escape from the island. The Mark IIIs with their machine guns and 20- and 40-mm cannons did an exemplary job of patrolling as the smallest surface combat ships to see action during Urgent Fury.

The *Achille Lauro* Hijacking

On Monday, October 7, 1985, a terrorist incident took place that involved SEAL Team 6 in one of their few publicly known operations. That morning, four members of the Palestine Liberation Front (PLF) left cabin 82 on the 23,629-ton Italian luxury liner *Achille Lauro*. The luxury cruise ship normally carried more than one thousand people, but many of the passengers were not on board. The terrorists had waited until most of the passengers had left the ship in Alexandria, Egypt, for a land tour before making their move.

Armed with AK-47s, pistols, and grenades, the four terrorists entered the main dining salon, where most of the remaining ship's passengers were gathered. Firing wildly as they entered, the gunmen injured two people before they stopped shooting. The terrorists then started separating the 320, mostly Italian, crewmen and 80 passengers into national groups. After placing the American and British passengers in a huddle on deck, the terrorists surrounded them with oil drums that they threatened to ignite. After assaulting Captain Gerardo de Rosa on his own bridge, the terrorists ordered the ship to steam to the Syrian port of Tartus.

Response by the U.S. was immediate, with President

Reagan dispatching units of the Delta Force and SEAL Team 6 to stand by at a U.S. base in Sicily. Since the terrorist action was taking place at sea, SEAL Team 6 was considered the primary action unit. The Italians were also reacting to the situation by placing units of their elite Commando Raggruppamento Subaqueri ed Incursor (COMSUBIN) and Gruppi Interventi Speciali (GIS) teams at a British military base in Cyprus to stand by and await developments. The COMSUBIN is a combat swimmer and commando group of the Italian armed forces similar to the U.S. SEALs, with a long history stretching back to World War I. The GIS is a specially trained unit of the Italian paramilitary police intended for counterterrorist work. Both units are well known to the U.S. military establishment, with cross-training being common, especially between the COMSUBIN and the SEALs.

The hijackers were demanding the release of fifty Palestinians held by the Israeli government and negotiations were ongoing Tuesday morning as the ship headed for Syria. The Syrian government, after consultation with representatives from the Italian and U.S. governments, refused the *Achille Lauro* permission to dock at Tartus. It is when these negotiations began to run against the hijackers that they shot a U.S. hostage.

Leon Klinghoffer was a sixty-nine-year-old retired Jewish businessman from New York who had been partially paralyzed by two strokes and confined to a wheelchair. Klinghoffer was taken away from the rest of the passengers, including his wife, who was traveling with him, and shot in the head and chest. Two of the crewmen were then forced to toss Klinghoffer's body and wheelchair overboard. After this heinous deed, the terrorists ordered the ship to sail for Port Said in Egypt, the ship's original destination, because attempts to dock in Cyprus had also failed.

Several days after the hijacking was over, Leon Klinghoffer's body washed up on shore in Syria. Autopsies established the time and manner of his murder.

A plan calling for the aid of the American SEAL Team was approved by the Italians and all that remained was the wait for darkness to fall. Recognizing the advantage the Americans had in technology and techniques for attacking a ship at sea, the Italian units had agreed to act as backup while the SEALs conducted the actual assault. After the successful rescue, the SEALs would leave the area, allowing the Italians to take the glory and the SEALs to retain anonymity.

Specific information on the terrorists' actions on board the *Achille Lauro* was very limited and little was available to any journalists. The United States did have sophisticated surveillance aircraft making overflights above the hijacked ship and were monitoring events on board. All of the information gathered by the planes still remains classified.

By Wednesday morning the *Achille Lauro* had arrived at Port Said in Egypt and was riding at anchor in the harbor. The American SEAL team gathered aboard the amphibious assault ship *Iwo Jima*, waiting at a distance from Port Said for darkness. The plan was for the SEALs to approach the ship under the cover of night in small boats with specially silenced engines. Using classified methods, the SEALs would climb aboard the *Lauro* and eliminate all of the terrorists on board. With the terrorists neutralized, the SEALs would silently slip away from the cruise ship and allow the Italian teams to come aboard and take the ship in.

The events that took place during the morning and early afternoon of Wednesday were to result in a radical change in the SEALs' operation and the cooperation between the United States, Egypt, and Italy. Acting as a supposedly "interested third party," Yasser Arafat, chairman of the Palestinian Liberation Organization (PLO), had sent in two emissaries to help negotiate a peaceful settlement to the situation aboard the *Achille Lauro*. One of the negotiators was Abbu Abbas, a high-ranking officer in the PLO and the leader of the PLF, whose terrorists had hijacked the *Achille Lauro* in the first place.

The two "negotiators," as well as the ambassadors from Italy and West Germany, went out to the cruise ship Wednesday morning, taking with them guarantees offered by President Hosni Mubarak of Egypt. The guarantees stated that the hijackers would receive safe passage out of Egypt and transportation to a country of their choice if they would release the liner and its passengers unharmed. It was later confirmed that the Egyptian government did not know of the murder of Leon Klinghoffer when it made the offers of safe passage.

Taking advantage of the guarantees, and probably under the orders of their superior, the terrorists accepted Egypt's offer. At 1630 hours in the afternoon the terrorists left the *Achille Lauro*. According to the Egyptians, the terrorists landed at Port Said and almost immediately left the country for an undisclosed location.

With the end of the hijacking and hostage situation the various special units in the area, both Italian and American, stood down from their positions of readiness. Some of the members were headed back home within a few hours.

The U.S. ambassador to Egypt, Nicholas Veliotes, went out to the *Achille Lauro* on Wednesday evening to speak to the U.S. citizens who had been held hostage. Upon learning of the cruel murder of Leon Klinghoffer, Veliotes flew into a rage and contacted his embassy in Cairo over the ship's radio.

The uncoded message sent by Veliotes was couched in somewhat undiplomatic language: "You tell the Foreign Ministry [of Egypt] that we demand they prosecute those sons of bitches."

It appeared to be too late to imprison the terrorists, as the Egyptian government insisted that the terrorists had already left Egypt. Later Wednesday night, U.S. intelligence agencies received hard intelligence from inside Mubarak's government that the terrorists had not left Egypt but were planning to fly to PLO headquarters in Tunisia the next day.

Lieutenant Colonel Oliver North was the man on the National Security Council responsible for the counterterrorism efforts of the United States. When North learned of the terrorists' location he suggested that they could still be captured. President Reagan gave his approval for the suggested plan of action and the wheels were set in motion.

On the morning of October 10, an Egyptian Boeing 737

left the Al Maza air base outside of Cairo. On board the airplane were the four hijackers, the PLO negotiators, and four men from the elite Egyptian military unit Force 777. On receipt of this information, the U.S. plan went immediately into effect.

F-14 Tomcat fighters were already in the air from the carrier U.S.S. *Saratoga,* which was sailing in the Aegean Sea. The F-14s set up a checkpoint south of Crete where an E2-C Hawkeye electronic surveillance plane was tracking the targeted Boeing 737. The 737 was refused landing permission at Tunis in Tunisia, where it was originally headed. Tripoli, Libya, next refused the terrorist plane permission to land, and, as the plane turned to fly toward Athens, the F-14s struck.

Four F-14s surrounded the Egyptian aircraft and ordered it to fly to the NATO air base at Sigonella in Sicily. Attempts by the 737 to contact Egypt, or anyone else, were completely blocked by the electronic warfare aircraft accompanying the F-14s. Unable to gain assistance, the 737 followed the F-14s to Sigonella.

The members of SEAL Team 6 had, the night before, been preparing to return to Gibraltar and from there home to the United States when they received orders that they had another mission. The team moved out to Italy, where they prepared to greet the arriving terrorists. Due to the need for absolute secrecy, the U.S. government had not informed the Italians that the Egyptian 737 would be landing at Sigonella until the entourage had actually entered Italian airspace. The air traffic controllers at Sigonella refused the Egyptian 737 permission to land until the pilot, in desperation, declared a low-fuel emergency.

As the 737 came to a stop it was immediately surrounded by the SEALs, who expected the Force 777 commandos aboard the plane to resist surrender. The Italian paramilitary Carabineri police unit at the airport quickly surrounded the SEALs, who were surrounding the captured aircraft. The Italians demanded the terrorists and the SEALs refused to turn them over. The situation became very tense and it appeared that the two armed units would open fire on one another.

At the beginning of the hijack situation, the State Department had sent an official from the Office for Combatting Terrorism to Rome to liaison with the Italians. This State Department official was at the Sigonella Airport when the terrorists arrived and was "eavesdropping" on the radio communication among the SEALs. "It was a crazy situation," said the official after the affair was over. "At one time we heard one of the SEAL officers discussing whether or not he should order his men to open fire on the Italians. That could have been very embarrassing."

The impasse came to an end without bloodshed when Secretary of State George Shultz received assurances from the Italians that the terrorists would be tried for murder. Shultz then ordered the SEALs to stand down and let the Caribineri have the prisoners.

After the situation had cooled and the Italians had the prisoners, the Egyptian commandos were sent home. The SEALs, however, were still not satisfied with the results. Not completely trusting anyone after the duplicity of the Egyptians, the commander of the SEALs did not want to let the prisoners out of his sight. Thinking that the Italians might release the terrorists, as they were known to do, as soon as they were out of sight, the SEAL commander, along with a small contingent of SEALs, shadowed the terrorists' plane all the way to Rome in a small plane of their own. The SEALs claimed engine trouble and were allowed to land right behind the terrorists' plane at the Rome airport.

The Italians did imprison and try the terrorists for murder, though they released Abbu Abbas, who had an Iraqi diplomatic passport. The interception of the aircraft angered Egypt and the military action on Italian soil strained U.S.-Italian relations. By and large, the operation was seen as a great success by the Americans, though few knew to what extent the operation's success had been dependent on the actions and determination of the Navy SEALs of SEAL Team 6.

Role Model*

Chief Nelson: A Role Model for New SEALs

Walking tall in his khakis, the SEAL enters the workspace at Team One. Although a large man, he moves with the lithe grace characteristic of athletes. His very demeanor speaks of control. He is a man in control of himself and his surroundings.

"The first time I saw the Chief, I knew it was right," says GMM1 Diederik "Didi" Molenaar, talking about Andrew Nelson, a newly frocked chief petty officer. "In my eyes, Andy has always been a chief wearing a 1st class crow. He's deserved the promotion for a long time now."

A demolition and weapons instructor, Nelson is a part of Team One's training cell. The Team is home-ported at Naval Amphibious Base, Coronado, Calif. "I see Andy as a role model," says Molenaar, a fellow instructor. "He doesn't even need to use a lesson guide when he conducts a class. Andy has forgotten more about demolition than I'll ever know. Whenever someone has a question or is looking for a better way to do the job, they call on Andy."

*Reprinted from U.S. Naval Publication, *All Hands*, December 1987.

Nelson attributes most of his knowledge to the training he received from the other SEALs. "I grew up in the old tradition," he says. Joining the teams right after Vietnam, Nelson was trained by men who drew their knowledge from actual combat experience.

"Rules were written in blood," Nelson says. They are rules that he sees as being forgotten by some of the younger team members. "I was taught by people who learned how to operate in life or death situations." With the passage of time, many of these veterans have retired, taking with them their first-hand knowledge. Nelson says he tries to keep those lessons fresh so they will not have to be rewritten in the blood of a new generation.

"All anybody has to do is express an interest in learning and Andy will immediately take the newcomer under his wing," Molenaar says. "He really enjoys training the new people." Another co-worker agrees. "Andy is always putting himself into situations where he can teach others."

Thirteen years ago, Nelson, a lumber grader in Tacoma, Wash., made a decision that forever changed his life. It was a payday Friday and he had just finished a long day rating the quality of wood at the local mill. "Just like every other payday, the guys I worked with were getting together to drink and gamble away their paychecks," Nelson says. Suddenly, in an older co-worker, he saw a reflection of himself 20 years into the future: two bucks in his pocket, waiting for payday Friday to roll around. "The very next day I was in the recruiter's office saying, 'Get me out of here.'"

The son of a retired Air Force master sergeant, why did Nelson pick the Navy? And why SEALs? The answer: a special friend, someone with whom he shared experiences dating back to high school. A good friend of Nelson's, Mitch Croft, had joined the Navy and volunteered for SEALs. Whenever Croft came home to visit, the two would get together, often for deer hunting. It was there, while stalking game deep into the forest, that Croft would tell Nelson of his latest SEAL adventures. "It just sounded pretty exciting to me," Nelson says. "Besides, SEALs can do everything other special warfare units can do and more—more because of our underwater capabilities.''

Nelson's mother, Joyce Nelson, says she was surprised at first when her son decided to volunteer for SEALs. "He was always such a gentle person, bringing home hurt animals and such.'' But, she says, she is not surprised that Nelson has become a demolition and weapons expert.

She remembers how Mitch and Andrew would gather up old garbage cans from around the neighborhood. "They took the garbage cans down to a nearby swamp and blew them up with firecrackers. Even way back then, Andrew loved making things go bang."

The two boys were always shooting, plinking away at something. "We're having a great time in the SEALs," Croft says, laughing. "We now have bigger toys, make bigger noises and have more responsibility."

When Croft heard that Nelson had joined the Navy and was attending BUD/S, he was happy for his buddy and pretty confident Andy would survive the training. "I remember Andy teasing me, 'If you can do it I can do it,' " he says. "It's not all that easy, but I figured Andy had the drive and good sense needed. Besides, it was probably a matter of pride—not only had I made it through, but he told everyone he would be a SEAL. So a SEAL he was going to be."

Determination is one trait Nelson has always had. "He doesn't give up," Joyce says. A member of his high school wrestling team, Nelson separated his sternum just before a big regional tournament. His doctor told him he was finished for the year. Joyce recalls, "Andrew just looked the doctor in the eye and told him he was wrong. 'Show my mom how to tape my shoulder. I'm going to regionals.' " Nelson went on, not only to win the tournament, but also to post the record for the fastest pin. "He pinned his man literally seconds into the match," Joyce says. "He later told me that the tape had blocked off his breathing and he had to pin his man fast or else."

According to Nelson, it wasn't just his determination that helped him through the BUD/S training, but rather an extreme fear of failure. "I never once thought of quitting," he says. "Out of the 125 guys that started in my class, only 25 of us graduated. I knew I wouldn't quit, but I was afraid of being dropped. I don't think I could have handled being told 'You're not good enough.'"

Nelson's determination and intense desire to be the best at whatever he undertakes are emotions he keeps to himself. To the world, he presents an easy-going image. Even those who know him best describe him as a laid-back kind of guy—someone who "doesn't sweat the load."

Master Chief James "K-bar" Kauber tells of an experience that would have rattled most men, but didn't seem to faze Nelson. During a C-130 jump in Okinawa, Nelson was jumpmaster. It was the first time a fixed-wing jump had been attempted at this DZ (drop zone), The DZ was surrounded by dense jungle that measured 200 by 100 meters. After landing half the squad safely, Nelson returned for a second drop. "Andy not only missed the DZ, but he landed four men in the trees." Andy's reaction—rather his lack of reaction—was "Whoops—guess I missed."

But Nelson, as jumpmaster, knows full well that there is always danger when jumping from a plane. As he says, "After you have put the men out of the plane, you don't really breathe again until you see all good canopies." He added that "landing in the trees can be very hazardous. All a jumper can do is make himself as small as possible and hope he slides through the branches." He really didn't feel relieved until he saw them all safe and walking. "After it was over and I learned everyone was OK, I took a lot of ribbing and verbal abuse from the guys. All the 'atta boys' in the world are erased by one 'oh # * @!!'" he says. "Whenever I feel down or bummed out, I jump free-fall to recharge the batteries. It's the ultimate high as far as I'm concerned," Nelson says. But it wasn't always that way. He can still remember asking himself just before his jump without a static line, "Do I really want to do this?"

SEALs are required to jump on a static line, but, even though they are not required to learn free-fall, almost all do. It's part of the image. Nelson felt he needed to cut the umbilical cord of that static line to fully join the fraternity. "I wanted to be free-fall qualified."

Off duty, Nelson is a very sociable guy. According to co-workers, he and his wife, Debbie, are always having team members over to the house for a barbecue and a couple of beers. A considerate host, Nelson warns first-comers in advance about his strange collection of pets. As a guest enters the Nelson's home he is likely to be greeted by an animal which appears to be all muscle and teeth. Don't worry, it's just Knuckles or J.W. (pronounced "J-dub"), one of his two Pit Bulls, looking for a scratch behind the ears.

Also scary to the uninitiated is his pet Red-Tailed Boa, "Mrs. Snake." Nelson enjoys snakes and sees nothing out of the ordinary in having one for a pet. However, it was just this fascination with snakes that earned him a permanent file in the drawer of stories SEALs like to dust off and share for a laugh among good friends.

It all started when a friend of Nelson's, Senior Chief Bill Nehl, was standing camp guard at a desert training camp in California. Nehl had caught and caged three rattlesnakes before turning the watch over to Nelson. "When I returned to camp, I heard that one of the guys had been bitten by a rattler. I just knew it had to be Andy. Sure enough, Andy couldn't keep away from the snakes. He had stuck his hand in the cage and gotten bit," Nehl says. Andy survived with no permanent damage, but the episode did put an end to capturing snakes at the camp.

Rattlers aside, Nelson has built himself a reputation as a "good operator." In 1986, he was named Team One's Sailor of the Year and, according to his Command Master Chief, Master Chief Petty Officer Girardin, "Nelson has been a cornerstone in his command. He's the type of guy we can always rely on."

A seriously injured SEAL found out just how reliable Nelson could be. During a jump that went awry, Nelson could see one of his fellow SEALs land in and become entangled in high-tension wires. Barely clearing the wires himself, he saw his buddy arc, catch on fire and fall to the ground. Quickly landing, he grabbed the first aid kit and raced to his buddy's aid, where he began an IV, treatment for shock and radioed for a medevac. "In our job, sometimes things go wrong. You try to avoid this but accidents are going to happen. All you can do is be ready to act," Nelson says. Nelson's quick action earned him a Navy Commendation medal, but more importantly to him, he saved his buddy's life.

Nelson's command values him not only for his coolness under pressure but also his expertise with demolitions and firearms. Nelson, a team sniper, is frequently called upon to give precise information on the team's firearms. "With Andy, you know that any information he tells you has first been thoroughly researched," Girardin says.

"I like to operate. I like doing SEAL things," Nelson says. "This is the kind of job where you can go as far as you want." Nelson sees one advantage the SEALs have over the rest of the Navy. In the teams, everyone has a voice, an idea worth listening to. It doesn't matter if it's a seaman's or master chief's, a good idea is a good idea. "Whoever has the knowledge, does the job. You're not stuck by an inflexible chain of command."

A man who likes to be on the road, involved in operations, "Andrew is just like his father," Joyce says. "If a job has to be done, they'll do it." She used to worry about Nelson because the job he felt he had to do was so dangerous. But one day he sat her down and told her to stop worrying. "He said, 'Mom, you must remember, I'm doing exactly what I want to do: what I love. And if I die doing something I love, well, how many people can say that?' "

Joyce has decided to place her son's safety in God's hands. "He's not foolhardy and he's had the best training available."

The SDVs

The Swimmer Delivery Vehicle (SDV) teams are the newest members of the SEAL community but are able to trace their lineage back to World War I and the Italian Human Torpedoes. The SDV teams (SDVTs) were commissioned on May 1, 1983, when the last of the UDTs decommissioned. SDVT 1, stationed on the West Coast, received its first complement of men from UDT-12, with SDVT 2, on the East Coast, receiving its original personnel complement from UDT-22.

The first SDV platoon was established by SEAL Team 1 in 1969 and consisted of two officers and ten enlisted men. Today, the SDV teams are built along the lines of the standard SEAL teams, with the teams being broken down into platoons, each capable of operating independently when deployed. Presently, each SDV platoon, when deployed in the field, would take with it at least one of each of the types of SDVs available to it, concentrating on the Mark VIII and Mark IX models. The platoon would have eight qualified operators for the SDVs, with four technicians, two mechanical and two electrical, completing the complement of enlisted men. The twelve enlisted men of a platoon would be supervised by two officers, usually of lieutenant rank.

The platoon's two officers would each act as navigator, with one of the eight operators acting as the pilot for a mission. During rehearsal dives the officers would alternate so there would always be a fresh, rested individual to go out on a mission. The two officers would each have a primary pilot, with a secondary pilot available in case one became ill or otherwise unable to go out on a mission. A tertiary pair of operators, with one of the enlisted men acting as navigator, would also be standing by in case a third dive pair was called for.

The SDVTs are receiving some of the SEALs' greatest financial support during the present expansion of the military's special operations forces. Out of all of the projected construction projects for the SEALs for the latter part of the 1980s, most of a budgeted $11.25 million will directly benefit the SDV teams. Increases in personnel will raise their strengths to a planned 20 officers and 120 enlisted men in SDVT 1, with 24 officers and 159 enlisted men in SDVT 2 by the end of fiscal year 1990. SDVT Detachment One in Hawaii is also being strengthened and is expected to have 5 officers and 36 enlisted men by the end of fiscal year 1990.

The reason for the increase of funds put into the SDVTs is the growing awareness of their effectiveness and value of their mission capabilities.

The primary advantages of the SDVs are their capacities for taking combat swimmers much farther and faster than they would be able to swim and still do it in a manner difficult to detect. The swimmers are also able to greatly extend their underwater time on station by using the breathing mixtures on board the SDVs, retaining their own portable breathing mix for the last swim to the target.

The SDVs are able to act as underwater "packhorses," transporting much larger quantities of material than swimmers could transport on their own for any major distance. The disadvantages of the SDVs include their need for large amounts of very specialized maintenance as well as the requirements for highly trained personnel to both perform the necessary maintenance and operate the vehicles effectively.

Using closed-circuit scuba while in the SDVs, especially the older model scubas, requires very close and consistent depth control. This level of training for both the maintenance and operation of the SDVs made it necessary to establish the SDV teams as separate units from the regular SEAL teams. The large allotment of funds and facilities available to the SDVTs increases their mission capabilities and limits or eliminates their disadvantages.

Today's SDVs are specially designed to perform their tasks in the most efficient manner and little resemble their ancestors, the slightly modified torpedoes used in World Wars I and II. The SDVs presently being used by the SEALs differ greatly from earlier models but still share most of the same general characteristics and basic designs.

All of the SDVs have some form of propulsion consisting of a power source, drive shaft, and propeller. They also have some method of ballast control that can be adjusted by the operator, a selection of instruments to indicate depth, direction, speed, time, and status of the SDV, and a hull to hold all of these systems together as well as protect the operators, passengers, and cargo from the force of the moving water.

All of the SDVs presently in use are of the "wet" type, that is, the hull allows the surrounding water in and does not protect its occupants from the water's pressure. In the wet-type submarine all of the occupants need to use some type of individual breathing equipment and protect all of their nonwaterproof equipment.

The first SDV, the Mark I, was a very simple device—little more than a motor with handles, operated by a single individual. The body of the Mark I was a cylinder only a few feet long with rounded ends and was less than eighteen inches in diameter. The rear of the body had two handles for the operator with a screened propeller blade beneath them. The motor and batteries in the body had enough power to tow one or two divers at speeds of three to four knots.

The Italian "Sea Horse" was the first wet-type submersible used by the UDTs and the SEALs. Used during the 1960s, the Sea Horse was a four-man SDV that carried two men in an open front compartment, seating one in front of the other, with the same arrangement for the two men sitting in the rear compartment. The experiments with the Sea Horse, including launching it underwater from the deck of a submarine, demonstrated the capabilities of the design and it was subsequently developed into the first U.S.-issue SDV.

The General Dynamics Convair Model 14 was the first U.S.-designed SDV and was used by the SEALs in developing their specific SDV program. The Model 14 was approved by the Navy for service as the Mark VII SDV. As adopted, the Mark VII was a four-man wet submersible powered by six sixteen-cell silver cadmium batteries. Though exact details are unavailable, the operational parameters put forward by the Navy called for the SDV to be able to travel at a maximum speed of 4.5 knots at depths of 200 feet at zero visibility. The Mark VII could hold its maximum speed for up to eight hours with a maximum range of up to forty nautical miles, equal to sixty statute miles. The cargo capacity of the Mark VII was fifty-five pounds (wet) of equipment in addition to the four swimmers.

The breathing system used in the Mark VII as adopted consisted of eight ninety-cubic foot aluminum air tanks feeding four Conshelf VI single-hose regulators. This commercial-based system was only used for training with the Mark VII. For combat operations, an N202 semiclosed system would be fitted to the SDV, giving it a much greater endurance and depth capacity while increasing its ability to make clandestine insertions. One other addition to the Mark VII was a sliding canopy, similar to those found on aircraft, to protect the crew from the pressure of the passing water

By the 1970s two new models of SDV had been developed and were in use by the SEALs and the UDTs. The Mark VII Mod 2 and Mark VII Mod 6 were the standard types of SDVs used. The Mark VII Mod 2 SDV has a fiberglass hull with most of the fittings made of nonferrous materials, thus minimizing the craft's acoustic and magnetic signature. The drive system is electric, using storage batteries to run a powerful electric motor that turns a single screw located at the rear of the craft. Instruments and electrical systems are contained in airtight, dry canisters that are water tight down to a depth of several hundred feet. The canisters and their contents are easily removable, simplifying maintenance.

The bow cockpit of the Mark VII Mod 2 has the controls at its front, with seating for two divers one in front of the other. The rear cockpit is arranged in the same manner as the front but does not have a duplicate set of controls. There are sliding canopies to cover both of the cockpits. A transparent viewscreen is at the front of the bow cockpit, allowing the pilot to see forward. The viewscreen was made from the same opaque materials as the rest of the hull in subsequent models. Control is managed by a vertical rudder at the rear of the craft and two bow planes at the front, which can be removed for stowage.

The Mark VII Mod 2 SDV is 212 inches long with a draft of 57 inches and a beam of 35 inches without the bow planes. The vehicle weighs 2,200 pounds fully equipped, but without crew.

The Mark VII Mod 6 SDV was modified from the earlier version to correct difficulties that were found after field use of the Mod 2. Deficiencies were found in the cargo capacity and electronic systems of the Mod 2. These were correctable without major changes in the basic design, but these changes were not able to be retrofitted to the Mod 2s already in use. The hull of the Mark VII was lengthened by eighteen inches to allow a greater cargo capacity, allowing the Mod 6 to have a greater weapons payload than the Mod 2. The nose and afterbody hull contours were changed to allow for the installation of new sonar transducers. Additional electronic subsystems added to the new sonar increased the Mod 6's accuracy in navigation and obstacle avoidance and also increased its capabilities for underwater rendezvous and docking.

The additions and necessary rearrangement of existing equipment inside the essentially unchanged hull envelope of the Mark VII Mod 6 required some installations to be redesigned to account for the new weight/buoyancy summary. A new motor canister, main ballast, open ballast, and bow buoyancy tanks were added. The volume of the ballast tanks was enlarged to compensate for the increased weight of the Mod 6, and a system was added to allow for an emergency blowing of the main ballast tank.

The transparent viewscreen on the front cockpit was eliminated as unnecessary and the sliding canopies over the compartments were made opaque, allowing lights to be used inside the cockpit to operate the craft while not allowing the light to be detected from the outside or the surface. Other than the changes listed, the Mark VII Mod 6 has the same general characteristics and operating parameters of the earlier Mod 2, which it replaced. The Mark VII Mod 6 is able to travel at speeds of four to seven knots for over five hours underwater.

New model SDVs were developed during the 1970s and are the standard models presently in use by the SEALs. The Mark VIII resembles the Mark VII series but has considerably greater capabilities. Known as the EX-VIII during its development, the Mark VIII is able to transport four combat swimmers in its rear compartment while being operated by a crew of two, pilot and navigator, in its forward compartment. The Mark VIII is propelled by an electric system that drives a five-bladed propeller located at the rear of the craft and is powered from rechargeable batteries. Steering is accomplished through the use of a vertical rudder and horizontal stabilizer at the rear of the craft, and buoyancy is controlled by two ballast systems, one closed and one open.

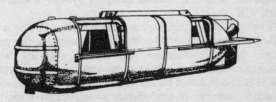

SDV Mark VIII. Both cockpit and cargo doors are open.

The main function of the closed ballast system is to adjust the water weight of the SDV to achieve neutral buoyancy during submerged operations under various load conditions. The open ballast system provides a rapid means for surfacing and diving the SDV while the closed ballast system stays adjusted to neutral buoyancy for the particular missions load. A trim subsystem maintains the SDV in a horozontal attitude, balancing any weight distribution that would cause the SDV to pitch up or down. Adjustment to the SDV's trim is accomplished by an assembly with a moveable lead weight that is located along the craft's centerline. By moving the position of the lead weight either fore or aft, the operator can adjust the craft's pitch, trimming the SDV.

The removable bow planes of the Mark VII have been retained in the Mark VIII SDV. The controls are operated manually by the pilot in the front cockpit, who sits side by side with the navigator rather than in the one-in-front-of-the-other arrangement found in the earlier SDVs. Sliding canopies are located over each crew member's position and may be opened or closed independently of each other. There are also two sliding canopies at the rear of the SDV, one on either side of the passenger compartment.

The Mark VIII has an on-board breathing system for use by the crew and the passengers and the system is fitted to allow free voice communications between the crew members. The Mark XV computerized, mixed-gas UBA is primarily used by the SDV operators as an individual breathing system because it can be taken deeper and last longer than the Drager LAR V system used by the SEAL combat swimmers. A full-face mask allows the Mark XV UBA to be compatible with the communications system aboard the Mark VIII.

A computerized Doppler navigation system (DNS) is installed on the Mark VIII and greatly simplifies the navigator's job and increases the SDV's accuracy when traveling. A specialized obstacle-avoidance sonar subsystem (OAS) is also installed on the Mark VIII. The OAS provides automatic warning of any obstacles—especially important since the pilot of the SDV is flying "blind" and is steering by instruments. A separate docking subsystem is used to rendezvous with a host platform or various insertion platforms, or may be used to locate a swimmer team. A standard type of naval radio is also installed on the Mark VIII and allows the surfaced craft to communicate with other ships.

All instruments and electrical or electronic subsystems aboard the Mark VIII are contained in removable, dry, airtight canisters capable of withstanding an ambient seawater pressure equal to a depth of over three hundred feet. Along the top of the Mark VIII is a lifting rail, allowing the SDV to be raised out of the water by a standard crane. Alongside the lifting rail is the antenna for the SDV's radio system. The radio antenna normally lies along the hull but can be raised above the surface of the water to extend the range of the radio.

The Mark VIII has a length of 254 inches with a beam of 52 inches and a draft of 52 inches. The relatively wide beam of the Mark VIII allows the crew to work in a side-by-side position and increased the SDV's combat swimmer capacity to four men while not greatly increasing the Mark VIII's length over that of earlier SDVs.

The newest SEAL SDV is the Mark IX, earlier known as the EX-IX. Of very unusual design, the Mark IX appears as a long flattened rectangle rather than having the "whale"

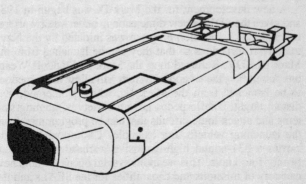

SDV Mark IX. Top view with hatches closed.

shape of earlier SDVs. Designed to carry two combat swimmers and their equipment or cargo, the Mark IX has unique capabilities.

When moving, the Mark IX is driven by an electric motor system turning twin, three-bladed propellers at the craft's stern and using rechargeable batteries for power.

The surfaced or submerged position of the SDV as well as its pitch attitude and buoyancy are controlled by a dewatering/ballast and trim subsystem. The Mark IX is manually controlled through the use of stabilizers added to the planes at the craft's stern along with a single horizontal stabilizer running the width of the stern. Two vertical control fins bracket the stern stabilizer and assist in dampening vibration while the Mark IX is under power. As in the Mark VIII, the Mark IX has a computerized Doppler inertial navigation subsystem to aid in guiding the craft. The Mark IX also carries an obstacle avoidance sonar subsystem as well as a separate docking subsystem for rendezvousing with the parent delivery vehicle.

Although it carries only two swimmers and their equipment, the Mark IX has a length of 233 inches with a beam of 76 inches—but a draft of only 32 inches. Weight of the Mark IX is around 5,000 pounds equipped. Both the Mark VIII and Mark IX have a speed of several knots when submerged.

A new development for the Mark IX was begun in 1985 and gives the SDVs a new dimension in underwater warfare. In 1985 a $12.5 million program was initiated by the Navy to convert torpedoes so that they can be launched from the Mark IX SDV. Referred to as the Mark 32 Standoff Weapons Assembly, the weapons system will allow the torpedoes to be launched from the Mark IX, while submerged, at a distant target. The torpedos have a variety of homing systems and attack logic circuits that can be programmed from the launching vehicle. For example, 1,400-pound torpedo carries a 331-pound high-explosive warhead at speeds of twenty-four knots. This weapons system opens a whole new category of missions and capabilities for the SEALs and the SDV teams.

The SDVs can all be delivered to the target area by a variety of means. The ASDV, a converted LCU-1610 Class Utility Landing Craft, is available to transport SDVs as well as lift them to and from the water. The distinctive appearance of the ASDV is such that it is normally used only for training or rehearsal missions. Three landing craft have been converted to ASDVs with ASDVs 1 and 3 being based in San Diego and ASDV 2 based at Little Creek. A simple wheeled trailer is used to move all the types of SDVs while at shore facilities and aboard aircraft.

An unusual method of transporting SDVs over water utilizes a form of sled that can be towed behind a suitable boat such as the Seafox or an LCPL. The sled has open sides and a large bow that raises the sled above the water into a planing position when towed at speed. When the towing craft slows down, the sled sinks down into the water to a point where it is held by its two flotation tanks, one on either side of the sled. When the sled is in the sunken or down position, the carried SDV can simply drive off the sled's open rear under its own power. The sled can also be used to recover launched SDVs by reversing the above procedure.

The most efficient and the best concealed method of getting the SDV within target range was first proven out during the 1960s. Experiments with launching the Sea Horse from the deck of a submerged conventional submarine established the viability of using a submarine as a base of operations for SDVs. Men were able to swim out of the submarine's escape hatch and detach the Sea Horse from the sub's deck for transportation. A major problem with the system was the need to surface to perform most of the needed maintenance and preparation of the SDV for an operation. As it turned out, a unique individual craft was becoming available that would solve most of the problems with sub launching and transporting of SDVs.

Commissioned at the Mare Island Navy Yard in California on March 7, 1958, the SSG-574 *Greyback* was the first of the U.S. Navy's submarines intended to carry the Regulus II sea-to-surface missile. The Regulus II missile was a cruise-type weapon with an overall length of more than fifty-seven feet and a wingspan of twenty feet, capable of carrying an atomic warhead for over one thousand miles. To transport the Regulus missile, the *Greyback* was designed to have two large hangars on her upper bow and to be able to sit on the ocean bottom for extended lengths of time. The two cylindrical hangars on the *Greyback* extend for seventy feet back from the bow and are each eleven feet high. Each hangar could contain two missiles riding on their transport dollies. The *Greyback*'s ability to surface and quickly prepare and launch up to four Regulus missiles made it an important part of the United States nuclear deterrent force. After logging over 130,000 miles while cruising on deterrent missile strike missions, the *Greyback* was decommissioned on May 25, 1964, when her mission was replaced by the more powerful Polaris missile submarines.

A conversion and refitting of the *Greyback* was begun at the U.S. Naval Ship Repair Facility at Yokosuka, Japan, in 1967. The refit included a new 504-cell battery system, a more modern radar package, and a complete overhaul of one main engine, the generators, the hydraulic system, trim and drain systems, the air-conditioning system, and evaporators. The primary change for the use of the SDVs was the conversion of the two bow missile hangars into giant pressure locks. One half of the hangars can be flooded and the outside door opened to the sea while the ship is either submerged or on the surface. The facilities for *Greyback*'s original complement of eighty-seven, nine officers and seventy-eight enlisted crewmen, were expanded to include an additional sixty-seven troops, seven officers and sixty enlisted men.

After the conversion was completed the *Greyback* was recommissioned as the LPSS-574, the first Amphibious Transport Submarine. Having a length of 334 feet with a beam of 30 feet and a draft of 17 feet, the *Greyback* displaced 2,935 tons submerged, making her the largest diesel/electric-powered submarine in the world. Assigned in January of 1970 to Subic Bay in the Philippines as her home port, the *Greyback* acted as the flagship for the commander of the U.S. 7th Fleet Submarine Force as well as the only unconventional warfare submarine in the U.S. Navy.

Each of the twin bow hangars could now carry either two SDVs on movable dollies or a single high-speed surface craft. The SDVs could be launched while the *Greyback* was submerged at depth or while she was surfaced with her decks awash in a wet-deck condition. While in the wet-deck condition the high-speed surface craft could also be launched in place of an SDV. The *Greyback* was also the first U.S. submarine to carry a fully accredited doctor as part of the ship's normal complement. The Navy's largest recompression chamber was installed on the *Greyback* to fully support divers' operations.

Oxygen and other breathing gases were carried aboard the *Greyback* as part of the ship's normal stores along with a large explosives magazine. Lastly, the *Greyback* was the only U.S. submarine that could bottom on the seabed for long periods of time and still be able to run her on-board machinery. The *Greyback* could do this because her seawater inlet valves were ten feet above her keel rather than along her bottom, as they are on other submarines. Altogether the conversion of the *Greyback* cost $4.7 million in 1968 and took 74,000 man-hours of time to complete. The *Greyback* continued in service with the Special Warfare community of the U.S. Navy until she was permanently decommissioned in 1984.

It was the age and length of service that resulted in the decommissioning of the *Greyback* and not any lack of need for her capabilities. A new program was developed to carry the SDVs in removable containers that could be mounted on suitably modified nuclear submarines. The Dry Deck Shelters (DDSs) each carry a single SDV in a dry hangar accessible from inside the submarine so that maintenance and pre-mission preparation can be conducted while the submarine is under way. The DDS is a three-chambered structure consisting of two large spheres and a cylindrical tank. The first spherical chamber is an access sphere that mounts directly to one of the submarine's escape hatches. The central sphere acts as a hyperbaric chamber for swimmer decompression after long dives at depth. The cylindrical chamber is the actual SDV hangar and as such can be completely flooded, with the end hatch opening to the sea. The hangar can also act as a lock-out chamber, allowing large teams of swimmers to leave the submarine at one time. Modifications required to mount a DDS to a submarine include changing the outer door and seals of an escape hatch to accept the access sphere that must be bolted to it. Some deck fittings are also added to firmly attach the DDS to the submarine's deck.

Launched in February 1972, the *Cavalla*, SSN-684, is a Sturgeon-class nuclear-powered attack submarine. From August to December of 1982, the *Cavalla* underwent conversion at the naval facilities at Pearl Harbor to carry troops and mount the first available DDS. The *Cavalla* proved out the DDS concept during sea trials while retaining her capabilities as an attack submarine. Most of the Sturgeon-class submarines, including the *Cavalla*, have been fitted with the Harpoon missile, launchable from the ship's torpedo tubes. The Harpoon can precisely deliver a five hundred-pound conventional high-explosive or small nuclear charge to a range of sixty-eight miles.

The *Cavalla* is 10 feet longer than the normal 292-foot length of the Sturgeon-class submarine. The extra length of the *Cavalla*'s hull is needed to give room for her special array of sonar equipment. Capable of diving to a depth of 1,320 feet, the Sturgeon-class submarines are driven at speeds of up to thirty knots underwater by their Westinghouse S5W reactors.

Six of the Sturgeon-class submarines are slated to receive the DDS conversions by 1992. When the DDS conversions are completed it is expected that three of the submarines will be attached to the Pacific fleet and three to the Atlantic fleet, giving maximum flexibility for SEAL and SDV deployments.

After the concept of the DDS was proven by the *Cavalla*, two submarines of the Ethan Allen class were slated for conversion to accept the DDS. Referred to as "Boomers" by members of the Navy, the *Sam Houston*, SSN-609, and the *John Marshall*, SSN-611, were originally Polaris missile submarines and carried sixteen nuclear-tipped missiles in individual launch tubes amidships, behind the sail. Age and advances in missile technology outdated earlier designs such as the Polaris missile, and it was considered to be too difficult and costly to convert the Ethan Allen-class boats to accept new model missiles.

The *Sam Houston* and the *John Marshall* were both decommissioned as part of the SLBM (Submarine Launched Ballistic Missile) force and were converted to a modified SSN configuration in the early 1980s. The conversion consisted of removing the missile fire control and other redundant systems as well as placing concrete ballast in the bases of some of the empty missile tubes to compensate for the weight of the removed Polaris missiles.

Conversion was continued on the *Sam Houston* and the *John Marshall* to place them in the amphibious transport status. Some of the missile tubes were completely removed and others were converted for equipment stowage or to act as air locks for swimmer exit. Facilities were enlarged to accept a further 67 troops in addition to the ship's normal complement of 143 officers and men. Modifications were made to the hatches and deck so that the submarines could each mount two of the DDS assemblies.

Changing the submarines to fit their new duties was done at the Puget Sound Naval Shipyard and took from September 1983 to September 1985 to complete. Both of the ships are capable of traveling at a speed of thirty knots while submerged to a maximum depth of 984 feet. The submarines also retained their normal armament of four twenty-one-inch torpedo tubes.

All in all, eight nuclear submarines are scheduled to be assigned to Special Warfare duties as DDS/SDV transports. Ten DDS shelters are planned to be constructed, allowing ten SDVs to be deployed with the fleet. SDV teams are to have had nineteen of the new model Mark VIII and Mark IX SDVs available to them by the end of fiscal year 1987. Requests to manufacturers for submissions for the new advanced Mark VIII Mod 1 SDV have gone out, with the vehicle to be available by the end of fiscal year 1992.

All SEALs who are assigned to SDVs after graduation from BUD/S receive their initial SDV training at the Coronado Naval Amphibious Base directly across the street from the Phil H. Bucklew Center for Naval Special Warfare and the BUD/S school. As assignments are passed out after BUD/S graduation, an occasional reaction to an SDV assignment is "What did I do wrong?" This attitude toward the SDVs is gradually disappearing as the importance of the SDVs and their mission becomes more commonly known.

Most observers see the SDV students as being the "cream of the crop" of SEAL graduates due to the highly technical nature of the work they do and the training they receive. As of 1989, eight SDV classes a year were being conducted, with at least one class having twenty-four students. Classes run for twelve weeks and the curriculum is a difficult one. Besides the obvious training in piloting an SDV effectively—no small task in itself—special attack and rendezvous methods are taught and practiced constantly. Further technical training includes the electrical and mechanical information and skills needed to maintain the SDVs in proper operating condition. Courses include ballast training, special sonar and communications gear, both operation and maintenance, and the use of specialized breathing equipment and advanced underwater navigation techniques.

The need for all the maintenance training is made clear with the realization that the SDV teams perform all their own servicing of these highly complex and classified vehicles themselves except for major work done at the manufacturers' facilities. Given the classified nature of the SDVs, and the dependence of their operators on their proper functioning, no general Navy mechanics are allowed near them. Most people outside of the SEALs are unaware even of the existence of the SDVs.

New models of underwater breathing apparatus (UBA) are taught to the SDV students. The computerized Mark XV mixed-gas rebreather is almost exclusively used by the SDVs over the regular SEALs' LAR-V Drager UBA systems. The Mark XV is antimagnetic and using it helps minimize the SDVs' sonar and magnetic signature, making the vehicle harder to detect. A full-face mask is used with the Mark XV aboard the SDV with a special microphone, earphone, and necessary electronics to allow the members of the crew to speak freely to each other. At present, the voice communications system aboard the SDV only allows the crew members to speak to each other, and the passengers. Surface personnel are able to speak directly to the crew. Though breathing mixture, referred to as "boat air," is available to the crew and passengers, personal UBAs are always worn in case of an emergency or need to exit the SDV.

Long before a student is put into the water with an SDV, hours must be spent studying their inner and outer workings, layout, and characteristics. Even after study the student must spend time in an SDV simulator that allows him to practice maneuvers in a safe environment before entering open water. The instructor is able to directly communicate with and coach a student while he is in the simulator. When the student finally enters the water with an SDV, strict safety procedures are followed at all times.

Since it is very hard to track an SDV when it is underwater, even when you know where it is supposed to be, a large red surface float is attached to the vehicle so that its location is easily detected. The safety boat, always used during training dives, follows the students and their SDV. The safety boats currently being used are twenty-two-foot utility boats built by Boston Whaler to the Navy's specifications. The safety boat is driven by twin 140-HP outboard motors and is quickly able to reach an SDV in case of an emergency.

Primary open water training by the SDV school is conducted in the enclosed waters of San Diego Bay, avoiding the difficulties that could arise in the open sea. Because there is a great deal of civilian and military boat traffic moving in the bay, a second boat, usually another twenty-two-foot utility boat, acts as a blocking boat, intercepting any craft that might stray into the training area. Even with all the precautions taken there are still dangers in simply training with the SDVs. When there are large craft moving near the training areas it is conceivable that an SDV could be struck by a ship or moving propeller, or even sucked up against an operating seawater induction system.

To prevent students from traveling outside the cleared training area, a simple signal device has been developed. A military M-80 firecracker is waterproofed and attached by the fuse to an M60 fuse igniter so that a simple pull on a ring will ignite the delay fuse and the signal can be tossed into the water. The sharp bang of the firecracker can be heard clearly for long distances underwater and is the signal for the SDV to immediately surface and contact the safety boat.

On board the safety boat is the Safety Observer, a coxswain, the Diving Supervisor, Diving Medical Technician (DMT) Corpsman, and a fully suited standby diver. This whole assembly is an impressive sight to drivers on the San Diego-Coronado Bay Bridge, who can look down and see them moving through the water.

After the students graduate from SDV school they are assigned to one of the SDV teams, where they will receive advanced training during their probationary period. The students will have already received their basic parachute training at the Army school at Fort Bragg even before they entered the SDV school, but refresher courses in weapons, tactics, and more sophisticated applications of the SDV await them at their prospective Teams.

Each SDVT is planned to eventually have at least five operational platoons and one or two specialized DDS platoons. Since the DDS system is still so highly classified no real information is available on the training its operators will receive.

After the buildup of the SEALs is completed in the early 1990s, the size and number of classes running through the SDV school will be cut back. Training given in the Coronado area will be expanded, with the SEALs intending to open their own parachute qualification school, among other projects.

Construction Projects

Besides the large number of students being trained for the SDVTs, a number of construction projects are also scheduled to aid the SDVTs and the SEALs in completing their missions. Some of the projects and start dates include the following:

P-145 NAB Coronado SDV ONE Facility
Cost: $2,100,000, Project Date: 1988

This project is to provide a waterfront operations and maintenance facility to support the mission of SDV Team One. The facility will provide pre/postoperational training and checkout of SDVs, SDV launch capabilities, and special warfare, advanced (SWA) operations and maintenance. The construction will be a masonry-walled two-story building on concrete slab with large bay doors, security lighting, and utilities.

P-374 NAB Little Creek SEAL Team Operations Facility
Cost: $5,100,000, Project Date: 1988

Approved Manning Level increases for SEAL Teams 2 and 4 and SEAL Delivery Vehicle Team Two require that additional facilities be provided to sustain training and operation increases. This project provides for the construction of facilities to accommodate the expanded functions of SEAL Teams 2 and 4 and SDV Team Two. The construction will be a one- or two-story, permanent building of masonry construction, pile foundation, concrete floor, steel-roof framing and deck with a built-up roof, utilities, fire-protection system, parking and paved work areas, with security alarms and fencing.

P-378 NS Pearl Harbor SEAL Training/Support Building
Cost: $3,240,000, Project Date: 1987

Naval Special Warfare Group One at Pearl Harbor will

receive two Dry Deck Shelters (DDS) and three SEAL Delivery Vehicles (SDVs) beginning in 1985. Since the DDSs are classified vehicles, special secure spaces are required for the vehicles, for the personnel who will perform maintenance and training, and for the support equipment, including cradles, training devices, lifting and handling devices, and trailer vans with equipment used for deployment. The construction will be a steel-framed building, masonry walls, concrete floor and pile foundation, bridge crane and hoist assembly, fire-protection system, air conditioning, mechanical ventilation, and utilities.

P-422 NS Roosevelt Roads (Puerto Rico) SEAL Team 4 Facility
Cost: $790,000, Project Date: 1987

This project will provide an SDV support building, which includes storage and premission preparation areas for the Mark 32 Standoff Weapons Assembly Trainer. This project will support introduction of the initial operational capability of this weapons system in the Caribbean operational area and will support training for worldwide operations. Included as add-on to this project are the existing Butler buildings (#787,#792, and #29), which require structural repairs and general upgrade in order to meet electrical and safety standards. These buildings are required for vehicle/equipment maintenance and storage, diving locker and storage area, and combat craft repair shop, and will support requirements of continuously deployed SEAL and SDV teams.

The result of all this construction and buildup of personnel is to give the SDVTs far greater capabilities for operations and for meeting the quick-changing conditions of the future than they have today. Though the SDV teams are the newest members of the SEAL family and have not yet seen combat, at least no action that is unclassified, they have a rich tradition from other units that demonstrates their possibilities. The Italians used the first SDVs to sink the Austrian dreadnought *Viribus Unitus* in World War I. During World War II other Italian SDV units effectively paralyzed the British navy in the Mediterranean, sinking the battleships H.M.S. *Valiant* and H.M.S. *Queen Elizabeth* among others. Also in World War II, the British used their midget submarines and combat swimmers to severely damage the German battleship *Tirpitz* and to sink the Japanese cruiser H.I.J.M.S. *Takao*. Today the Swedish government has been able to report the many incursions into their restricted waters by Soviet naval *Spetsnaz* in their own SDVs.

Today's SEALs and SDV teams are many times more competent than those early SDV users and are at least as formidable as their "opposite numbers" in foreign navies.

Behind Enemy Lines*

The Life of a "True Warrior"

Lured by surf, sand and the stunning Pacific sunset, throngs of tourists flock to the Silver Strand of Coronado in San Diego, California, vacationing in leisure and comfort at the massive, red-roofed Hotel del Coronado.

Occasionally, the view from the hotel's stacks of white Victorian balconies is interrupted by a small offshore swarm of what appear to be seven-legged black water bugs with orange polka dots. As the "bugs" fan out and draw nearer to the cluster of rocks at the surf's edge, illusion transforms into reality.

The legs become paddles and the polka dots become kapok life preservers strapped around the occupants of a black inflatable raft.

These men are drawn to the beaches of Coronado by a different lure, pursuing a life far from leisurely and comfortable. They are training to become members of one of the most demanding special warfare units in the world—U.S. Navy SEALs.

*Reprinted from US Naval Publication, *All Hands*, December 1987.

A mile down the Strand from the landmark hotel lies the newly dedicated Phil H. Bucklew Center for Naval Special Warfare. The center houses basic and advanced SEAL schools and is home to the Navy's top special warfare planners. The largest division within the center is dedicated to Basic Underwater Demolition/SEAL training.

Every six weeks, a BUD/S class starts its first phase of the three-part school. Most of the students will not graduate. "Anything less than excellence is unacceptable," said the center's executive officer, Commander Bob Nelson. "Consequently, only the strongest survive the rigors of training."

BUD/S students are forced to expand their physical and mental limits while raising their self-confidence and learning teamwork. The center's motto: "The only easy day was yesterday."

According to Nelson, the commitment necessary to complete the BUD/S program requires all the desire, ingenuity, dedication and integrity an individual can muster.

With those ideals in mind, the center honored retired Navy Capt. Phil H. Bucklew, who served with distinction as a special warfare officer in three wars. His achievements, spanning 40 years of active and reserve service, have inspired "wanna-be" BUD/S students and seasoned tacticians alike.

At the dedication of the Bucklew Center for Naval Special Warfare, the 72-year-old Bucklew was described as a "legendary" naval officer by Commanding Officer Capt. Larry Bailey, (Co from 1985 to 1988). And, according to Vice Adm. Joseph Metcalf, III, Assistant Chief of Naval Operations for Surface Warfare, Capt. Bucklew is a "true warrior" symbolizing the dedication of today's Navy SEALs.

At the ceremony, a bronze plaque, which will become a permanent monument at the special warfare school, was unveiled honoring Bucklew. Inscribed on the plaque is the following:

DEDICATED IN HONOR OF CAPTAIN
PHIL H. BUCKLEW FOR HIS HEROIC AND
LASTING CONTRIBUTIONS TO THE INCEPTION
AND PERMANENCE OF NAVAL SPECIAL WARFARE.

THIS CENTER OF EXCELLENCE IS A
LASTING MONUMENT TO HIS COURAGE,
FORESIGHT AND LEADERSHIP.

With his wife, Helen, at his side, Bucklew, now confined to a wheelchair, expressed his appreciation for the dedication: "I'm very proud of the honor extended to me." In referring to Metcalf and Bailey and all the SEAL/UDT personnel at the school, Bucklew added, "These guys always keep me up to date on what's happening in the special warfare teams. I love 'em all."

Adventure and high drama are the main ingredients that made up Capt. Bucklew's life, always spiced with a pinch of the unconventional. He was born in Columbus, Ohio, on Dec. 19, 1914. While still a student attending North High School in Columbus, he joined the Naval Reserve at the age of 14. Graduating from high school in 1932, Bucklew went on to attend Xavier University in Cincinnati, Ohio.

While at Xavier, Bucklew excelled as a football player. His prowess on the gridiron was such, that after graduating from college in 1936, he turned pro, playing for the old Cleveland Rams. Bucklew would later go on to coach the Columbus Bulls of the American Football League and would be named in 1961 to Sports Illustrated's Silver Anniversary All-American Team.

Shortly after the Japanese attacked Pearl Harbor, Bucklew cut short his coaching career with the Bulls and reported for active duty as a Chief Boatswain's Mate. In 1943 he received his commission as an Ensign.

Serving in both Europe and the Pacific, Bucklew was an original member of the U.S. Navy Scouts and Raiders for Special Operations, the forerunners of today's SEALs. It was the mission of the Scouts and Raiders to act as guides for Army assault troops prior to invasion landings by scouting, locating and maintaining a position at a designated beach, hours before a landing.

While with the Raiders, Bucklew collected intelligence, conducted beach reconnaissance and helped plan the invasions of North Africa, Sicily, Italy and Normandy.

During the invasion of Sicily, code-named Operation Husky, in July 1943, Ensign Bucklew was awarded his first Navy Cross for his part in the landing. The mission called for a night reconnaissance of the beach from a submarine-launched kayak. He had to locate the designated beaches for each wave of landing boats and guide them in. In spearheading the invasion, Bucklew met withering machine gun fire from the enemy as he moved in under the glare of searchlights. Disregarding the hail of bullets that repeatedly slammed into his scout boat, Bucklew and his men made it ashore and guided the invading waves of assault craft to their designated beaches.

In the invasion of Italy in September 1943, Bucklew and his men were again the first on the beach, this time at Salerno, to guide in General Mark Clark's 36th Infantry Division, of the U.S. Fifth Army. During this invasion, Bucklew and his men were forced to maintain an exposed position in a hail of enemy lead while directing the landing craft in.

For his role at Salerno, Lt. J.G. Bucklew was awarded the Silver Star. His citation read in part, "by his brilliant leadership and thorough training of scout boat gun crews prior to the invasion, Lieutenant, Junior Grade, Bucklew contributed materially to the high combat efficiency of our forces during the successful assault in this vital war area."

Bucklew was also on the Normandy beaches six months before the invasion of June 6, 1944. Operating at night and often under the noses of German guards, his mission was to scout the beaches and gather sand samples. The buckets of sand collected were sent back to England to be tested and analyzed to determine if the beach could support heavy vehicles, an important factor in the invasion planning.

During the actual Allied invasion on D-Day, Bucklew was a scout boat officer, embarked on one of the first craft to approach the heavily defended coast. Again, it was his job to locate the assigned beaches for the waves of assault boats and guide them in. This perilous mission was carried out in a rough surf under continuous enemy gunfire.

After leading in the first wave of tanks to the beach, he fired his boat's rockets over the tanks at enemy targets in support of the landings and also directed his guns at German machine-gun nests in houses along the beach. As subsequent waves of landing craft came in to hit the beach, Bucklew and his men continued to cover the assault troops against heavy enemy fire. At the same time, they rescued wounded soldiers from burning landing craft and directed the flow of traffic to the beachhead. A gold star in lieu of a second Navy Cross was awarded to Bucklew as a testimony of his courage that day on the beaches of Normandy.

In 1945, a second gold star in lieu of a third Navy Cross was recommended for Bucklew in recognition of his heroism during a three-day recon behind Japanese lines in China. Disguised as a Chinese peasant, he set out to make an amphibious reconnaissance in the vicinity of Japanese-held Kitchioh Wan on the southeast coast.

Playing the role of one of the local rustics required that Bucklew walk with a stoop in an attempt to conceal his six-foot, two-inch frame, which would be a dead giveaway in a land occupied by considerably smaller people. Because of this feigned physical characteristic, Bucklew would later be referred to by his comrades as "Big Stoop." The exploits of Bucklew behind enemy lines would become the basis of the "Big Stoop" character in the popular syndicated comic strip of that time, "Terry and the Pirates."

Traveling through extremely rugged country and under constant danger of capture or ambush, Lt. Cmdr. Bucklew skillfully penetrated the Japanese lines about 35 miles from Kitchioh Wan to bring information needed by General MacArthur.

Once during this scouting adventure Bucklew found himself surrounded by Japanese as he lay hidden in a haystack. Twelve Chinese guerrillas who were traveling with Bucklew and protecting him sat in a circle around the stack with their arms folded, Lugers hidden under their arms, as a Japanese patrol scoured the area looking for the lone American.

Capt. Bucklew left active duty in 1946 to coach football at his alma mater, Xavier University. A year later, in 1947, he returned to active duty as NROTC instructor and football coach at Columbia University, in New York City. While at Columbia, Bucklew also found time in his busy schedule to earn his Ph.D.

In 1951, Bucklew became the first commanding officer of Beach Jumper Unit II.

Bucklew remained as C.O. of Beach Jumper Unit II until 1956 when he was reassigned to Commander, Naval Forces Far East, in Yokosuka, Japan, as Officer-in-Charge of Korean Special Operations. He remained at this post until 1958, when he was ordered to Coronado, Calif., to take over the reins as commanding officer of the Amphibious Intelligence School.

Following his duties at the intelligence school, Bucklew served as Intelligence Officer for Amphibious Group I, also located at Coronado, and then in 1963 he broke new ground by becoming the first commanding officer of the Naval Operations Support Group in Coronado. This group was consolidated under one headquarters and included Underwater Demolition Teams 11 and 12, Beach Jumper Unit One, SEAL Team One and Boat Support Unit One.

It was during this tour, in 1964, that Bucklew led a study team tasked with investigating communist infiltration and guerrilla activities in South Vietnam. The information for the study was gathered first hand as the team traveled throughout the Republic of South Vietnam, especially in the Mekong Delta region.

With all the information in, Bucklew compiled what came to be known as the Bucklew Report, an important narrative that laid the groundwork for early U.S. action in assisting the Republic of Vietnam.

Bucklew's last assignment began in 1966 when he went to work at the Pentagon in the Special Warfare and Special Operations Division. His active military duties ended there in 1969 upon his retirement. And, until a recent illness

limited his activities, he worked in the civilian community
as a consultant on small-craft design and sales in Washington, D.C.

During his distinguished military career, Bucklew has
been awarded several of the highest military awards. These
include the Navy Cross with a gold star in lieu of a second
award, the Legion of Merit, Silver Star and Joint Service
Medal, the Croix De Guerre with Palm (France), the Ulchi
Medal (Korea), commendations from the Republic of China
and Great Britain, and the Navy League Meritorious Citation, which is the highest Navy League award that can be
made to uniformed men or women of the Department of
Defense.

At the dedication in San Diego, retired Capt. Del Giudice,
who commanded the first SEAL team at Coronado in 1962
and is now a defense consultant in Washington, D.C., said,
"SEALs perform well under duress, but Bucklew was a cut
above that. He was not a 'shouter' or 'screamer' like some
of the officers I've known." And in a statement that may
well summarize Bucklew as a man and officer, Del Giudice
added that Capt. Bucklew "was calm in the field or here
at the center and one of the truly great leaders."

Training

Train verb; 1: to form by instruction, discipline, or drill. 2: to teach so as to make fit, qualified, or proficient.

Long, hard hours spent training. Train to learn a skill, train more to master that skill, and then train even further to master that skill and make it a part of you before moving on to another skill, even more advanced. This is the basic credo of the SEALs and one each individual SEAL follows throughout his career in Special Warfare. Everything about what the SEALs are and what they are able to accomplish is directly attributable to their training, and BUD/S is where that training begins.

BUD/S, Basic Underwater Demolition/SEAL, Navy training course A-431-0024, is the proper name for what is considered by many military experts to be the most difficult and demanding course offered anywhere in the U.S. military. BUD/S is the heart and soul of what a SEAL is and is the most obvious binding factor among SEALs visible to the outside observer. A common identifier used by both past and present SEALs or UDT men, outside of their team number, is their BUD/S class number. The statement ''I was in class XX or XXX'' immediately identifies the individual as a member of a very small fraternity of elite fighting men, graduates of BUD/S.

The physical appearance of the BUD/S training center is rather plain and unprepossessing. A medium-sized cluster of gray concrete buildings, just across Highway 75 from the Naval Amphibious Base and south of the well-to-do town of Coronado, make up the primary offices and facilities of the BUD/S school. To the immediate south of the school's buildings stands the obstacle course made up of log structures that simply look puzzling to the passersby on Highway 75 but are soon very familiar to the trainees at BUD/S. Extending far to the south of the training center is a long stretch of sandy beach constantly pounded by the surf of the Pacific Ocean. Though Coronado is known for having a mild climate, given its location in sunny Southern California, the Pacific waters running along the beaches are kept cold by the California current running close offshore. The surf crashing onto the shores of the training base stay at an average temperature of 55°F throughout the year.

The Naval Special Warfare Training Detachment that runs BUD/S is based out of the Phil H. Bucklew Center for Naval Special Warfare, which is the primary building around which the rest of the training area is centered. Kept in the Quarterdeck, the main hall by which visitors enter the complex, is a collection of photographs of all of the classes that have graduated BUD/S at Coronado. Along with the photos are mementos that each class has given to the school since the early 1960s. One of these mementos, from Class 70, is a large wooden plaque hanging over the door leading to the training area. The plaque has two carved wooden seals, one standing and one diving, with the inscription above them: ''The more you sweat in peace, the less you bleed in war.'' The importance of that simple inscription stays with you as you pass into the training area.

Going through the doors takes you into the central courtyard of the complex. Other mementos of earlier classes bracket the doors on either side. On one side is a full-sized statue of the Creature from the Black Lagoon. The Creature has a large sign on his chest inscribed: "So you wanna be a frogman?" The statue is courtesy of a SEAL class in 1963. On the opposite side of the door is a more recent acquisition, a "Wheel of Misfortune." The wheel, from Class 154, is spun to give interesting "awards" such as "Wet and Sandy," "The Zone," a rather mundane "120 Push-ups," an ominous "Mouthful of———," and the smallest section of the wheel: "Easy Day."

These objects, along with a large blue sign stating "The only easy day was yesterday," from Class 89, all face the center courtyard, known affectionately as "The Grinder."

The Grinder is a large square expanse of asphalt where normal daily calisthenics are performed. At one end of the area stands a raised platform where the instructor leading the class would stand. On the front of the platform are the symbols for both the UDTs and the SEALs. Facing the platform are 143 sets of white "footprints" in the shape of swim fins painted on the concrete in a staggered pattern. In is on these prints that the would-be SEAL trainees start developing the strength and stamina they will need to complete BUD/S.

Standing at the far corner of the Grinder, secured to a post, is the brass quitting bell. Ringing this bell is the fastest way to quit BUD/S and is an admission that you can't take any more. Lying along the ground next to the bell is a line of helmets from the most recent trainees who have quit, mute testimony to the level of difficulty and the demands made at BUD/S. The walk to that bell is the longest walk some men have ever taken.

Overlooking the entire complex is the dive tower. Easily the tallest building at the school, the dive tower is a very unusual and ominous structure. Consisting of a square building sitting atop a thick steel cylinder, the dive tower contains a fifty-foot deep tank of water. In this tank trainees will learn free ascent and submarine lock-out techniques in a safe, controlled environment.

Looking to the west of the tower are the beach and the Pacific Ocean, just a hundred yards away. Near the beach is a rack holding more than a dozen of the soon-to-be-hated rubber boats known as IBSs. On the beach near the boat rack is a fifty-foot-tall stand holding six climbing ropes ready to help new trainees build their upper body strength.

To the south of the entire complex is the collection of constructions known as the obstacle course. Over the twenty-six weeks of BUD/S, trainees will become intimately familiar with the course and its carefully designed obstacles. The obstacles have a variety of colorful names such as the Balance Logs, Cargo Net, Barb Wire Belly, and the Dirty Name. Past the obstacle course are bleachers for outdoor classes and a seemingly harmless pile of loose telephone poles. Beyond this stretch miles of sandy beaches broken occasionally by patches of rough rock, perfect for the distance runs BUD/S instructors are so fond of.

What is most memorable about BUD/S is not its interesting layout but rather what happens to each trainee. As Commander Larry Simmons, Executive Officer of the center, put it: "This course stretches each individual's personal 'rubber band' right to the limit and then eases off. Then does it again, and again. This course does that [stretching] both physically and mentally." CDR Simmons went through BUD/S Class 38 in 1966 and has dedicated part of his twenty-four years in Navy Special Warfare to improving the quality of the training at BUD/S.

Teamwork is *the* main lesson taught at BUD/S. While at the school students learn that a seemingly impossible goal can be reached through the common focusing of effort by a highly trained, confident group. Individual achievement is stressed at BUD/S but only to the point that each student is always putting forward his maximum effort. The phrase "It pays to be a winner" is often used at BUD/S, but winning can be accomplished only as part of a team.

Though the level of physical exertion at BUD/S is staggering it is a student's mental attitude and personal resolve that are most tested. Without "fire in the gut" an individual will not make it through the trials of First Phase. As one instructor put it: "They [the public] say that BUD/S is 90 percent physical and 10 percent mental and I say that it's the other way around. If you have the motivation and the drive you can overcome anything. And if you did not bring that with you, then you'll never get through this training."

Quoting CDR Simmons again: "Any one day [of training] most people could do. But when it's twenty-six weeks long and it's so simple to quit, you just ring the bell and it's over, not many people can stay the course. But if he does stay the course, he's the kind of individual that will also stay the course on some of the most difficult missions our nation might send us on."

Fourth Phase

Fourth phase is a new idea being implemented by the Navy to help decrease the number of dropouts from BUD/ S due to injuries or inadequate preparation. With the ongoing increase in the number of active SEALs, as well as a constant view toward fiscal economy—it costs about $80,000 to put a man through BUD/S—a way is needed to raise the number of class graduates while still keeping the necessary high SEAL standards intact. The addition of a fourth phase to the training schedule seems to be helping in solving the graduation problem.

Fourth phase, which lasts four to seven weeks, has replaced the former two-week indoctrination period before training starts. When men arrive at Coronado to begin training there is a certain amount of slack time as men come in from different areas. In fourth phase these men are given a thorough introduction to the specific types of activities they will be expected to perform once they begin BUD/S training in earnest. The nature of each exercise performed during calisthenics is taught and the men are given the opportunity to break in new footwear for running. Running is the most common exercise done while at BUD/S, with the majority of it being done in loose beach sand.

At BUD/S, running is considered one of the best ways to build up leg strength and endurance, as well as a way to force a man to "reach way down inside himself and keep going." The drawback with the amount of running done at training was the number of medical rollbacks and dropouts due to injuries, especially stress-related fractures. Though the trainee had to pass a distance/time running test to be accepted for BUD/S, many of the men, especially those just coming off a long ship cruise, were not adequately acclimated for distance running before arriving at Coronado. Fourth phase allows the trainees to be given that very important third week of rest, no running, after an initial two-week period of distance running. The "rest" period allows the bones of the lower limbs to become adapted to the level of stress that they will be exposed to. The adaptation has been found to greatly cut down on the number of stress fractures and subsequent medical rollbacks.

The "rest" time is a misnomer, since all of the prospective SEALs are kept constantly busy. Exposure to the obstacle course allow the trainees to learn how they must pass through, over, around, and under the twenty-one obstacles to complete the course and the times for completion they will be expected to meet. Swimming is also a primary component of BUD/S, and during fourth phase they will learn the strokes they will use during training. The basic sidestroke, breaststroke, and crawl are backed up by innumerable flutter kicks and flotation board swims to help build up the leg muscles.

At the end of the fourth phase, the students are much better prepared for the beginning of their actual BUD/S training. Those men who needed to "lose a few pounds" have been given the chance to do so. Particular individual weaknesses at certain activities have been discovered and the trainee strengthened at those points. The time spent in fourth phase also allows new testing procedures to be tried out, identifying those individuals who are most likely to not pass BUD/S. The weaknesses of these individuals can be analyzed and new requirements to qualify for BUD/S can be added. Now, with the proper number of men available, the group "classes-up" and begins BUD/S.

A new BUD/S class completes fourth phase and classes-up every seven weeks. About 5 percent of the original class that starts training together will graduate at the same time. Much of any given graduating class is made up of rollbacks out of earlier classes. Rollbacks are students who, for one reason or another, were unable to complete BUD/S with their original group. Those students whom the instructors feel are worthwhile are started back in training with a class at the same point they were in when they rolled back. Students who are rolled back before completing Hell Week start at the beginning of a training cycle.

It is easy to see where students stand in training. Those trainees who are pre-Hell Week (normally the fifth week of training) wear white T-shirts. After successfully completing Hell Week, the students wear green T-shirts for the remainder of their training.

Colored helmet liners are worn by students who have classed-up and begun training. Green helmet liners indicate first phase trainees, red liners are worn by second phase students, and blue liners are worn by third phase students. Each liner also has the student's name and class number stenciled on it in white paint.

On the average, there are four classes in different phases of BUD/S training at any one time, including fourth phase. At the time of this writing, eight classes are being run a year, each class being twenty-six weeks long.

FIRST PHASE

First phase is a seven-week basic conditioning program in which students learn basic skills while undergoing a strenuous program of running, swimming, calisthenics, and drills. The fourth week of first phase is the infamous Hell Week, where students will be pushed beyond what they consider their physical and mental limits. Those who complete Hell Week will continue with an additional three weeks of training in hydrographic reconnaissance, beach surveying, and underwater mapping.

Lessons or tasks—whether physical or mental—are referred to as "evolutions," which each student must pass to successfully complete BUD/S.

The physical evolutions are the most numerous during first phase, and include weekly four-mile timed runs, swimming of up to two miles, and timed runs of the obstacle course. The required minimum times to complete certain evolutions in order to pass first phase are as follows:

PHYSICAL EVOLUTION	REQUIRED TIME
1/2 mile pool swim without fins	30 min
3/4 mile pool swim without fins	45 min
1 mile pool swim without fins	60 min
1 mile bay swim without fins	70 min
1 mile pool swim with fins	50 min
1 mile bay swim with fins	50 min
1 1/2 mile ocean swim with fins	75 min
2 mile ocean swim with fins	95 min
obstacle course	15 min
2-mile timed run	16 min
4-mile timed run	32 min

Besides the physical evolutions, academic standards also are high. Each student must pass all of his written tests at 70 percent and above for enlisted men and at 80 percent and above for officers. Tutoring in some subjects are given to students in need of help to pass academic standards after Hell Week is completed.

A steadily increasing regimen of exercise gives each student the maximum chance to pass all evolutions. Running is, of course, the prime building agent for budding SEALs, with the trainees moving everywhere in the training area at the double-time during first phase. All the running quickly adds up with the students normally covering up to 30 miles perweek.

Swimming training starts early during first phase. Students spend much of their early morning time in the NAB pool across the road.

The pool is the Mike Collins Swimming Memorial. Lieutenant Collins was a member of SEAL Team One who was killed in action in South Vietnam in March of 1971. Collins had been the captain of the Naval Academy swim team and an All-American swimmer.

The pool itself is a large one measuring 50 meters long by 22.9 meters (25 yards) wide. New techniques are first taught to the trainees in the protected environment of the pool. While in the pool, it is easier to concentrate on the task at hand, and the instructors are able to better ensure the safety of the students.

Besides simple swimming, drown-proofing also is taught to the trainees. Among the drown-proofing exercises is one in which students must swim the length of the pool with their arms and legs tied, "dolphin-style." Other exercises include retrieving objects such as a face mask from the bottom of the pool—a depth of nine feet—legs and arms tied behind the student's back. Good teeth are also a prerequisite at BUD/S.

One of the first major evolutions for trainees is to swim the width of the pool underwater. This type of evolution is considered a "confidence builder" by first phase instructors.

"Once they do that, their confidence starts building. If we can get them to do a 50-yard swim (underwater)—and in most cases we can—their confidence is way up again," said one BUD/S instructor.

Building the trainees' confidence is important to help minimize the number of unnecessary dropouts. It is relatively easy to simply break a man with the amount of physical activity and miserable conditions trainees face at BUD/S. The instructors prefer to convince the men that they are able to complete the training with the proper attitude and "intestinal fortitude."

Fortitude is what's needed when standing in line at 0530 in the morning, waiting your turn to continue swimming laps in a pool. A cold fog, along with a chilling onshore breeze from the Pacific, combine with the darkness to make the situation thoroughly miserable for a wet trainee shivering at poolside in trunks and swim fins. The same situation applies in Southern California in July during a hot spell.

Besides running, swimming, calisthenics, and classroom work, instructors always find time to introduce their trainees to unique traditions found at BUD/S. Though sounding very strange at first, students quickly learn to follow instructions immediately and perform whatever task required. Trainees are ordered, while in the wet conditions after a dip in the nearby Pacific, to roll along the dry portion of the sandy beach before performing other actions. Rolling in the sand quickly coats the wet trainee with a fine layer of abrasive, irritating sand, creating the "sugar cookie" effect. Later, the trainees will find that this exercise has hardened them so that they can operate effectively while possibly crawling along an enemy-held beach.

Another traditional exercise is one where the trainees—usually individual boat crews—sit in a circle, with their backs to the center and throw fistfulls of sand into the air over their heads while shouting "I'm a volcano." Although it may look very peculiar to the outside observer, this exercise shows the trainees that they can still see in an environment filled with flying sand, such as that found on a beach while under fire.

As the difficulty of evolutions and exercises increases, so do the levels of physical performance by the students. Often individuals find themselves completing tasks of strength and endurance they did not consider possible earlier, and these accomplishments soon become commonplace.

The amount of activity is so great and demands are so high as to make BUD/S seem almost punitive. Treatment during punishment in the regular Navy is nowhere near as harsh as some of the training SEAL candidates receive. Historically, the drop-out rate is 60 percent of a class with one class, number 78, having disappeared entirely during Hell Week.

In earlier classes students are constantly reminded that they are volunteers and can quit at any time. Simply removing your helmet in earlier training cycles or ringing a brass bell three times during the first phase, signals an individual's resignation from BUD/S.

Instructors actively encourage men to quit and constantly deride students in earlier training cycles. However these actions have ended in today's BUD/S training. The training is no less severe and demanding, but the instructors have more of a positive "can-do" attitude. This attitude is instilled in the instructor's students along with constant reinforcement of the need for cooperation and teamwork.

Teamwork is the basic tenet taught at BUD/S and the most active element in SEAL philosophy. Though tremendous effort may be required from an individual at any time, it is the actions of a closely-knit team that are the strength of the SEALs. It is this strength that has given the SEALs and earlier UDTs the ability to accomplish the mission in the face of almost impossible conditions.

Close cooperation is taught early at BUD/S through such actions as log and Inflatable Boat Small (IBS) drills. The ability to do sit-ups is a requirement to enter BUD/S. Doing sit-ups while along side six of your fellow trainees with a two- to three-hundred pound log lying across your collective chests is a very new experience. Without equal concentrated effort on the part of all seven men simultaneously, the drill is impossible; but as a team with teamwork it is merely very difficult.

The Physical Training Log, as it is properly called, is the length of thick telephone pole weighing at least several hundred pounds. Considered just the thing for instilling the need for teamwork on the part of the trainees, log PT has a variety of exercises besides sit-ups.

Push-ups can be done with the toes of the trainees feet on top of the log to increase the amount of strength needed to raise the upper body. Other exercises include bench presses with the trainees lying down as in the sit-up position, but they must push the log up off themselves and hold it there with their arms. Press-ups are a particularly grueling exercise as the men must push the log up over their heads from the standing position. Taller men have a hard time, as they must keep their arms slightly bent so that the shorter men can also press with the team.

Log races are run over long distances of up to 14 miles with boat crews carrying the log on their shoulders. Other races include one where the trainees race over the sand dunes carrying the log on their shoulders, drop the log into the surf, flop down into the surf themselves, get up and race back across the beach with the wet log. After this the men get to raise the log end over end, covering a distance of 100 yards, and then drag the log back to the start between their legs.

Exercises with the log build strength and teamwork, both of which are needed for boat drills. Early in training the class was broken down into boat crews, usually seven-man teams, and issued a complete IBS. The IBS, Inflatable Boat Small, is designed to carry seven men along with 1,000 pounds of equipment. Issued with an emergency repair kit, large air pump, paddles, sea anchor, manual, CO_2 cylinder, and ropes, the IBS weighs 289 pounds, is 12 feet long, and 6 feet wide.

The boat crew will carry the IBS everywhere with them, always keeping it inflated and in good condition. Any crew that allows their boat to become damaged or deflated— something the instructors are always looking to do—will be punished strongly. A single man from the boat crew always guards his crew's boat while the others are at chow. The first member of the crew to finish eating immediately goes out and relieves the guard so that he can eat.

Boat drill consists of a variety of exercises besides using the boat in the water. The IBS can be carried at a run of course resting on the heads of the boat crew. Occasionally instructors will consider a crew's boat too light and climb aboard. Carrying these boats overhead is no small feat, especially when it contains one large, "healthy"—read that "heavy"—instructor who does anything except lay quiety in the boat.

Besides the log drills, boat drills, and physical training, the trainees have other activities to help fill their days. Running, swimming, and calisthenics take up a great deal of the time, but classroom lessons are also given.

Subjects taught in First Phase include basic first aid, lifesaving, and hydrographic reconnaissance techniques.

Twelve-hour days are easily the norm during the first few weeks of first phase. Students are well-fed with a studied diet and kept under constant medical supervision. Corpsmen are always on the alert to catch injuries before they become severe enough to roll a student back to another class.

All of this training is given in the early portion of first phase to help prepare a student for his greatest trial while at BUD/S—Hell Week.

Officially referred to as "Motivation Week," Hell Week traces its lineage back to the early part of World War II and the original Navy Combat Demolition units, Navy/Marine Scouts, and Raiders.

The philosophy behind Hell Week has been proven sound by years of testing in combat of the graduates from BUD/S. From the islands of the Pacific and the sweltering swamps of Vietnam to the frozen shores of Korea, many SEALs and UDT men have stated that it was the accomplishment of passing Hell Week that made all other obstacles seem small in comparison.

Hell Week is where the primary idea behind SEAL training—that a man is capable of ten times the effort he thinks he is—is proven. The long hours of physical exertion, lack of sleep, and overwhelming obstacles and noise come as close as possible to simulating the worst of a combat environment and its effects during peacetime.

The level of stress and cold of the training—especially during Hell Week—eliminates those volunteers unable to surpass them. This prevents those same individuals from being put into combat situations where they would have to fight in a location where the environment is more hostile than the enemy.

Hell Week

Trainees are told that Hell Week will begin on Monday morning and last six days. As far as the instructors are concerned, Monday morning starts at one minute past midnight, and this is when the trainees are awakened. This is also where the "real" SEAL training begins. Scheduled classes are referred to as being pre-or post-Hell Week. Hell Week is the time when a class's size will change the fastest.

During the week, trainees are accompanied by the brass bell normally kept at the Grinder. If he rings the bell a trainee can be clean, warm, and dry again. The desire to

quit can be great; in the past, more men have dropped out
of BUD/S than have passed the course. Only a very few
classes, numbers 114 and 147 among them, have completed
a "no-bell" Hell Week. It takes a solid group of men with
good leaders and top-notch instructors to complete Hell
Week without a single man quitting, and quitting during
Hell Week can be a tremendous temptation—that is in part
what makes passing it so very important. The level of stress
and confusion placed on a trainee is carefully calculated.
This training is the result of years of experience, but this
sophistication matters little to an exhausted man struggling
to complete one more "evolution," a task or exercise.

Some exercises seem intended to simply confuse the trainees, though they complete them as best they can. As one
trainee put it: "They kept blowing the whistle and we kept
falling down every thirty yards [during a run], covering our
ears, opening our mouths, and crossing our legs." Later,
the class learned that this was the proper position to take
to protect themselves from a nearby explosion.

Exercises such as the above are combined with small boat
drills, log PT, and other evolutions to keep the trainees
moving. "Breakout," the Monday morning wakeup call for
Hell Week, sets the pace for the upcoming week. Trainees
jerk awake at the sounds of instructors screaming commands, smoke grenades and explosive simulators going off,
and automatic weapons being fired nearby. Over all this
confusion an amplified voice is heard welcoming the men
to Hell Week.

Marathon and other distance runners talk about "the
wall," the point at which your body has used up its energy
stores (glycogen depletion) and makes you feel as if you
cannot go another step. Those same runners state that you
can pass the wall with training and the will to succeed.
During Hell Week, instructors will force every man up
against his own "wall." Those men who pass through it
will continue on to complete tasks far beyond anything a
marathon runner could even conceive of.

The lack of sleep and resulting mental confusion are what
gets to many men who attempt to pass BUD/S. Some reports

list trainees as receiving only four to six hours of sleep during the entire week. Captain Mike Jukoski, a twenty-four-year SEAL veteran who attended Class 38 in 1966, recounted some of his experiences during Hell Week in an interview with the author.

"The instructors' staff, after having been with you for six weeks, has a pretty good feel for the class," remembers Jukoski. "They act like ogres but they're really professionals now that I look back on it. What they would do is occasionally have you in an evolution and shout 'Okay, everybody get down,' like something was going to happen. And then [they] go away for like half an hour, something like a catnap."

Another personal experience related by Captain Jukoski referred to one of the many IBS drills and evolutions conducted during his Hell Week. This particular reference was to a boat race conducted in the IBS. "My boat got finished before the tide shifted," remembered Jukoski. "Normally these evolutions are planned so that you do not win but just survive them."

"The boat race was planned so that you approached the beach just as the tide shifted and you would have to paddle the hardest to finish the last distance. We happened to get through before they had planned it.

"Just because I think we had a good boat crew we just got way ahead of the schedule and got through that last obstacle before the tide changed. The next boat came in four hours later. We got to lay out for four hours. That day we made out."

All of the exercises with the boats are preparations for future operations that the trainees will conduct with them. The basic surf passage and rock portage the trainees learn in first phase will later be used by the future SEALs during beach landings in Combat Rubber Raiding Craft (CRRCs) with tactical equipment loads.

During all this training, the men help each other to pull through Hell Week. This is where the future bond between SEALs is forged. Shorter men will be seen placing a can on their heads so they can carry their share of the load when doing overhead IBS carries. Steady men will reach out and support their fellow trainees when they start to wobble from exhaustion. Cursing quietly at the instructors helps ease the mens' torment. No one passes BUD/S alone; the loner does not exist in the SEALs and could not have passed Hell Week.

Classroom training also takes place between bouts of intense physical activity. Attention must be paid to what is being taught. More than one nodding trainee has found himself moving out for a quick bracing plunge in the nearby cold Pacific waters.

Instructors are not limited in using their imaginations to devise ways to help keep individual trainees awake and attentive. One instructor tapped a nodding trainee awake to get his attention, then handed him a live smoke grenade to hold, minus the safety pin. For the remainder of the lesson, neither the trainee with the grenade, nor the other trainees around him, had trouble staying awake.

Trainees are tested on what they were instructed in during class. It does not matter if the lesson being given was on the care of a weapon or the reading of a grade school primer, future SEALs will learn to get it right the first time.

Some trainees will be able to correctly answer questions while some others will not. As the incorrect trainees drop to the deck to begin one thousand push-ups, the total for the class, the correct trainees drop alongside their fellows and begin pushing the deck. Each man's work takes off from the total for the class—SEALs work together.

All of this leads up to the last days of Hell Week and the infamous mud pits far to the south of Coronado. It is at these pits where most of the well-known mud-covered trainee photos have been taken. The trainees will spend hours in the mud, doing push-ups or performing headstands and somersaults according to the instructors' orders. Officer or enlisted man, all trainees work together.

During the last day of Hell Week, once known as "So Solly" day from World War II, the trainees will be pushed to the absolute limit. The instructors will try to duplicate the noise and confusion of an actual beach landing during wartime. While literally hundreds of pounds of explosives are detonated all around them, the trainees will crawl through the mud. Instructors will be keeping a close eye on the trainees, not only for safety's sake, but to see if any man hesitates or shows fear of the explosions.

More strange exercises will be performed in the mud. Caterpillar races will be run with the men moving backward. In the caterpillar race, all the members of a boat crew will sit in a line in each other's laps. With their arms and legs interlocked, the men will have to move as a unit through the mud. If they do not work together, the team cannot move, and the instructors are there to insist.

In the middle of all of this the trainees are fed lunch. They eat standing hip-deep in a water-and-mud-filled shell hole while explosions rain mud and slime down on them.

It is at the end of this day that the staggering, exhausted men hear one last command: "BUD/S class XXX, secure from Hell Week."

They have made it. Some men laugh, or cry, or cheer. Those who cannot move out on their own are helped by their fellow students. The next day is reserved for the cleaning of equipment and holding Field Day. There will never be anything quite the same for these men as this time. The students now wear green T-shirts; they have passed Hell Week.

The last three weeks of first phase are spent learning hydrographic survey techniques and chart sketching. The students receive practical experience in hydrographic reconnaissance where a pair of student swimmers move ashore from the water to recon a beach. The students learn to collect the critical information that is needed to conduct a successful amphibious landing.

Training Phase Two

The second phase of BUD/S concentrates on land warfare and demolition techniques. This is also the time when students will learn the different insertion and extraction techniques, both traditional and new. During the first five weeks of second phase, which is nine weeks long total, students will spend a lot of time in the classroom. Safety is constantly stressed and woe betide the student who makes a safety error. Hands-on instruction insures that a student will know exactly what is expected of him and how to accomplish his task.

The land warfare instruction is very involved. During second phase, each student will be expected to learn forty-five different skills. The skills to be learned include, but are not limited to, the following: rappelling, small unit tactics, compass (land) navigation, map reading, the essentials of basic marksmanship, combat shooting techniques, RTO procedures, use of pyrotechnics, night firing, cast and recovery techniques, demolitions, rock climbing, grenades, booby traps, patrolling, ambush techniques, military explosives, reconnaissance, sabotage, infiltration, prisoner abduction, sentry removal, first aid, survival, river and stream crossing, camouflage, intelligence collecting and reporting, prisoner and building searching, POW handling, weapons and equipment maintenance, and exfiltration.

These lessons and more are reinforced during the last four weeks of second phase. During that time the students will be on San Clemente Island for live firing and field exercises. San Clemente is a rocky chunk of land sticking up out of the Pacific about ninety miles north of San Diego. During their time on the island, the students will conduct practical exercises on all of the subjects they were instructed in at Coronado.

The weapons that students will be taught to use and maintain include the following: the M16A1 rifle and its variations, M60 and M60E3 machine guns, the 9-mm pistol, the Smith & Wesson Model 686 revolver (for basic pistol marksmanship training only), the MP5 submachine gun and its variations, the M14 rifle, and the M203 and M79 grenade launchers. Future plans include training on foreign weapons such as the AK-47 family.

As a graduation exercise from second phase, the students will conduct several large-scale exercises. A full, simulated wartime beach recon will be conducted, including a live demolition of emplaced underwater obstacles. An inland demolition raid will also be conducted where the students will be able to pit themselves against their instructors.

Physical evolutions are not forgotten during second phase. Each student will be expected to match or surpass the following times to graduate from second phase.

PHYSICAL EVOLUTION	REQUIRED TIME
Obstacle course	12 mins
4-mile timed run	31 mins
2-mile ocean swim with fins	75 mins
5½-mile ocean swim with fins	completion

Third Phase

Third phase is seven weeks long and consists of underwater training. Physical training is continued, but the completion times for evolutions become shorter. Concentration is placed on combat scuba training. Students learn first in a pool how to use the various breathing systems, and then they move out into open water (San Diego Bay).

Standard open-circuit scuba is taught to the students to give them a secure background on which to base future training. Later, the students will learn the more complicated Draeger closed-circuit breathing system. The Draeger is the most common breathing system used in the teams.

Emphasis is placed on long-distance underwater compass swims. Student pairs swim about in the bay on set courses, towing behind them a red buoy with their number on it. Instructors follow closely behind, keeping an eye on the students' safety. The goal is to make the students into competent combat divers who will be able to swim in from a launch point to their objective without exposing themselves above the water. Students are placed into swim pairs and taught to *never* leave a fellow swimmer. Safety is the primary emphasis at all times.

During the past twenty years of BUD/S training, only three students have been lost due to accidents. Two of the deaths were due to a single accident that took place in the water. One student panicked during an open-water exercise and caused the drowning death of himself and his swim buddy. The students were with Class 42 and had been free-diving without scuba at the time of the accident. Changes in procedures were implemented to prevent such an incident from happening again. The third student death occurred when a trainee succumbed to hypothermia and a heart attack during training. There is now even closer medical super-vision of trainees during the initial phases of training. New medical screening procedures were also implemented.

Besides learning scuba techniques, free buoyant ascent, and submarine lock-in/lock-out procedures, the students conduct mock attacks on nearby ships. The attacks become increasingly more difficult as time goes by, but the students have learned how to persevere and complete their assign-ments.

Last, the students have to complete their final timed phys-ical evolutions. The times seem incredibly short when com-pared to those they faced during first phase. The evolutions and their times are as follows:

PHYSICAL EVOLUTION	REQUIRED TIME
Obstacle course	10 mins
4-mile timed run	30 mins
14-mile timed run	110 mins
2-mile ocean swim with fins	70 mins

With the successful completion of their final tasks, the students graduate BUD/S. However, they are still not yet SEALs. First, all graduates attend basic parachute training, usually at the Army Airborne School at Fort Benning, Geor-gia. The time at airborne school seems almost like a vacation to recent BUD/S graduates. The airborne requirement of a three-mile run in twenty-seven minutes is easy to men used to running for miles in deep beach sand.

After Airborne School, individual students go on to a SEAL team or to SDV school before reporting to an SDV team. The students will undergo a six-month probationary period of training at their final assignments. At a SEAL team, the probationary SEALs will undergo STT (SEAL Tactical Training). During STT, new SEALs will learn the combat techniques and procedures used by the SEALs during active operations. As these are their operational techniques, the SEALs do not discuss them at any length with outsiders.

At the end of their probationary period, prospective SEALs go before a board that will judge if they have become qualified as SEALs. Those students who have successfully passed this training, begun more than a year before, will be able to wear the Naval Special Warfare insignia, the SEAL trident.

Putting it in its simplest terms, SEAL training and BUD/S are the most arduous and demanding regimens offered by any U.S. military unit. Maximum possible demands, both physical and mental, are placed on all volunteers. The end result is a supremely confident and fit individual, able to take on almost any task and, as part of a well-organized team, accomplish that task.

Commander Larry Simmons, the Executive Officer at BUD/S, put his definition of a warrior and a Navy SEAL in this way: "To be a warrior—a SEAL—is to be someone special. The spirit of the warrior is geared toward the struggle. The warrior aims to follow his instincts, to choose consciously the items that make up his world; to be exquisitely aware of everything around him, to attain total control—and then act with totally controlled abandon. He seeks—in short—to live an impeccable, exciting life.

Standing on the ramp of a MC 130 at over sixteen thousand feet is not for the weak at heart; nor is knowing that if you screw this up you are going to die. The warrior says to himself "@ *%," and just goes for it. The warrior takes calculated risks and tests himself repeatedly. He does not have a love of violence, but is at home with it. He is human—not a robot. He doesn't love war. But there is no question that he wants to be where the action is. Being a SEAL warrior is about war and peace, and preparing for the common defense. It's about being ready for the most difficult of operational environments, the sea—on it, in it, and under it; one foot in and one foot out of it."

Panama

Just before midnight on Tuesday, December 19, 1989, sleeping guests at the Marriott Hotel in the south end of Panama City were suddenly awakened by the sound of gunfire. At the nearby Paitilla Airfield, U.S. Navy SEALs were engaging Panamanian forces in the opening acts of Operation Just Cause.

Panama is a small Central American country only slightly larger than the state of West Virginia. The strategic importance of Panama has nothing to do with its size but with what it contains. The Panama Canal, built by the U.S. and opened in 1913, connects the Pacific and Atlantic oceans. By using the canal, cargo ships are able to pass directly from one ocean to another rather than taking the long trip around Cape Horn, far to the south.

General Manuel Antonio Noriega, Commander of the Panamanian Defense Forces, had been the de facto ruler of Panama since 1981. Overturning the results of a May 7, 1989, national election, Noriega, a virtual military dictator, kept a tight grip on his control of the reins of power in Panama. A major opponent to Noriega's dictatorship had been the United States government. Scheduled to turn over control of the Panama Canal to the government of Panama in 1999, the United States has a right to defend the canal from outside threats according to treaties signed in 1979.

Noriega had been under U.S. criminal indictment since February 1988 on charges of drug trafficking and money laundering. Recognizing the threat the United States posed to his dictatorship, Noriega had been staging a long campaign over the last several years to stir up anti-American feeling among the Panamanian people. The situation reached its peak on December 15, 1989, when Panama's National People's Assembly, virtually all hand-picked Noriega appointees, declared a state of war to exist between Panama and the United States. At the same meeting, the assembly named Noriega the Maximum Leader and installed him as the head of the government.

On December 16, Panamanian troops shot and killed a U.S. Marine officer who had become lost while driving with some fellow officers to a local restaurant. The shooting of Marine 1st Lieutenant Robert Paz was witnessed by another U.S. officer on the scene, this one accompanied by his wife. PDF soldiers quickly arrested the lieutenant and his wife.

Over the next several hours, the PDF men beat the lieutenant severely and brutalized his wife, slamming her head against a wall and threatening to rape her. Before midnight that same day, President Bush had received a briefing on the treatment of the Navy couple and their subsequent release. Quietly stating "Enough is enough," President Bush ordered the military to implement a planned option. The United States could no longer guarantee the safety of its 35,000 citizens living in Panama. To make matters worse, intelligence reports had been received indicating a threat to the canal itself. It was now time for the U.S. military to act.

During the Reagan administration, Operation Blue Spoon had been designed for a massive military takeover of Panama. General Colin Powell, Chairman of the Joint Chiefs of Staff, and General Thomas Kelley, Director of Operations for the JSOC used Blue Spoon as the basis for a military operations plan against Panama. The plan had been prepared since an aborted coup attempt against Noriega in October

1989. President Bush accepted the plan and ordered its immediate implementation. Defense Secretary Dick Cheney came up with the new name for the planned operation, Operation Just Cause.

The plan outlined for Just Cause had three basic goals:

1. The quick neutralization or removal of any military resistance to the U.S. forces. This was directed primarily at the Panama Defense Force, but Noriega's so-called Dignity Battalions were also targeted.
2. The capture of Manuel Noriega himself.
3. The installation of a stable, democratically elected government and the restoration of order to the country. The government intended for installation by the United States was headed by Guillermo Endara as President. Ricardo Arias and Guillermo Ford would be Vice-Presidents. These were the men a team of observers had declared the winners of the May elections that had been overthrown by Noriega.

Opposing the U.S. forces would be the 15,000 men of the PDF. These PDF forces included army, navy, and air force units as well as the entire Panamanian Police Force and National Guard. In addition to the PDF were the 8,000 members of Noriega's Dignity Battalions. Referred to as "Dig Bats" by the Panamanians, the Dignity Battalions were made up of eighteen civilian militia groups ranging in size from 24 to 250 men each. In reality nothing more than armed thugs, the Dignity Battalions were very loyal to Noriega, the man who had given them their power. Dismissed as not being of significant military capability by U.S. Intelligence, the Dignity Battalions were to prove costly to Operation Just Cause.

Just Cause would consist in part of a 3,000-man airborne jump into Panama. Backed up by forces already in Panama as well as Marines and Special Operations Forces, the paratroopers would be part of the largest U.S. airborne operation since World War II. Airborne and infantry units would do the bulk of the fighting for the invasion. Army Rangers,

Special Forces, and Marine units would capture and hold strategic targets throughout the Panama City area. The Navy SEALs were assigned to help prevent Noriega's possible escape and to help in capturing him.

One SEAL objective was the capture of the Paitilla Airfield in southern Panama City. Noriega was known to keep a Lear jet at the Paitilla Airfield for his personal use. The SEALs would insure that Noriega could not use the jet for escape. Additional SEAL units would capture or disable boats kept by Noriega at various locations in the Bay of Panama, cutting off his escape by that route.

During the late evening hours of Tuesday, December 19, the SEALs took off as part of the largest U.S. military airlift since the Vietnam War. Two platoons from SEAL Team 4 would conduct the capture of Paitilla Airfield. Using the "rubber duck" method of insertion, modified since the difficulties encountered with the technique at Grenada, the SEALs jumped into the darkness over the Pacific Ocean to the west of Panama City.

Climbing from the water into their Combat Rubber Raiding Craft (CRRC), which had been air-dropped along with them, the SEALs started in to the beaches at the edge of Paitilla Airfield. With the strong U.S. military presence already in Panama, the SEALs had been given the unique opportunity to plan their assault of the airfield at the actual location only a few weeks before the operation. The SEALs expected to be able to slip into the airfield, disable the planes, and slip back out without being detected. Such was not to be the case.

Twenty-four hours before the SEALs attacked the airfield, an airlift was going into Panama. U.S. military aircraft were landing at the U.S. bases in Panama in much larger than normal numbers. The planes were carrying equipment and personnel for the upcoming operation. Such indications can be easily interpreted by experienced intelligence personnel, and Noriega's men had such experience.

Expecting to encounter only minimal resistance, the SEALs landed at Paitilla Airfield armed with only light weapons. Instead of the few troops they expected, the

SEALs ran into large numbers of heavily armed troops supported by armored vehicles. In the fierce firefight that followed the SEALs defeated the Noriega forces and took the airfield, but not without cost. Eleven SEALs were casualties, with four of their number having been killed in the assault.

Killed during the Paitilla Airfield raid were Lieutenant (j.g.) John Patrick Connors, 25; Chief Petty Officer Donald McFaul, 32; Petty Officer Christopher Tilghman, 30; and Petty Officer 2/c Isaac Rodriguis III, 24. These SEALs were the first official casualties of Operation Just Cause.

At the boat docking facility in Balboa, another team of SEALs conducted further operations in support of Just Cause. High-speed patrol boats were stored at the heavily guarded harbor. To prevent General Manuel Noriega from using one of these crafts to escape, a team of SEALs moved in to disable the boats. This operation ran smoothly, with the SEALs infiltrating the harbor from the sea in a classic action reminiscent of the heroic activities of the UDTs. This was, in fact, the first such mission involving U.S. forces since the close of World War II.

Eventually, 24,000 U.S. troops, including Military Police and support units, were committed to the operations in Panama. After a long chase, Noriega surrendered to U.S. authorities. Out of the special operations forces involved in Just Cause, ten were killed and ninety-three wounded. These figures include the Rangers and Special Forces as well as the SEALs. In the first three days of the operation, twenty-one servicemen were killed and over two hundred wounded. The Dignity Battalions conducted a hit-and-run battle over all of Panama City. Widespread looting and sniper activity was also caused by these leftovers of the Noriega regime.

The SEALs once again proved capable of the tasks assigned them. It is hoped that in future operations the SEALs will not be forced to work with large numbers of conventional forces. The SEALs proved their abilities in Vietnam with their successful operations in the swamps and waterways. It is when the SEALs are taken out of their element and made part of a large conventional force that they suffer their worst casualty rates, but it is the nature of the SEALs to tackle any job assigned to them. From the bullet-swept beaches of Normandy to the dark runways at Panama, the SEALs always go in.

Becoming a SEAL*

Recruiting Sailors for SEALs

There are a number of basic qualifications for sailors applying for the SEAL program. These qualifications can be waived in certain circumstances, except the physical fitness requirements. The specific qualifications are:

- Pass a diving physical examination—This exam is more stringent than regular physical examinations.
- Meet vision standards—Your vision must be correctable to 20/20, within certain limitations. Color blindness is disqualifying.
- Have a good overall performance record—Evaluations of 3.6 or higher are required.
- Have your 1306/7 endorsed by your commanding officer.
- Have minimum Armed Services Vocational Aptitude, Basic scores—You need a minimum combined score of 104 on the ASVAB test in arithmetic reasoning and verbal expression.
- Have source ratings—You must be a member of a source rating for SEALs (examples include specialties in engines

and machinery, electrical and electronics work, supply and medical care). Or, you must convert to a source rating within one year of graduation from the SEAL program.

- Have minimum obligated service—At the class convening date, you must have obligated services for 36 months, or extend/reenlist to 36 months.
- Be under maximum age—The age cutoff for the program is 28 years.
- Men only apply—Because of laws prohibiting women from combat assignments, only men are eligible.

To apply for the SEAL program you must submit a package to: Commander, Naval Military Personnel Command (NMPCN-401D), Washington, D.C. 20370-5000. The package must be forwarded by your commanding officer with an endorsement, and include an enlisted personnel action request (1306/7) from you requesting to enter the SEAL program. It must also contain your PT scores, diving physical and certified ASVAB scores. Keep in mind, your application is processed at NMPC and the determination to accept you into the program is made there. A negative endorsement by your CO is not an automatic disqualifier.

For further details, consult MilPers Manual 1410380 and the Manual of Medicen, chapter 15-36. Most issues of *Link* magazine also contain further information about SEAL, explosive ordnance disposal and fleet diver programs.

Personnel known as "SEAL/EOD/Diver Motivators" are available at each of the three Recruit Training Commands, Orlando, Great Lakes and San Diego, to provide information and assist with screenings. Their commercial telephone numbers are: RTC Orlando, (305) 646-4725; RTC Great Lakes, (312) 688-4643; RTC San Diego, (619) 225-3520.

Also, if you meet the criteria, you can use the Selective Training and Reenlistment program to get into Basic Underwater Demolition/SEAL training. Your career counselor or command master chief can help you get more information or you can call the SEAL detailer, Autovon 224-1091, commercial (202) 694-1091.

The U.S. Navy SEALs Today*

SEAL Team Program Expands

The Navy SEAL—rough and tough, ready for any mission, anytime, anywhere. Armed with only cunning and a knife, he can single-handedly overcome the odds!

It's an exciting "Rambo" portrait, but not exactly accurate. In fact, in the current drive to increase the number of personnel in Sea-Air-Land Teams, if you're a Rambo, the SEALs aren't looking for you.

"We're looking for someone who is mature, well-motivated and anxious to do a professional job," said Capt. Michael Jukoski, Director of the Naval Special Warfare Division in Washington, D.C.

He emphasized that the Rambo image, the lone warrior taking on all comers, is not a realistic one for SEALs. "In fact," he said, "Rambo wouldn't be able to complete SEAL training. We're looking for a team member—you have to be a member of a fairly small group, people who are highly dependent on one another, to accomplish the job. We have no need for a person who isn't mindful of being part of that team," Jukoski said.

*Reprinted from US Naval Publication, *All Hands*, December 1987.

"Can you think how scary it would be during a parachute drop in the middle of the night and 'Rambo' wants to take off on his own? There's just no place for that," he pointed out, "because, number one, he would compromise the success of the mission—everyone is interdependent on one another—and number two, he would imperil the rest of the members."

Teamwork is the key to SEAL training and operations. "Our people are taught to function as a group," Jukoski said, "and the greatest rewards come from accomplishing success as a group."

The standards that prospective SEALs must meet are high, and the drive to recruit more SEALs hasn't changed that. "We will not sacrifice quality for quantity," said Jukoski. "We've had a tough time making our personnel goals because of that. However, we have maintained very high standards and in the long run, that pays off."

He said attitude is an essential part of the successful SEAL. "Mental attitude is one of the real determinants. . . . We have a group of well-motivated people who are willing to give the extra 10 percent to get the job done," Jukoski explained. "You have to have a person with the mind-set toward always making that effort—he's not satisfied with just getting the job done, but doing the best possible job consistently."

The present recruiting drive is part of an effort which began in 1982. After U.S. forces encountered difficulties in the attempted rescue of hostages in Iran, the Reagan administration wanted to revitalize the special operations forces in all the armed services. For the naval special warfare force, this meant doubling the number of personnel in the program between 1982 and 1990, with a goal of more than two thousand enlisted men and officers. Jukoski said SEALs are eventually expecting a 60 percent growth from present levels.

The majority of new SEALs are being drawn from the civilian community. "Our present emphasis is on recruiting through the Divefarer program," Jukoski said, "which guarantees you a shot at Basic Underwater Demolition and

SEAL training if you meet the basic requirements." Active duty personnel can also apply for SEALs. "There are lots of good people in the fleet. In many cases, they are more mature, have a more informed opinion about what they want to do in life."

One of the attractions of the SEAL community is the close-knit, almost family atmosphere. Some SEALs express concern that the increased numbers in their community will change that.

"We have been very small," Jukoski said. "I can remember when I knew every officer in the community by name. Now we're going through a period of transition from a small family to a larger one. . . . We will still be small enough that we are not going to lose our identity as team members. We'll still have the same name."

The Navy SEAL—rough and tough; ready for any mission, anytime, anywhere. Armed with cunning and a knife, ready to overcome all odds . . . not as a lone "Rambo," but as part of a highly organized team.

Divefarer:
Tailored for New Recruits*

If you are young, fit, and willing to spend six years in one of the most challenging jobs in the world, the Navy Divefarer program may be for you.

The Divefarer program brings people directly into the Navy's programs for SEAL combatant swimmers, Explosive Ordance Disposal, and second-class divers.

In return for a six-year enlistment, Divefarer offers you guaranteed assignment to one of these three diving programs. This also includes entry into an appropriate class "A" school or apprentice training.

You must volunteer for diving duty, which requires a more stringent physical screening than other ratings. The initial physical exam for entry into the Navy will be rechecked for diving qualifications. Also, a physical fitness test is administered during recruit training and at the selected dive school.

Specific requirements you must meet to qualify for Divefarer are:

*Reprinted from US Naval Publication, *All Hands*, December 1987.

- Age—The maximum age for applicants is 27.
- Test scores—In addition to ASVAB scores required for your rating, you must meet minimum scores in arithmetic reasoning, word knowledge/verbal expression and mechanical comprehension. See box below.
- Medical—You must meet the medical standards outlined in the Manual of the Medical Department, U.S. Navy, article 15-36.
- Physical fitness—Same standards as in-service recruitment.
- Drug usage—Because of the hazards inherent to these programs, use of controlled or illegal substances can result in disapproval of an application. Drug waivers will be considered on a case-by-case basis for applicants who have experimented with drugs.
- Character—Those applying for SEAL and EOD programs must be judged trustworthy enough to have access to classified information. You must meet reliability standards for the Personnel Reliability Program according to Bureau of Personnel Instruction 5510.11 paragraph 7.
- Prior service—If you have prior service, you can apply for Divefarer, depending on your reenlistment code.
- Service schools—You will be assigned to a class "A" school appropriate to diver, SEAL and EOD programs. Only certain Navy ratings are used in these fields. Called "source ratings," these include specialities in engines and machinery, electrical and electronics work, gunnery, supply and medical care.
- Training cycle—Divefarer personnel begin with recruit training in Orlando, Fla., continue with class "A" school, and then take part in appropriate diver training. Duty assignment is made in accordance with the needs of the Navy.
- Term of enlistment—You must enlist for four years and concurrently sign an agreement to extend for two more years, for a six-year total commitment. You will also be required to sign a form acknowledging that you understand the exceptional physical and medical requirements of the program.

• Advancement opportunities—Applicants accepted into Divefarer are usually enlisted in pay grade E-1 with accelerated advancement to E-2 when recruit training is completed successfully. In some cases, individuals are enlisted in pay grades E-2 or E-3. Advancement to pay grade E-4 is authorized after completion of class "A" school and diving training.

For further details, talk to your Navy recruiter.

Diving
AR + WK/VE = 104
MC = 50 (second class divers)

SEAL
AR + WK/VE = 104

EOD
AR + WK/VE = 110

The Organization of the SEALs

The SEALs today have been undergoing a buildup in forces. Individual SEALs graduating from BUD/S are assigned to either SEAL teams or SDV teams. The teams are in turn assigned to groups. There are also four Navy Special Warfare Units assigned to different locations throughout the world.

Each SEAL team and its support units are attached to one of two Navy Special Warfare Groups (NAVSPECWAR-GRU). One of these groups is on the West Coast and one on the East Coast of the United States.

NAVSPECWARGRU-ONE, Naval Amphibious Base (NAR), Coronado, California, is assigned the following:

> SEAL Teams 1, 3, and 5
> Swimmer Delivery Vehicle Team One
> Special Boat Squadron One, made up of
> > Special Boat Unit 11 (NRF)
> > Special Boat Unit 12
> > Special Boat Unit 13 (NRF)
> Navy Special Warfare Unit One, Subic Bay, Philippines
> Helicopter Attack Squadron, Light-Five, the Blue Hawks

NAVSPECWARGRU-TWO, NAR, Little Creek, Virginia, is assigned the following:

SEAL Teams 2, 4, and 8
SEAL Team 6, administrative only
Swimmer Delivery Vehicle Team Two
Special Boat Squadron Two, made up of
  Special Boat Unit 20
  Special Boat Unit 22 (NRF)
  Special Boat Unit 24 (NRF)
Navy Special Warfare Unit Two, Machrihanish, United Kingdom
Navy Special Warfare Unit Three, Roosevelt Roads, Puerto Rico
Helicopter Attack Squadron, Light-Four, the Redwolves
SEAL Team 6 is under the command of JCS/DOD

Each SEAL team is made up of operational platoons, which are assigned to detachments as needed. Each platoon has two officers and twelve enlisted men. The platoon is broken down into two squads of one officer and six enlisted men. The team also has a headquarters "platoon" of two officers, the commander and his executive officer, and six enlisted men.

The group also has a staff section of fifteen officers and seventy enlisted men.

At the end of the 1990 fiscal year, the SEAL teams should each have an allotment of thirty officers and one hundred eighty-one enlisted men. Each SEAL team will have about fourteen operational platoons and a headquarters unit.

Glossary

Antiterrorism: Defensive measures used to reduce the vulnerability of individuals or property to terrorism. Also called AT (approved definition by JCS Pub 1).

Beach Landing Site (BLS): A geographical location selected for across-the-beach infiltration/exfiltration/resupply operations.

Beacon Bombing: Bombing operations using Radar Beacon Forward Air Controller (RABFAC) AN/PPN-18 and AN/PPN-19 transponders to aid aircraft in the conduct of close air support missions. Often used in conjunction with ground laser devices to deliver precision-guided munitions.

Blind Transmission: Transmission that is without expectation of a receipt or reply.

Brown Water: An unofficial term, generally used to encompass riverine, inshore, and coastal operations. "Riverine" is an inland or coastal area, characterized by both land and water, with limited land routes and extensive water surface and/or inland waterways. "Inshore" relates to coastal areas and is generally used to indicate activities adjacent to the shore (that is, in very shallow water). "Coastal" is the least defined term, generally taken to mean over the continental shelf (that is, a depth of six hundred feet or less).

Civil Affairs: Those activities conducted during peace and war that facilitate relationships between U.S. military forces, civil authorities, and people of the nation in which the U.S. forces are operating.

Clandestine Operations: Operations to accomplish intelligence, counterintelligence, and other similar activities sponsored or conducted by governmental agencies in such a way as to assure concealment of identity of sponsor.

Combat Control Team: A team of Air Force personnel organized, trained, and equipped to locate, identify, and mark drop/landing zones, provide limited weather observations, install and operate navigational aids and air traffic control communications necessary to guide aircraft to drop/landing zones, and to control air traffic at these zones.

Combat Search and Rescue: Combat Search and Rescue (CSAR) is a specialized task performed by rescue forces to effect the expeditious recovery of distressed personnel from a hostile environment during wartime or contingency operations.

Combined Operation: An operation conducted by forces of two or more allied nations acting together for the accomplishment of a single mission.

Command and Control: The exercise of authority and direction by a properly designated commander over assigned forces in the accomplishment of the mission. Command and control functions are performed through an arrangement of personnel, equipment, communications, facilities, and procedures employed by a commander in planning, directing, coordinating, and controlling forces and operations in the accomplishment of the mission (JCS Pub1).

Communications: A method or means of conveying information of any kind from one person or place to another (JCS Pub 1).

Compact Laser Designator (CLD): The compact laser designator is a target marking device with a rangefinder. The man-portable target marker will be used by a ground operator for target handoff to laser-guided ordnance and laser tracker-equipped aircraft. The CLD is a Class IV neodymium yttrium aluminum garnet (ND:YAG) laser. It weighs sixteen pounds and has a range from fifty to one thousand meters. The primary power source is a lithium battery, although rechargeable nickel cadmium batteries are available for training.

Compartmentation: Establishment and management of an intelligence organization so that information about the personnel, organization, or activities of one component is made available to any other component only to the extent required for the performance of assigned duties.

Compromise: The known or suspected exposure of clandestine personnel, installations, or other assets, or of classified information or material, to an unauthorized person.

Counterguerrilla Warfare: Operations and activities conducted by armed forces, paramilitary forces, or nonmilitary agencies against guerrillas.

Counterinsurgency: Those activities that are concerned with identifying and counteracting the threat to security posed by hostile intelligence services or organizations or by individuals engaged in espionage, sabotage, or subversion (JCS Pub 1).

Counterterrorism: Offensive measures taken to prevent, deter, and respond to terrorism. Also called CT (approved definition by JCS Pub 1).

Cover: Protective guise used by a person, organization, or installation to prevent identification with clandestine activities.

Covert Operations: Operations that are so planned and executed as to conceal the identity of, or permit plausible denial by, the sponsor under the provisions of Executive Order 12036. They differ from clandestine operations in that emphasis is placed on concealment of identity of the sponsor rather than on concealment of the operation.

Deception: Those measures designated to mislead the enemy by manipulation, distortion, or falsification of evidence to induce him to react in a manner prejudicial to his interests.

Denial Operation: An operation designed to prevent or hinder enemy occupation of or benefit from areas or objects having tactical or strategic value.

Direct Action Mission (DAM): A specified military or paramilitary operation involving a commando-style raid into a hostile or denied area. DAMs are usually conducted covertly or clandestinely by SPECOPS forces in order to rescue, strike, reconnoiter, or destroy a target behind enemy lines.

Diversion: The act of drawing the attention and forces of an enemy from the point of the principal operation; this can be an attack, alarm, or feint that diverts attention.

Drop Altitude: Altitude of an aircraft in feet above the ground at the time of a parachute drop.

Drop Zone (DZ): A specified area upon which airborne troops, equipment, or supplies are air-dropped.

Electronic Intelligence (ELINT): The intelligence information product resulting from the collection and processing, for subsequent intelligence purposes, of foreign noncommunications electromagnetic radiations emanating from other than atomic detonations or radioactive sources.

Encipher: To convert plain text into unintelligible form by means of a cipher system.

Encode: 1.) That section of a code book in which the plain text equivalents of the code groups are in alphabetical, numerical, or other systematic order. 2.) To convert plain text into unintelligible form by means of a code system.

Encrypt: To convert plain text into unintelligible form by means of a crypto system.

Espionage: Actions directed toward the acquisition of information through clandestine operations.

Evader: Any person who has become isolated in hostile or unfriendly territory who eludes capture.

Evasion and Escape (E & E): The procedures and operations whereby military personnel and other selected individuals are enabled to emerge from an enemy-held or hostile area to areas under friendly control.

Evasion and Escape Net: The organization within enemy-held or hostile areas that operates to receive, move, and exfiltrate military personnel or selected individuals to friendly control.

Evasion and Escape Route: A course of travel, preplanned or not, that an escapee or evader uses in his attempt to depart enemy territory in order to return to friendly lines.

Forward Operating Base (FOB): In unconventional warfare, a base usually located in friendly territory or afloat that is established to extend command and control or communications or to provide support for training and tactical operations. Facilities are usually temporary and may include an airfield or an unimproved airstrip. The FOB may be the location of The Joint Unconventional Warfare Test Force (JUWTF) component headquarters or a smaller unit that is supported by a main operating base.

Foreign Internal Defense: Participation by civilian and military agencies of a government in any of the action programs taken by another government to free and protect its society from subversion, lawlessness, and insurgency (JCS Pub 1).

Guerrilla Warfare: Military and paramilitary operations conducted in enemy-held or hostile territory by irregular, predominantly indigenous forces (JCS Pub 1).

Harassment: An incident in which the primary objective is to disrupt the activities of a unit, installation, or ship rather than to inflict serious casualties or damage.

Human Intelligence (Humint): A category of intelligence derived from information collected and provided by human sources.

Infiltration: 1.) The movement through or into an area or territory occupied by either friendly or enemy troops or organizations. The movement is made, either by small groups or by individuals, at extended or irregular intervals. When used in connection with the enemy, it infers that contact is avoided. 2.) In intelligence usage, placing an agent or other person in a target area in hostile territory. Usually involves crossing a frontier or other guarded line. Methods of infiltration are: black (clandestine); gray (through legal crossing point but under false documentation); white (legal).

Insurgency: An organized movement aimed at the overthrow of a constituted government through the use of subversion and armed conflict (JCS Pub 1).

Intelligence: The product from the collection, processing, integration, analysis, evaluation, and interpretation of available information concerning foreign countries or areas (JCS Pub 1).

Interdiction: Preventing or hindering by any means enemy use of an area or route.

Logistics: The science of planning and carrying out the movement and maintenance of forces. It incorporates supply and services, maintenance, transportation, ammunition, construction, and medical services (modified JCS Pub 1).

Low-Intensity Conflict: A limited politico-military struggle to achieve political, social, economic, or psychological objectives. It is often protracted and ranges from diplomatic, economic, and psychosocial pressures through terrorism and insurgency. Low-intensity conflict is generally confined to a geographic area and is often characterized by constraints on the weaponry, tactics, and level of violence. Also called LIC (approved definition for JCS Pub 1).

Marker: A visual or electronic aid used to mark a designated point.

Marking Panel: A sheet of material displayed by ground troops for visual signaling to friendly aircraft.

Meaconing: A system of receiving radio beacon signals and rebroadcasting them on the same frequency to confuse navigation. The meaconing stations cause inaccurate bearings to be obtained by aircraft or ground stations.

Military Assistance Advisory Group: A joint service group, normally under the military command of a commander of a unified command and representing the Secretary of Defense, that primarily administers the U.S. military assistance, planning, and programming in the host country. Also called MAAG (JCS Pub 1).

Military Civic Action: The use of preponderantly indigenous military forces on projects useful to the local population at all levels in such fields as education, training, public works, agriculture, transportation, communications health, sanitation, and others contributing to economic and social development, which would also serve to improve the standing of the military forces with the population. (U.S. forces may at times advise or engage in military civic actions in overseas areas.) (JCS Pub 1)

Net Authentication: An authentication procedure by which a net control station authenticates itself and all other stations in the new system, systematically establishing their validity.

Net, Chain, Cell System: Patterns of clandestine organization, especially for operational purposes. "Net" is the broadest of the three; it usually involves (1) a succession of echelons, and (2) such functional specialists as may be required to accomplish its mission. When it consists largely or entirely of nonstaff employees, it may be called an agent net. "Chain" focuses attention upon the first of these elements; it is commonly defined as a series of agents and informants who receive instructions from and pass information to a principal agent by means of cutouts and couriers. "Cell system" emphasizes a variant of the first element of the net; its distinctive feature is the grouping of personnel into small units that are relatively isolated and self-contained. In the interest of maximum security for the organization as a whole, each cell has contact with the rest of the organization only through an agent of the organization and a single member of the cell. Others in the cell do not know the agent, and nobody in the cell knows the identities or activities of other cells.

Overt Operation: The collection of intelligence openly, within concealment. Operations that are planned and executed without attempting to conceal the operation or identity of the sponsoring power.

Paramilitary Forces: Forces or groups that are distinct from the regular armed forces of any country, but that resemble them in organization, equipment, training, or mission (JCS Pub 1).

Peacetime Contingency Operations: Politically sensitive military operations normally characterized by the short-term rapid projection or employment of forces in conditions short of conventional war (for example, strike, raid, rescue, recovery, demonstration, show of force, unconventional warfare, and intelligence operations). (TRADOC Pam 525-44)

Propaganda: Any form of communication in support of national objectives designed to influence the opinions, emotions, attitudes, or behavior of any group in order to benefit the sponsor, either directly or indirectly (JCS Pub 1).

Radar Beacon: A receiver-transmitter combination that sends out a coded signal when triggered by the proper type of pulse, enabling determination of range and bearing information by the interrogating station or aircraft.

Raid: An operation, usually small-scale, involving a swift penetration of hostile territory to secure information, confuse the enemy, or destroy his installations. It ends with a planned withdrawal upon completion of the assigned mission.

Recovery Site: An area within or outside a SAFE (E&E) area from which an evader/escapee can be evacuated. The area is selected for its accessibility by ground, sea, or airborne recovery personnel.

Sabotage: An act with an intent to injure, interfere with, or obstruct the national defense of a country by willfully injuring or destroying, or attempting to injure or destroy, any national defense or war material, premises, or utilities, including human and natural resources.

Safe Area: A designated area in hostile territory that offers the evader or escapee a reasonable chance of avoiding capture and of surviving until he can be evacuated.

Search and Rescue: The use of aircraft, surface craft, submarines, specialized rescue teams, and equipment to search for and rescue personnel in distress on land or at sea.

Sensitive: Requiring special protection from disclosure which could cause embarrassment, compromise, or threat to the security of the sponsoring power. May be applied to an agency, installation, person, position, document, material, or activity.

Sensitive Area: Specific location that has become a center of activity of intelligence interest.

Signal Panel: Strip of cloth used in sending code signals between the ground and aircraft in flight.

Special Activities: Indicates activities conducted abroad in support of national foreign policy objectives that are designed to further official United States programs and policies abroad and that are planned and executed so that the role of the United States government is not apparent or acknowledged publicly, and functions in support of such activities, but not including diplomatic activity or the collection and production of intelligence or related support functions.

Special (or Project) Equipment: Equipment not authorized in standard equipment publications but determined as essential in connection with a contemplated operation, function, or mission.

Special Forces Operational Base (SFOB): In unconventional warfare, a provisional organization that is established within a friendly area by elements of a Special Forces group to provide command, administration, training, logistical support, and intelligence for operational Special Forces detachments and such other forces as may be placed under this operational control. (*Note*: CINCPAC adds: "The SFOB also provides logistical support for indigenous UW forces sponsored by those detachments. The Commander, SFOB will normally be the Army component commander of the JUWTF if only one SFOB is utilized".)

Special Operations: Operations conducted by specially trained, equipped, and organized DOD forces against strategic or tactical targets in pursuit of national military, political, economic, or psychological objectives. These operations may be conducted during periods of peace or hostilities. They may support conventional operations or they may be prosecuted independently when the use of conventional forces is either inappropriate or infeasible.

Strategic Intelligence: Intelligence that is required for the formation of policy and military plans at national and international levels. Strategic intelligence and tactical intelligence differ primarily in level of application but may also vary in terms of scope and detail (JCS Pub 1).

Tactical Intelligence: Intelligence that is required for the planning and conduct of tactical operations. Tactical intelligence and strategic intelligence differ primarily in level of application but may also vary in terms of scope and detail (JCS Pub 1).

Target: 1.) A geographical area, complex, or installation planned for capture or destruction by military forces. 2.) In intelligence usage, a country, area, installation, agency, or person against which intelligence operations are directed.

Target Acquisition: The detection, identification, and location of a target in sufficient detail to permit the effective employment of weapons.

Target Folders: The folders containing target intelligence and related materials prepared for planning and executing action against a specific target.

Terrorism: The unlawful use or threatened use of force or violence against individuals or property to coerce or intimidate governments or societies, often to achieve political, religious, or ideological objectives.

Theater: The geographical area outside the continental United States for which a commander of a unified or specified command has been assigned military responsibility.

Transponder: A transmitter-receiver capable of accepting the electronic challenge of an interrogator and automatically transmitting an appropriate reply.

Unconventional Warfare: A broad spectrum of military and paramilitary operations conducted in enemy, enemy-held, enemy-controlled, or politically sensitive territory. Unconventional warfare includes, but is not limited to, the interrelated fields of guerrilla warfare, evasion and escape, subversion, sabotage, and other operations of a low-visibility, cover, or clandestine nature. These interrelated aspects of unconventional warfare may be prosecuted singly or collectively by predominantly indigenous personnel, usually supported and directed in various degrees by (an) external source(s) during all conditions of war or peace.

SEALS

THE WARRIOR BREED

by H. Jay Riker

The face of war is rapidly changing, calling
America's soldiers into hellish regions where
conventional warriors dare not go.
This is the world of the SEALs.

SILVER STAR
76967-0/$6.99 US/$8.99 Can

PURPLE HEART
76969-7/$6.50 US/$8.99 Can

BRONZE STAR
76970-0/$6.50 US/$8.99 Can

NAVY CROSS
78555-2/$5.99 US/$7.99 Can

MEDAL OF HONOR
78556-0/$5.99 US/$7.99 Can

MARKS OF VALOR
78557-9/$5.99 US/$7.99 Can